THIRD CULTURE COOKING
Classic Recipes for a New Generation

Zaynab Issa

Photographs by Graydon Herriott

ABRAMS, NEW YORK

*To Sakina, Fatema,
and Mikaeel*

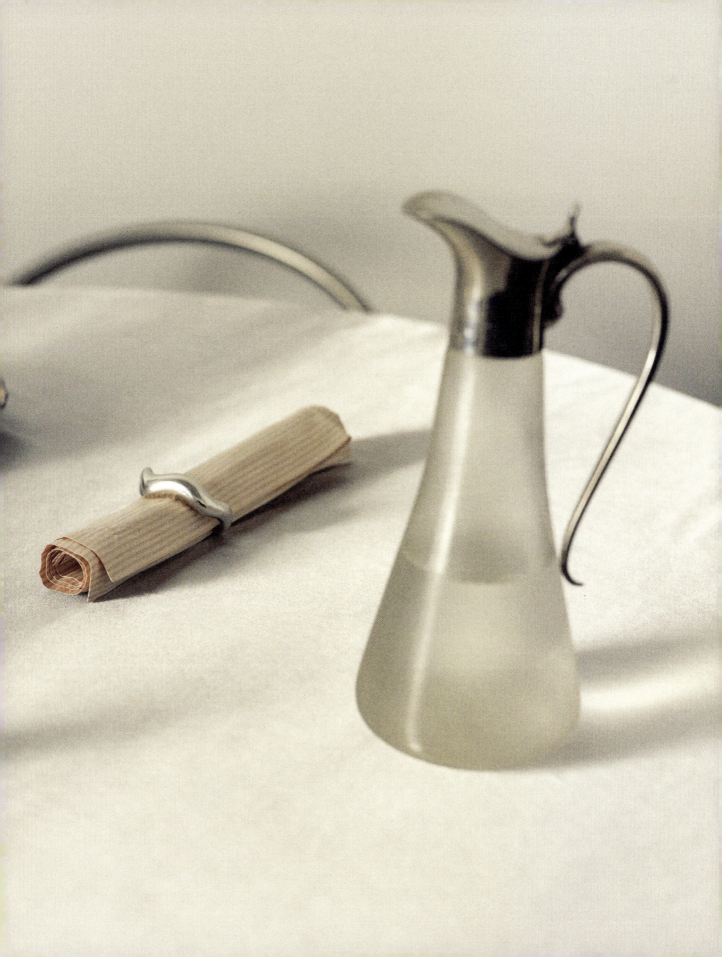

CONTENTS

10	Cook Like an American?
14	Set Yourself Up for Success
18	Pantry Staples
20	Fridge Staples
21	Tools
22	Salt, Namely Diamond Crystal Kosher Salt
24	I'm Super Particular in a Very Flexible Way
26	Eating with Your Eyes
29	On Food and Feelings
32	Host with the Most

RECIPES

38	Start Small
84	Fill Up
186	Make It Better
204	Something Sweet
250	Sips
264	Acknowledgments
266	Index

START SMALL

- 40 Batata Vada (Kachori)
- 42 Chevro Chips
- 44 Coconutty Corn
- 46 Coronation Chicken Pastries
- 48 Cucumber and Chutney Sandwiches
- 50 Fruity Fattoush
- 52 Grape and Fennel Salad
- 54 Gyoza with Garlicky Labneh and Chili Butter
- 56 Herby, Garlicky Pasta Salad
- 58 Hot and Sour Tomatoes
- 60 Lemony Cucumber Salad with Salted Yogurt
- 62 Za'atar and Maple Kettle Corn
- 64 Peppery Potato Pakoras
- 66 Rumina's Kebabs and Coconut Chutney
- 68 Salty Little Hearts
- 70 Samosas Two Ways
- 75 Shawarma-Spiced Carrots
- 76 Summer on a Plate
- 78 Red, Hot Tandoori Wings
- 80 Tarka Olives
- 80 TGIF Artichoke Dip

FILL UP

- 89 Achaar, Egg, and Cheese
- 90 An Iconic Chicken Pot Pie
- 92 Arrogant Tomato Toast
- 94 Ashraf's Tomato Saag
- 96 Smashed Black Bean Burgers
- 99 B-L-D Tomatoes and Eggs
- 100 Calabrian Chili Chicken with Caper Raita
- 103 Carthage Must Be Destroyed
- 104 Chicken Kitchri
- 106 Cumin Fried Rice
- 108 Farzana's Biryani
- 112 Fish Fillet
- 114 French Onion Ramen
- 116 Super-Savory Chicken Noodle Soup
- 118 Gochujang Tahini Noodles
- 120 Green Eggs and Hummus
- 122 Gully's Gajjar Chicken
- 124 Halal Cart Salad
- 126 Koobideh Meatballs with Minty Yogurt
- 128 Last-Minute Tahdig
- 130 Lemony, Herby Shrimpies
- 132 Not So Norma Pasta
- 134 One Pan(try) Pasta
- 137 Pasta Day Pasta
- 138 Red Curry Orzotto with Mushrooms and Peas
- 141 Riffat's Kuku Paka
- 143 Rishma's Pilau
- 146 Roasted Eggplant Sandwich
- 148 Samosa-Spiced Burgers
- 150 Shawarma Salad Wrap
- 152 Shenaz's Chicken Haleem
- 156 Spicy Lamb and Cumin Noodles

158	Spiced Chickpea Soup		**SOMETHING SWEET**
160	Spiced Short Ribs and Potatoes		
164	Steak Sandwich with Date Chutney	208	Ashraf's Baklava
		212	Baklava Granola
166	Sukayna's Omelet	214	Banana Cake with Tahini Fudge
168	Sungold and Saffron Spaghetti	216	Chewy Ginger Cookies
170	Tandoori Tacos	219	Chocolate Cake with Chai Buttercream
173	Thai-Style Crispy Salmon and Rice	222	Mall Cinnamon Rolls
174	A Great Tuna Melt	225	Coconut and Cardamom Cake
176	Tortellini en Preserved Lemon Brodo	228	Coffee Cake Muffins
		230	Date and Dark Chocolate Cookies
179	Turkish-ish Eggs	233	Fruit and Nut Biscotti
180	Udon Carbonara	234	Gahwa Sundae
182	Wali Ya Mboga, Sorta	236	Gulzar's Sugar Puffs
185	Weeknight Daal	238	Almond Mocha Blondies
		240	Jugu Scones with Butter and Jam
		242	Melon Sorbet
	MAKE IT BETTER	245	Pineapples and Ghee
		246	Salted Brown Butter Pecan Shortbread
190	Carrot Sambharo	248	Strawberry Delight
192	Chili Crisp		
194	Chutney Butter		
195	Date Chutney		
196	Green Chutney		**SIPS**
197	Homemade Hot Sauce		
198	Pickled Kachumber		
202	Shortcut Lemon Achaar	252	A Different Date Shake
203	White Sauce	254	Ginger Lime Spritz
		256	Karak Chai
		260	The Pink Drink
		260	Preserved Limonata
		261	Slightly Salty Mango Lassi

Pickled Kachumber (198)

COOK LIKE AN AMERICAN?

Almost everything you need to know about me can be learned through the way I eat, and this cookbook is much like a memoir, but of my memories of food. The recipes to come reflect my experiences with different foods throughout my life living as a first-generation American. You'll find a variety of inspirations, some taken from American classics, some from my East African and South Asian roots, and others still from somewhere in between—the throughline is the third culture lens.

The term *third culture* describes the result of growing up in a combination of the culture of my parents' homeland and the place we now call "home." My own mixed identity is this third culture, and my recipes reflect this perspective.

Both my parents were born in Tanzania, my mother on the mainland and my father on the island of Zanzibar. Their Khoja ethnicity reflects their cultural customs as tradespeople from India and the longstanding migration to East Africa, along with their religious ties to Islam and Middle Eastern practices. What comes with all of that is a food culture so rich and nuanced, it's impossible not to be inspired by it.

As a child growing up in suburban New Jersey, I wanted near-nothing to do with my parents' culture; the American way was better, and whatever I didn't know about it needed to be learned. I watched so much Food Network, learning the ways of the country I call home through food in ways my parents couldn't teach me—looking to Ina Garten, Rachael Ray, and other hosts to show me how to cook like an American.

As I've grown up and lived here, my perspective on American food has shifted to reflect a new understanding: America itself is a third culture nation; especially considering many of us who've ended up here and planted roots can't actually trace our bloodline to this land. Most of us have a story of migration—if not you, then maybe your great-great-grandparents, but this reality remains: the culture of your homeland has mixed with the culture of others here, creating an entirely new one.

I no longer think "American food" can be reduced to "burgers and hot dogs," or "pasta and pizza," or "apple pie and strawberry shortcake," all of which have roots in different countries around the world (Germany, Italy, and England respectively) but have been incorporated into American culture just the same. And, to some extent, intrinsically, even when making something traditional, one could argue it undergoes a metamorphosis, reflecting the place it's cooked in. Coconut milk in some places is made at home, from readily available fresh coconuts, and here, in New York City, a 13.5-ounce sealed tin can of it is close to as good as it's going to get. This example may feel like a small departure, and it is, but it's also reflective of time and place, two things that affect the integrity of a dish.

So, American food is also *my* food—it might have origins elsewhere, but it belongs here equally. These recipes take inspiration from global cuisines, and I've tried to acknowledge the inspiration and origins of certain flavors, dishes, and ingredients, as I view that as essential to cultural preservation.

You'll notice a select group of recipes in this book aren't like the rest. And that's because the third culture is nothing without the first culture—my Khoja heritage. My community-centered upbringing exposed me to the wonderful world of food, and I probably wouldn't have ever turned to Food Network in the first place if it wasn't for the way I was fed in my early life and the way food played a role in my day-to-day. My grandmother Ashraf and my mother, Rishma, are both incredible cooks who are constantly feeding their very involved extended families. For them, food is everything, and they make sure it is in abundance. Each meal is an excuse to get together, and the same is true for preparing it. I have never once been turned away from the kitchen.

As I grew up and learned the reality of the patriarchy, some of the romance in cooking was stripped from me. I couldn't unsee it as an act of forced selflessness. I turned away from it in my late teenage years, afraid of what it could mean to be in the kitchen, for the fear of being trapped into the same expectation—to feed the men in our lives. But these women were so much more than that, and I feel guilty for ever even making that assertion—for diminishing the skill and intention they exerted on a daily basis, often because they loved cooking and what it meant, just the same way I do. I wish they were the ones writing cookbooks; I know they could if only they wanted to. Blessed to be empowered to be in the kitchen without obligation, I saw this opportunity to offer the women who fed me this honor that I, too, have: to share their recipes with an audience who will cherish and appreciate them and endeavor to cook them.

Who better to teach you about the food I love to eat than the women who taught me to love food in the first place. Sprinkled throughout the book's five main recipe chapters, you'll notice recipes titled with a woman's name before the name of the dish. That is *their* recipe, not mine. I simply recorded the expertise they've spent years honing—The same expertise that taught me, and continues to teach me, how to love eating, cooking, and feeding.

And so, to preserve that spirit, while watching and recording their cooking, I resisted any urge I may have had to "food edit" their recipe. I didn't change it to follow the culinary "rules" I've learned over the years, like adding salt to baked goods or streamlining the method to use fewer tools. After all, the method in a recipe is just as important as the ingredients used to prepare it. So, the food editor in me sat down and just observed, frantically reminding them to let me measure their every move. I documented exactly what they did, noting every tip they may have mentioned along the way and weighing every ingredient. In the final recipe, I offered information only for what I saw them do. Some of those recipes feed a metaphorical army, some have an extensive ingredient list, and some take hours to prepare, but if that's the way she cooks, I'm not going to tell her otherwise.

On the other hand, much of my own formal recipe development experience happened in the *Bon Appétit* test kitchen, where I was drilled to consider the average weeknight home cook. As soon as I stepped foot onto the twenty-third floor of One World Trade Center in New York City, anything I made was fine-tuned by a talented team of seasoned food editors. Together, we developed "useful" recipes, ones that solve problems. And that's what most of the recipes in this book are: streamlined methods with minimal ingredients that deliver big on flavor. There may be some unfamiliar ingredients or methods, but almost never both. If you do see an unfamiliar method or ingredient, know that it's there to push you to be a better home cook. As is true with many other parts of life, dabbling in the uncomfortable is essential to growth.

At my core, I'm busy, hungry, intentional, nostalgic, lazy, and a little fancy. These qualities transfer to the way I eat and, more importantly, the way I cook. While I love the elaborate, I don't always have the time or patience for it, and because of that you'll find these recipes to be simple and straightforward while maintaining a wow factor I can appreciate. Inspired by the food or flavor profiles I've experienced, many of the dishes are attached to a memory or story that I re-created for comfort, but with a twist. As for the recipes that are more involved or unfamiliar, know that they deliver, and I wouldn't encourage you to embark on that journey for anything less than exceptional.

xx Zaynab

SET YOURSELF UP FOR SUCCESS

"Set yourself up for success," Chris Morocco, *Bon Appétit*'s food director, said to me as he walked down the length of the pass to my station, handing me a rubber grip to place under my cutting board as I began to remove the firm, thick skin of a fish fillet. This was something I had never done before, and I suspect he knew that, although I never explicitly admitted it. He talked me through it, and I did pretty well for a *Bon Appétit* newbie. It would have been much more challenging if my cutting board hadn't been secured in place from that rubber grip—all the best cooks know preparation is important.

This entire guide is dedicated to giving you the information you'll need to make these recipes successfully. I don't use a ton of unusual ingredients and tools, so I listed some of the more uncommon ones I think you absolutely should have. These are the things present in my kitchen that make it mine—I reach for them over and over again, and they will do some heavy lifting in the recipes to come. I consider these items personal pantry and fridge essentials—they all appear several times over in my recipes, so I've provided some context around each. Some of them may be easy to source and some might require you to play find-and-seek. Regardless, here's everything you'll need to know to convince you to use them.

PANTRY STAPLES

ALEPPO CHILI FLAKES

From the Halaby pepper, Aleppo chili flakes offer a subtly spiced, fruity flavor with a gorgeous reddish burgundy hue and are commonly used in Middle Eastern cuisine.

BASMATI SELLA RICE

Basmati sella rice is a variety of parboiled long-grain rice that's slightly more forgiving during the cooking process than regular basmati rice, and more nutritious (thanks to its grain layer that adds to its fiber content), too. I cook it using the pasta method almost every time: I bring a large pot of salted water to a boil and cook the rice until tender. I purchase Shahzada Extra Long Grain Basmati Sella Rice most often (Zebra and Royal are two other brands I like); it offers me the luxury of not having to soak the rice, which the procrastinator in me loves. That said, soaking certainly helps with texture, so if I remember to soak, I will. If you can't find sella, regular extra-long-grain basmati rice will work well.

BREAKFAST TEA

You'll notice many of my recipes reference serving with chai (meaning tea). I make chai at least once a day, and when I'm hosting people or feeling a little more indulgent, I'll make my Karak Chai (page 256). I rely on strong, black tea bags for any type of chai, and my preferred ones are PG Tips and Tetley's Orange Pekoe or British Blend. I'll usually make a simple quick-steeped cup with a splash of milk and sometimes sugar.

BROTH

Making broth at home is ideal, but when I can't (which is most of the time), I'll use Knorr Halal Bouillon Cubes—either chicken or beef. For readers who are unfamiliar with the term, "Halal" refers to an animal slaughter standard followed by many Muslims that prioritizes the animals' well-being. Needless to say, if a good-quality carton of broth is at your disposal, use it. Unfortunately, finding cartons of halal beef or chicken broth is near impossible, but the bouillon cubes are great for a good-enough-to-drink alternative. And for vegetarian cooking, Better Than Bouillon Sauteed Onion and Seasoned Vegetable bases are my go-to.

CHICKPEA FLOUR

Also called gram flour or besan, it's a great gluten-free flour to keep on hand. It's the result of grinding down dried chickpeas into a powder and is perfect for thickening, binding, and making batters.

CITRIC ACID

Oh, I love this one. It's basically lemon juice in powder form, used mostly when a tart citrus-sour flavor is required without additional moisture.

CURRY POWDER

A blend featuring a medley of spices, usually including, but not limited to, turmeric, coriander, cumin, cinnamon, and cayenne. It's aromatic, relatively mild, and somewhat citrusy. My favorite one is Spicewalla's

Madras Curry Powder. Madras varieties are considered a bit spicier than regular curry powder.

DATES

Because dates are generally sold off the shelf, not from the refrigerator case, people tend to think of them as a dried fruit. But they are in fact fresh—just very ripe. Sweet, plump, and jammy in texture, Medjool dates are the variety I usually call for in recipes because they're the most common, but Barhi dates are my favorite to snack on. I like Bateel and Rancho Meladuco brands.

DIAMOND CRYSTAL KOSHER SALT

There's a lot to be said for this one. In short, start using it—you'll be a better cook for it. So many of the recipes to come call for a measured amount of this particular variety of salt. See page 22 if you need even more convincing.

DUTCH-PROCESS COCOA POWDER

Most of the time the cocoa beans used to produce this specialty variety of cocoa powder are fattier and higher in quality. It's also darker in color, resulting in a richer visual.

GARAM MASALA

Another aromatic spice blend, garam masala is very commonly used in South Asian cooking, and it often includes cumin, coriander, cloves, and cinnamon, among others. Most serious home cooks in my community will make it from scratch, but when I don't have my mom's homemade blend on hand, I use Spicewalla's.

INDIAN RED CHILI POWDER

Also called lal mirch (meaning red chili), this spice is similar to cayenne pepper but typically a little more vibrant in color. There are many different types with varying heat levels, but I prefer Kashmiri.

KASHMIRI CHILI POWDER is a mild variety of Indian red chili powder. It's bright red in color, floral, and kind of smoky. When I can't find this one, I'll buy deggi chili powder, which is similarly mild and smoky.

OLIVE OIL

While not the traditional cooking fat in most South Asian cooking, olive oil is so flavorful and readily available stateside that it's become the go-to for many. I usually have two varieties on hand—one high-quality, super-flavorful extra virgin olive oil that I use for dressings and finishing and one more affordable that I don't need to be precious about and can pan-fry, saute, and roast with comfortably. Right now, my go-tos are Flamingo Estate's Heritage Extra Virgin Olive Oil for finishing and California Olive Ranch's Everyday Medium 100% California Olive Oil for cooking, or I'll buy a set of Graza's Sizzle and Drizzle Olive Oils. And, if you feel like splurging on art for your kitchen, Tacapae olive oil is as delicious as it is beautiful.

POMEGRANATE MOLASSES

A deep, slightly sweet, and very tangy syrup made from concentrated pomegranate juice, akin to a very-good-quality thick balsamic vinegar (acidic and sweet).

SAFFRON

Harvested from the saffron flower, these reddish, thread-like strands impart a uniquely sweet and earthy flavor and a bright orange hue when used in cooking. While this stuff is expensive, a little goes a long way, and it can be used in both sweet and savory applications. I find that Iranian and Kashmiri saffron are the most vibrant in color and flavor.

SUMAC

Dried ground berries from the sumac shrub. There are so many varieties of this citrusy, tangy spice, but I prefer using Turkish or Iranian sumac—it's lemony and rich in color and flavor.

WHOLE GREEN CARDAMOM PODS

I've never known a pantry without these. I usually purchase a bag of them from the South Asian supermarket, and even though I use them very often, it lasts me quite a while. My Karak Chai and Gahwa Sundae recipes (pages 256 and 234) call for whole pods, smashed to reveal the seeds, but many of my other recipes call for ground cardamom. Yes, you can purchase it pre-ground (Spicewalla brand would be my recommendation here), but grinding the seeds down yourself in a spice mill or mortar and pestle will almost always yield a more aromatic result.

ZA'ATAR

It's both an herb and a homonymous herb blend, but in my recipes I'm always referring to the blend. It features the herb, along with salt, sesame seeds, and sumac in most cases. Olive Odyssey's Palestinian Za'atar Mixture is my favorite, and when I can't get that I'll reach for Z&Z Za'atar.

FRIDGE STAPLES

ACHAAR

Achaar is a spicy South Asian pickled condiment, usually preserved in salt and oil and made with chilis alongside a variety of different fruit or vegetable options, like mango, lemon, carrot, or, my favorite, ginger. It lasts years, both in the pantry unopened and in the fridge after opening. For my Achaar, Egg, and Cheese recipe (page 89), I use my personal favorite, AKI-brand Chilli and Ginger Pickle, which can be found in Canada or ordered online. It's the perfect accompaniment to add a fiery and punchy bite and pairs well with most savory dishes. If you want to make one at home, check out the Shortcut Lemon Achaar on page 202, which relies on preserved lemons to help jump-start the process.

GREEN BIRD'S-EYE CHILIS

These little green chilis, also commonly referred to as Thai chilis, are quite spicy and incredibly flavorful with a grassy, fruity heat. These are interchangeable with small Indian green chilis.

CALABRIAN CHILI PASTE

One of my favorite spicy chili pastes, it's what reminds me most of an achaar. Most varieties are made with salt and vinegar, taking it to a flavorful, pickle-y place. I also love that I can use it generously before the heat gets the better of me.

CASTELVETRANO OLIVES

My favorite variety, these green olives are buttery and mild.

CHILI CRISP

I prefer to make my own (page 192). That being said, you can find this pretty easily at the grocery store now. I love to keep it on hand for a final finish of spicy, aromatic flavor.

FISH SAUCE

Fish sauce adds saltiness and an instantaneous depth. I think of it as similar to anchovies but in liquid form. Red Boat is the brand I prefer; I find it tastes clean and pungent.

LABNEH

Technically a cheese, I wouldn't quite describe it as one in the commonly understood sense. It's less funky, and more acidic and has a super-lush texture thanks to all the strained-out whey. If you want to make it at home, you can simply add older whole-milk plain yogurt to a cheesecloth set over a strainer and let the whey strain out for 1 to 2 days (a technique I learned from Homa Dashtaki of the White Mustache). The resulting labneh will be tangy and thick, like it should be.

PRESERVED LEMON

I cannot praise preserved lemon enough. It's so dynamic and surprisingly not all that lemony (it's saltier and brinier). It lasts forever and is quite versatile in both savory and sweet preparations. When paired with fresh lemon, the resulting flavor is stellar.

KEWPIE MAYO

This Japanese mayo that uses only egg yolks is richer and more flavorful than Hellmann's or Duke's, thanks to those extra yolks. It functions similarly and can be swapped out at a 1:1 ratio in most cases.

TOOLS

A GREAT PEPPERMILL
For me, it's the Unicorn Pepper Grinder because it just offers so much pepper with each turn. Plus, I love the gloss black finish—very chic.

"MICROPLANE" MICROPLANE
I've tried other non-Microplane-brand "microplanes," and they're fine—good, in fact—but not ideal. If you are going to buy one, buy the branded one. It's great and really lasts—I've had mine for over five years and haven't even thought of replacing it. It's great for finely grating garlic and ginger and for zesting citrus.

SHARP KNIFE
I thought about not including a knife in the list, considering a knife is an ordinary kitchen tool. But having a well-sharpened knife makes a real difference to the cooking experience as a whole, while a dull knife can create a burden out of it. If you're new to the vast world of knives, I always recommend Victorinox Swiss Classic Knife Set, 5 Pieces. They're sharp and comfortable.

CITRUS JUICER
I swear by manually juicing lemons, limes, and oranges using the OXO 2-in-1 Citrus Juicer—the juice accumulates in a small liquid measuring cup, which makes it so much easier to measure for recipes.

CLIP-ON STRAINER
I'm not typically an advocate for kitchen gizmos. This one, however, I can't believe I ever lived without. It's a worthwhile addition if you find yourself constantly making noodles, pasta, or rice (using the pasta method).

DELI CONTAINERS
This might seem like a random addition, but a set of deli containers is essential to storing the food you make. They're reusable and microwave and dishwasher safe, and the best part: you can stack them easily in your refrigerator and freezer to maximize space.

DIGITAL SCALE
Akin to a digital thermometer (see "instant-read thermometer" below), a digital scale takes the guesswork out of cooking and preparing ingredients, allowing for precision without too much brainpower. If you like baking, you absolutely *need* to buy one—you'll thank me later.

DUTCH OVEN
I know, they can cost an arm and a leg. I bought my first one using credit card points, which is objectively dumb (points go much further as airline miles), but I'd do it again. A good Le Creuset, Staub, or Great Jones Dutch oven will last years, if not a lifetime. They're durable, chic, and oven-safe. Is a Dutch oven worth more than a weekend trip to Miami? Unequivocally, yes.

INSTANT-READ THERMOMETER
Great for when you want to turn your brain off during cooking. Knowing for sure your meats are cooked to the correct temperature and doneness without setting timers or needing to cut into them is a luxury you can get used to.

MINI FOOD PROCESSOR
I don't actually own a full-size food processor. Between my blender and my KitchenAid cordless mini food chopper, I've done pretty well in the kitchen. A full-size one would certainly make things easier on occasion, but the mini is so convenient for my day-to-day cooking.

MORTAR AND PESTLE
I love my mortar and pestle. I find myself reaching for it so often, whether to crack open cardamom pods or crush up some nuts. They're widely useful and can be a beautiful countertop staple.

SALT, NAMELY DIAMOND CRYSTAL KOSHER SALT

I am a firm believer in salt. So much so that I carry a tiny tin of flaky sea salt in my purse.

I'm not sure I can adequately even begin to explain the importance of salt in cooking, but I'll try: It's often the difference between food that's good and food that's great, and one of the reasons food at restaurants tastes so good—professional chefs know how to use salt, and their food is better for it. Once you recognize the significance salt plays in the final taste of your dish, be it savory or sweet (yes, you read that correctly), it'll change the way you understand flavors and give you a newfound value for the ingredient.

This is also a plea to purchase Diamond Crystal kosher salt, specifically. If you ask me, it's the superior brand of easily accessible salts. I know many home cooks use table salt, and I did consider developing recipes using that, but ultimately I decided that convincing you to buy and use Diamond Crystal would be more beneficial in the long run.

Kosher salt is coarser and less salty than table salt, making it more forgiving to work with, and it's just more intuitive for cooking. You don't run the risk of oversalting through an even surface sprinkling, which is ideal for adequate seasoning without measuring.

If my mother, an avid table salt user for more than forty years, converted, you can, too.

SALT, NAMELY DIAMOND CRYSTAL KOSHER SALT

I'M SUPER PARTICULAR IN A VERY FLEXIBLE WAY

And so are these recipes.

Recipes are a lot like instruction manuals—they exude an air of precision and accuracy. The reality of cooking is much different. The way I see it, cooking is much more individualized than a recipe, in that no two people will cook any given recipe the exact same way (and that's very much OK). I've designed these recipes to reflect that fundamental truth—with as much precision as possible, while recognizing that cooking isn't always quite that precise.

Whenever I think about cooking, I make myself aware of the who, what, when, where, why, and how: who am I feeding, what is the purpose of this meal, when will I make it, where am I eating it, why am I cooking in the first place, and how do I make sure I have the time and energy to execute the task ahead. Knowing the answers to these questions helps me decide what to make and aligns my thoughts and actions. Reading recipes also helps guide the answers to these questions.

Here you'll find a guide to how I write my recipes and what you can expect from them. I wrote these recipes in the hope that you'd read them, and I recommend you *do* read each one entirely at least once (the more you read it the better, honestly) before beginning to cook from it. When you do this, the margin of error decreases significantly.

RECIPE TITLE   This is what I think best describes the dish, either in concept or through flavor.

HEADNOTE   This is where I offer context for the recipe through anecdotes, notes on inspiration, or more information on the method and ingredients to come.

SERVINGS   This is my best interpretation of how many people can eat from this dish. It's an assumption and should be taken as such; you know how much or how little you and who you're feeding can eat.

TIME   This is the total amount of time it'll take to make the dish including prep time, but not always including rest or chill time. This section is even more subjective than "Servings," because it really depends on how efficient and skilled you are in the kitchen. These recipes have been cooked through many times by many different cooks, and this number represents the average. Do with it what you will, but I love to see it there as a guide for planning ahead, and I wouldn't have included it if I didn't think it could be useful.

INGREDIENTS   This is everything you need, from a food perspective, to make the dish, along with how it needs to be prepared to execute the method. For ease, it's all written together, but if you follow my advice above about reading the entire recipe ahead of time, you'll be able to piece together exactly how much ingredient prep needs to be done beforehand and how much of it can be done while something else is happening.

INSTEAD OF...   This is where I offer alternatives for ingredients above that have an asterisk next to them, meaning there's a reasonable swap for the ingredient. That's not to say the dish will turn out the same if you use the alternative, just to say it can be done. The way I've written the recipe is the way I think it's best and the way I've tested it, but sometimes life gets in the way, and one missing ingredient shouldn't stop you from making a dish.

METHOD   This is where everything comes together, where the list of seemingly random things becomes a dish. I've done my best to include as much detail as possible, especially in recipes that I think might trip you up (because they've tripped me or my cross-testers up at one point or another during testing). You'll also find notes on serving and storage in this section.

EATING WITH YOUR EYES

If you're anything like me, the way your food is presented makes a difference to whether or not you want to eat it. Naturally, I take this notion into consideration when recipe developing and cooking. I'll do small things to improve the visual of a recipe so it's more appealing to me and the people eating it; I imagine the finished dish and make adjustments accordingly.

In the hope of inspiring you to do the same, I've noted the principles I tend to consider when thinking about food from a visual perspective. Style is extremely subjective and, therefore, like human nature, is constantly changing and evolving. These principles don't *always* apply, and I won't *always* follow them, but I'll definitely think about them.

When it comes to styling (a plate, or even an outfit for that matter), my philosophy generally consists of these five elements:

USE BALANCE AND CONTRAST

Contrast in flavors helps to balance the flavors. In salad dressing, an acidic component exists to balance the fat, and vice versa. In desserts, adding some salt will balance the sweetness; not to overwhelm the sugar, but to make it really shine. There's something magical in balance and something interesting in the juxtaposition of balance and contrast. Consider the visual on An Iconic Chicken Pot Pie (page 90). The suggested vessel is a round, black cast-iron skillet; the beige puff pastry that sits on top offers contrast to the visible black handle, resulting in some color balance. The suggested shaping of the pastry, which is to lay it directly on top without trimming or crimping, allows the squared-off edges to remain—the rounded edges of the pan get interrupted by the sharp corners of the pastry, adding further contrast. I'd argue that because of these choices, this pot pie is a lot more interesting and dimensional to look at than your average pot pie.

CONSIDER PREPARATION

It might seem obvious, but beauty isn't just in the final product. Thinking about it through the process is essential for me. This is the time to consider quality. If I'm making a recipe with lots of fresh ingredients, I'll look for the nicest produce I can find—greens that look plump and hydrated, berries with a saturated exterior flesh, etc. And taking it a step further, when I prep the ingredients according to the listed mise, I'll take creative liberties to make something more interesting to look at. For example, a recipe might read "cucumber, chopped," and instead of simply just cutting it into rounds, I might opt for a roll cut, a technique that results in a more visually interesting shape with a pointed edge that contrasts the natural curve of the cucumber. This may or may not be necessary depending on the recipe and whether I want to relish its simplicity or attempt to be more decorative.

CHOOSING SERVEWARE

Deep bowls and foil trays might make things easy and fast, and believe me, I know there's a time and place for that, but they don't necessarily make things super beautiful. That's not to say they can't make things appealing—seeing food in such abundance can certainly be impactful and joyous (see Pasta Day Pasta, page 137). But when I'm down to do some extra dishes and have the time to care for aesthetics, using dishes that complement the color and texture of the food can make it look extra appetizing. If you're serving something super bitsy, made with lots of small things, it may not be the best idea to serve it in a vessel with a very intricate pattern, but if you're serving something one dimensional, it'll offer contrast and visual interest. If you're serving white rice, a white bowl or platter might make things look flat, and depending on what else you've got happening on the table, that's not ideal. Also consider what's happening around the dish. Are there other dishes being served? Take the concept of balance and contrast here and apply them similarly, mixing up the colors, sizes, and shapes accordingly.

ADD A FINISHING TOUCH

This probably reminds you of garnishing. I don't love that word. For some reason, when I picture a garnish, I see a singular sprig of parsley lying on top of something that does not actually have parsley in it at all. That should tell you exactly what I'm guided by when it comes to finishing: the ingredients that are actually in the recipe. Accompaniments are also great for sprucing up a dish's visual, without garnishing. Serving a big chunk of roast or a homogenous pot of haleem with a bunch of smaller dishes filled with things it'll taste good with is a great way to shift the focus off of just that one dish. I also like to consider the surface, especially with something like a salad. If and when possible, if there's an ingredient I should be able to see, I want to see it. There's usually olive oil and salt in my recipes—those are great finishers, too, adding a final sheen and a touch of texture. This is also something that can happen naturally in a recipe, if it's designed that way. Like the caramel in my Pineapples and Ghee (page 245). Instead of just making enough caramel to cook the pineapples, I increased the amount so there'd be some left for serving.

LOOSEN UP

Cliche, I know, but don't get caught up in seeking perfection—that's not fun—and instead seek interest. As with any art, make something worth looking at, for better or worse. Even after considering all of these "rules," at the end of the day, what you're making is yours, and it should look like it. Looking for inspiration is fine, but your natural instincts will take you where the dish needs to go, and honoring them will leave you with a dish that looks uniquely yours.

This is all part of how I approach food, and while I'm not solely guided by the way it looks, I'd be lying if I said I don't judge a recipe by its photo, even just a little.

ON FOOD AND FEELINGS

The cooking happening in cookbooks like this one is often portrayed in the most romanticized way. I love it. I wish I could cook from cookbooks every day, the way so many authors tell me to, and I hope that one day I can. But the reality is, while cooking is an activity I, and probably you since you're reading this, enjoy, it's also a necessity—in my case, for work, and in most cases, after work. As an everyday task, it's seldom an activity we can revolve our entire day around, even if we'd like to. And so when I cook not-for-work, I'm likely led by the way I'm feeling on any given day. Some days I'm more adventurous, have a few extra hours, or have mentally prepared myself to make something fun, but some days, I have twenty minutes and a bare fridge, and I'm far too exhausted to do all that much.

Below you'll find a framing of some of my favorite recipes in this book, reflective of the way we *really* cook, the way you'll likely end up using this book—guided by a mood and how much time is at your disposal to dedicate to cooking. And as far as the nostalgia category goes, that one's for me.

COZY	*perfect for cozying up with on the couch*	*< 30 minutes* *Under 1 hour* *1 to 2 hours* *2+ hours*	Udon Carbonara Spiced Chickpea Soup Banana Cake with Tahini Fudge Wali Ya Mboga, Sorta

---

LAZY	*for when very active cooking is the last thing you want to do*	*< 30 minutes* *Under 1 hour* *1 to 2 hours* *2+ hours*	One Pan(try) Pasta Tortellini en Preserved Lemon Brodo TGIF Artichoke Dip Spiced Short Ribs and Potatoes

CELEBRATORY	*best enjoyed with good company*	*< 30 minutes* *Under 1 hour* *1 to 2 hours* *2+ hours*	The Pink Drink Peppery Potato Pakoras (with caviar) Chocolate Cake with Chai Buttercream Farzana's Biryani
BORED	*something fun, when there's nothing else to do*	*< 30 minutes* *Under 1 hour* *1 to 2 hours* *2+ hours*	Za'atar and Maple Kettle Corn Chewy Ginger Cookies Chili Crisp Mall Cinnamon Rolls
AMBITIOUS	*up for a challenge, a project bake, or a multi-step meal*	*< 30 minutes* *Under 1 hour* *1 to 2 hours* *2+ hours*	Melon Sorbet Batata Vada (Kachori) Rumina's Kebabs and Coconut Chutney Samosas Two Ways
NOSTALGIC	*dishes that scratch an itch and remind me of home*	*< 30 minutes* *Under 1 hour* *1 to 2 hours* *2+ hours*	Achaar, Egg, and Cheese Pasta Day Pasta An Iconic Chicken Pot Pie Rishma's Pilau
ROMANTIC	*best by candlelight*	*< 30 minutes* *Under 1 hour* *1 to 2 hours* *2+ hours*	Gahwa Sundae Shawarma-Spiced Carrots Sungold and Saffron Spaghetti Spiced Short Ribs and Potatoes
CURIOUS	*hoping to try something new, maybe learn a new skill or flavor combination*	*< 30 minutes* *Under 1 hour* *1 to 2 hours* *2+ hours*	Carrot Sambharo Samosa-Spiced Burgers Jugu Scones with Butter and Jam Shenaz's Chicken Haleem

MOODY	*when you're craving a little escape*	< 30 minutes Under 1 hour 1 to 2 hours 2+ hours	Gochujang Tahini Noodles Red Curry Orzotto with Mushrooms and Peas Fruit and Nut Biscotti Ashraf's Baklava
GENEROUS	*for feeding a crowd*	< 30 minutes Under 1 hour 1 to 2 hours 2+ hours	Chevro Chips Grape and Fennel Salad Red, Hot Tandoori Wings Gully's Gajjar Chicken
PRACTICAL	*for a functional weeknight meal*	< 30 minutes Under 1 hour 1 to 2 hours 2+ hours	B-L-D Tomatoes and Eggs Thai-Style Crispy Salmon and Rice Halal Cart Salad Rishma's Pilau
CLASSICS	*finding comfort in familiar flavors*	< 30 minutes Under 1 hour 1 to 2 hours 2+ hours	A Great Tuna Melt Fish Fillet Salted Brown Butter Pecan Shortbread Coconut and Cardamom Cake
DEPLETED	*call a loved one or order takeout*		

HOST WITH THE MOST

Cooking a meal requires intention, time, and effort. That's why I'm a firm believer that cooking for yourself is one of the highest forms of self-care. That being said, over the years, I've come to realize there *is* something equally fulfilling about cooking for other people. As an act of nurture and care, we have a responsibility to one another as humans with the same basic needs (food being one of them).

In the following pages you'll find menu suggestions for occasions when you might find yourself hosting friends, family, loved ones, and strangers alike. They're more elaborate than what you might actually be willing to take on, but I think it's nice to have options so you can adjust each section to reflect how many people you're feeding and how much time you've got. I've prioritized flavor pairings and offered a few appetizer, main, and dessert recommendations for each. It's safe to say, though, that Karak Chai (page 256) has a place at every occasion.

If you're up for the task of executing these menus as suggested, first, yay! and second, planning is your friend. Assuming you'll be feeding a crowd, know your home kitchen can function akin to a restaurant if organized similarly. For me, that means I'll usually print all the recipes I plan to tackle, make a grocery list of everything I could need, shop my pantry and fridge first (crossing things off the list as I gather them). Then I'll purchase everything else I need to execute them about three days before I plan on hosting. After reading all the recipes, I'll rely on "do-aheads" and my intuition to break up preparing the mise en place (gathering of the prepped ingredients) for all the recipes among the coming days. Splitting up tasks over the course of a few days means on the day of, you're really just assembling and laying things out.

If you care for tablescaping, try to visualize how you'd like to see the dishes in their final form, as individual servings or family style, and pull dishes from your collection to support that vision (or head to the flea market or thrift store if that's in the cards; it's my favorite place to find unique serveware on a budget). Then, write the name of each dish on a Post-it note or tape and label the dishes. Arrange them where they're meant to go and in a way that's visually pleasing to you, and leave them be until it's time to plate up. This tried-and-true method has gotten me through hosting and making Thanksgiving dinner for twenty-plus people since I was fifteen years old.

TEATIME
a cute catchup

—

Cucumber and Chutney Sandwiches
Coronation Chicken Pastries
Salty Little Hearts
Gulzar's Sugar Puffs
Jugu Scones with Butter and Jam
Karak Chai

COCKTAIL EVENING
dress up to go nowhere

—

Peppery Potato Pakoras (with caviar)
Tarka Olives
Rumina's Kebabs and Coconut Chutney
Za'atar and Maple Kettle Corn
Chevro Chips
Chewy Ginger Cookies
Date and Dark Chocolate Cookies
Melon Sorbet
Ginger Lime Spritz
The Pink Drink
Karak Chai

FAMILY FEAST
family-style dinner party

—

Samosas Two Ways
Batata Vada (Kachori)
Lemony Cucumber Salad with Salted Yogurt
Coconutty Corn
Rishma's Pilau
Wali Ya Mboga, Sorta
Shenaz's Chicken Haleem
Shortcut Lemon Achaar
Date Chutney
Green Chutney
Chocolate Cake with Chai Buttercream
Ashraf's Baklava
Slightly Salty Mango Lassi
Karak Chai

BRUNCH
basically an excuse for breakfast in the afternoon

—

Peppery Potato Pakoras
Ashraf's Tomato Saag
Turkish-ish Eggs
Sukayna's Omelet
Green Eggs and Hummus
Coffee Cake Muffins
Fruit and Nut Biscotti
Pineapples and Ghee + Baklava Granola
A Different Date Shake
Karak Chai

A SUMMER AFFAIR
a warm-weather get-together

—

Hot and Sour Tomatoes
Summer on a Plate
Lemony, Herby Shrimpies
Tandoori Tacos
Preserved Limonata
Slightly Salty Mango Lassi
Melon Sorbet
Coconut and Cardamom Cake
Strawberry Delight

DATE NIGHT
make an impression

—

Shawarma-Spiced Carrots
Grape and Fennel Salad
Thai-Style Crispy Salmon and Rice
Spiced Short Ribs and Potatoes
Ginger Lime Spritz
Karak Chai
Gahwa Sundae
Date and Dark Chocolate Cookies

VEGETARIAN
a plant-based party

—

Coconutty Corn
Fruity Fattoush
Peppery Potato Pakoras
Tortellini en Preserved Lemon Brodo
Smashed Black Bean Burgers
Gochujang Tahini Noodles
Roasted Eggplant Sandwich
Weeknight Daal
Ginger Lime Spritz
Karak Chai
Coconut and Cardamom Cake
Salted Brown Butter Pecan Shortbread
Fruit and Nut Biscotti

MOVIE NIGHT
*in lieu of "game day," since
I'm not that into sports*

—

TGIF Artichoke Dip
Red, Hot Tandoori Wings
Za'atar and Maple Kettle Corn
Samosa-Spiced Burgers
Fish Fillet
Almond Mocha Blondies
Date and Dark Chocolate Cookies

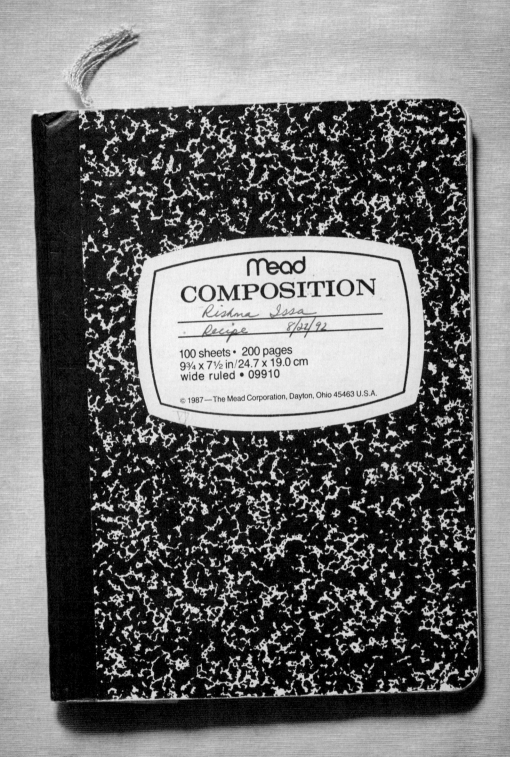

Date and Dark Chocolate Cookies (230)

START SMALL

(40–83)

Appetizers, snacks, and light bites

BATATA VADA (KACHORI)

Makes 25
1 hour

FOR THE FILLING

5 medium russet potatoes (about 2½ pounds/1.15 kg), peeled

1 tablespoon olive oil*

¾ teaspoon black mustard seeds

1 small yellow onion,* finely diced

1 green bird's-eye chili,* halved lengthwise

2 garlic cloves, finely grated

5 to 8 curry leaves, depending on size

3 to 4 tablespoons fresh lemon juice, from 1 lemon

½ teaspoon ground turmeric

¼ teaspoon Kashmiri red chili powder*

1 tablespoon Diamond Crystal kosher salt

FOR THE BATTER

⅔ cup (60 g) chickpea flour, plus more as needed

¼ teaspoon Diamond Crystal kosher salt

⅛ teaspoon Kashmiri red chili powder,* optional

Vegetable oil, for frying

Green Chutney (page 196), for serving

*INSTEAD OF...

Olive oil, use vegetable oil

Yellow onion, use red onion or spring onion

Green bird's-eye chili, use 1 jalapeño or serrano chili

Kashmiri red chili powder, use a pinch of cayenne or Indian red chili powder

Batata vada, meaning "potato fritters," are lemony, spiced mashed potato balls, lightly battered and fried. Pronounced "ba-tay-ta wa-ra," although referenced in my household as *kachori* (a Zanzibari tradition), these potato fritters are a family favorite. My dad loves these cute little round snacks so much, he used the name *kachori* as a term of endearment for my siblings and me when we were young (think honey or sweetheart, but savory).

Interestingly enough, these aren't traditional kachoris as they would be found in India (similar visually, but entirely different in taste and texture). No one's quite sure why Zanzibaris refer to batata vada as kachori, but here we are. In Mumbai, you'll find sandwiches made with these guys as the patty, known as *vada pav* ("fritter bread" in Hindi) served with sweet and sour tamarind chutney (similar to the Date Chutney on page 195), Green Chutney (page 196), and batter-dipped and fried green chilis. A tasty combo for sure, and you should definitely try them, but the fritter itself is delicious as is.

P.S. They're gluten-free.

METHOD

To make the filling: Bring a large pot of water to a rapid boil over high heat. Add the potatoes and boil until fully cooked and fork tender, about 25 minutes.

Meanwhile, heat the olive oil in a small saucepan over medium-high heat. Add the mustard seeds and cover. After about 1 minute, the mustard seeds will begin to pop. Remove from the heat and carefully stir in the onion, chili, garlic, and curry leaves. Return to the heat and cook, stirring frequently, until the onions are translucent, 2 to 3 minutes. Stir in the lemon juice, turmeric, and chili powder and cook until the spices are fragrant, about 1 minute. Remove from the heat and set aside.

Transfer the cooked potatoes to a medium bowl and smash them using a fork or potato masher. There should be a few bigger pieces and some that are entirely mashed. Add the spice mixture and salt. Using a rubber spatula or your hands, mix until the potatoes are evenly coated in the spice mixture. You can discard the curry leaves and chili, if you'd like; I usually keep them in.

Separate the potato mixture evenly into 3 tablespoon-sized portions and roll each portion into balls using your palms, making sure to tightly pack the potatoes to prevent breaking while frying.

Prepare the chickpea flour batter: In a small deep bowl, stir together the chickpea flour, ⅔ cup (160 ml) water, salt, and chili powder, if using, until well combined. The batter should be looser than pancake batter but slightly thicker than crepe batter. Use more water or chickpea flour as needed to achieve that texture.

Heat 4 to 6 inches of vegetable oil in a large pot or high-sided skillet over high heat or until it reaches somewhere between 350 and 400°F (175 and 205°C); you can test this by dribbling in a teaspoon or so of the batter—it should quickly float to the surface. Drop the potato rounds into the batter to evenly coat. Remove them using a fork or between your fingers to drain off excess batter, then place them directly into the hot oil, making sure not to overcrowd. Fry until light golden, 1 to 2 minutes, flipping halfway if needed so all sides are even in color. Use a slotted spoon or spider to remove the kachoris from the hot oil and place them on a paper towel–lined plate to drain excess oil. Serve immediately with green chutney.

Store leftovers in an airtight container in the refrigerator for up to 7 days. Reheat in a toaster oven, or in the microwave in 30-second bursts.

CHEVRO CHIPS

Serves 2 to 4
30 minutes

1 (8-ounce/224 g) bag salted Cape Cod Kettle Cooked Potato Chips*

3 tablespoons vegetable oil*

1 green bird's-eye chili,* thinly sliced

14 fresh curry leaves, from 2 sprigs

1 teaspoon fennel seeds

2 teaspoons coriander seeds

5 whole cloves

1 teaspoon black mustard seeds

¾ teaspoon ground turmeric

½ teaspoon Kashmiri red chili powder*

Diamond Crystal kosher salt

¼ teaspoon citric acid,* plus more as needed, optional

1 teaspoon sugar, plus more as needed

*INSTEAD OF . . .

Cape Cod–brand potato chips, use any salted kettle-cooked variety

Vegetable oil, use any neutral, flavorless oil

Green bird's-eye chili, use 1 jalapeño or serrano chili, or ½ teaspoon more chili powder

Kashmiri red chili powder, use another green chili or ¼ teaspoon cayenne

Citric acid, use a squeeze of lemon juice just before serving

A popular South Asian snack, chevro (or chewra) is made up of lots of crunchy fried bits and bobs tossed in a turmeric-stained, whole spice-infused oil. Essentially, it's a savory fried trail mix.

Making traditional chevro is too involved a process to be casual, so if you're taking the time to make it, you're making it to share it. When I think of chevro, I immediately picture my mom, my grandmother, and her sister gathered around a large stainless-steel pot (it's giving Sanderson sisters), frying and seasoning each individual component in bulk during my sisters' weddings. It's perfect and necessary to have on hand in the house as a snack for peckish guests.

Among all the different lentils and grains that are fried and added to traditional chevro, my grandmother would include a bag of kettle-cooked potato chips. In every gallon-sized zip-top bag filled with chevro, there were only a handful of potato chips. As the best ingredient in the mix, I would shuffle through the bag, find them, eat them all, and put the bag right back in the pantry, uninterested in anything other than those ultra-crunchy, flavorful chips.

Now I keep gallon-sized bags of just the seasoned chips in my pantry, and you should, too.

METHOD

Empty the potato chips into a large bowl.

Heat the vegetable oil in a small pot over medium heat. Add the chili, curry leaves, fennel seeds, coriander seeds, cloves, and mustard seeds. Swirl to coat, cover, and cook until the mustard seeds have stopped popping, about 2 minutes. Remove from the heat and add the turmeric, chili powder, salt, and citric acid, if using. Stir to combine and pour over the chips. Sprinkle with the sugar and toss vigorously to coat the chips in the spiced oil and chilis. Taste and add more salt, sugar, and/or citric acid to your preference. Let stand until completely cooled and the chips have absorbed the oil, about 15 minutes.

Store in an airtight bag or container for up to 1 month.

START SMALL

COCONUTTY CORN

Serves 2 to 4
25 minutes

1 (10-ounce/284 g) bag frozen sweet corn kernels*

2 jalapeños,* halved lengthwise, seeds removed for low spice tolerance

½ teaspoon ground turmeric

1¾ teaspoons Diamond Crystal kosher salt

1 (13.5-ounce/398 ml) can full-fat coconut milk

1 tablespoon fresh lemon juice,* from about ½ lemon

¼ cup (10 g) roughly chopped fresh cilantro leaves and tender stems*

*INSTEAD OF...
Frozen sweet corn kernels, use 3 ears fresh corn on the cob (1½ pounds/680 g), cut into 1½-inch segments (you can also use frozen corn on the cob segments or one 11 to 15-ounce [310 to 430 g] can sweet corn kernels, drained)

Jalapeño, use 2 or 3 green bird's-eye chilis or ⅛ teaspoon cayenne pepper

Lemon juice, use lime juice

Cilantro, use ⅛ teaspoon ground coriander, to be added with the turmeric

This side dish—perfect for your next barbecue—is inspired by makai paka, a classic East African dish made with corn (*makai* in Swahili) and a turmeric-spiced coconut curry (*paka* in Swahili). Traditionally made with corn on the cob segments that require butcher-level skill to cut, this version keeps things simpler and less dangerous by relying on a humble bag of frozen corn. Try to buy organic, high-quality corn to avoid that spongy texture cooked frozen corn often has. As with all minimal recipes, ingredients matter.

Instead of the traditional bird's-eye chilis for heat, I opted for halved jalapeños that braise in the coconut milk alongside the corn to impart heat and add an unexpected element of texture (don't discard these; they're my favorite part).

Reserving the herbs and lemon juice for finishing keeps the flavors bright, but otherwise the magic happens all together in one pot.

METHOD
Transfer the corn kernels to a medium pot with a lid. Top with the jalapeños, turmeric, and salt, then pour in the coconut milk. Cover and bring to a simmer over medium heat. Cook for 18 to 25 minutes, stirring halfway through, until the coconut sauce has thickened but is still saucy and the corn is tender. If using corn on the cob segments, flip the pieces of corn halfway through to ensure even cooking. Remove from the heat and stir in the lemon juice and cilantro. Serve warm or at room temperature.

START SMALL 45

CORONATION CHICKEN PASTRIES

Makes 18
1 hour 15 minutes

3 scallions,* thinly sliced
3 cups (585 g) shredded cooked chicken
⅓ cup (75 ml) mayonnaise
½ cup (70 g) dried cranberries, chopped *
2 tablespoons Dijon mustard*
2 tablespoons extra virgin olive oil
1 tablespoon curry powder
1 (17.3-ounce/490 g) package frozen puff pastry, thawed
All-purpose flour, for the work surface
1 large egg,* beaten
Flaky sea salt

*INSTEAD OF...
Scallions, use 1 small red onion
Cranberries, use dried cherries or raisins
Dijon mustard, use whole-grain mustard
Egg, use heavy cream

A fascination with the British royal family is just something innate in most South Asian families. Like many others of her time, my grandmother's captivation with Diana, Princess of Wales, introduced me to English traditions, the monarchy, and the inspiration for this dish.

As its name suggests, the chicken salad filling for these pastries is influenced by the dish served at Queen Elizabeth II's coronation luncheon. The signature creamy curry base remains true to the classic, but the addition of dried cranberries gives this filling a unique sweet bite to balance the spicy tanginess. While typically used to make sandwiches (which you can and should do, too), baking this chicken salad filling in a flaky, buttery puff pastry hand pie (referred to by Brits as a *pasty*) results in a perfect snack for entertaining, a picnic lunch, or even a full-on dinner.

METHOD

Place racks in the upper and lower thirds of the oven and preheat to 375°F (190°C). Line 2 baking sheets with parchment paper.

Place the scallions, shredded chicken, mayonnaise, dried cranberries, and mustard in a medium bowl and set aside.

Heat the olive oil and curry powder in a small skillet over medium heat, stirring often, until foaming and fragrant, 30 to 60 seconds. Pour the oil into the bowl with the chicken and mix well.

Working with one sheet at a time on a lightly floured surface, unfold the thawed puff pastry and roll out to a 12 × 12-inch square. Cut it into nine 4 × 4-inch squares with a knife.

Place a heaping 1 tablespoon of filling in the bottom corner of a square. Press down on the filling to spread it out, making sure to leave a ¼-inch border around the edges. Fold the dough in half on a diagonal up and over the filling to make a triangle, then lightly pinch the edges together to seal. Crimp the edges with a fork, then cut 3 slits across the top. Repeat this process with the remaining pastry squares and filling.

Transfer the pastries to the prepared baking sheets, spacing them about 1 inch apart. Brush the tops with the beaten egg and sprinkle with salt. Bake, rotating the baking sheets top to bottom and front to back halfway through, until golden brown and puffed, 30 to 35 minutes. Let the pastries cool slightly before serving.

Do-ahead: The pastries (without egg and sea salt) can be assembled up to 3 months ahead. Freeze on baking sheets until the pastry is solid, about 45 minutes, then transfer them to resealable plastic bags or stack in airtight containers between sheets of parchment paper. Brush with egg and sprinkle with salt, then bake for 35 to 40 minutes.

CUCUMBER AND CHUTNEY SANDWICHES

Makes 4 sandwiches
30 minutes

FOR THE CHUTNEY

1 medium bunch cilantro, leaves and tender stems, coarsely chopped*

1 jalapeño,* stem removed

2 garlic cloves

3 tablespoons fresh lemon juice, from 1 to 2 lemons

1 teaspoon extra-virgin olive oil

1 teaspoon Diamond Crystal kosher salt, plus more as needed

FOR ASSEMBLY

½ cup (115 g) whipped cream cheese,* divided

8 (½-inch-thick) slices white sandwich bread, such as Pullman, crusts removed if desired

1 English hothouse cucumber, sliced

Diamond Crystal kosher salt

*INSTEAD OF...

Cilantro, use any tender-stem herbs, like basil, mint, or parsley

Jalapeño, use 1 to 2 green bird's-eye chilis

Whipped cream cheese, use cream cheese (at room temperature)

On its own, a spoonful of green chutney's lemony, herbaceous flavor makes the glands behind my jaw tighten in the best way, but as an accompaniment or ingredient in a dressing or marinade, it adds brightness and flair. Case in point: this popular South Asian take on a basic teatime cucumber sandwich. Green chutney gets slathered onto a slice of fluffy white bread, topping another slice of bread with salted cucumber and tangy cream cheese. I like using whipped cream cheese because it spreads easily straight from the fridge without tearing the bread. Oh, and if you've inherited the "cilantro tastes like soap" gene, swap it for another tender herb, or a blend of tender herbs.

METHOD

To make the chutney: Combine the cilantro, jalapeño, garlic, lemon juice, olive oil, and salt in a blender and blend until smooth.

To assemble the sandwiches: Spread 2 tablespoons cream cheese over 1 slice bread and top with an even layer of cucumber slices (4 to 6 slices). Season with salt. Spread 2 tablespoons cilantro chutney over the second slice of bread. Close the sandwich and cut it in half. Repeat for the remaining 3 sandwiches. Store any remaining chutney in the refrigerator for up to 1 week.

FRUITY FATTOUSH

Serves 2 to 4
30 minutes

FOR THE DRESSING

¼ cup (60 ml) fresh lemon juice, from 1 to 2 lemons

2 tablespoons extra virgin olive oil, plus more as needed

2 tablespoons pomegranate molasses*

1 garlic clove, finely grated

1 teaspoon sumac*

1 teaspoon Diamond Crystal kosher salt

Freshly cracked black pepper

FOR ASSEMBLY

2 tablespoons roughly torn fresh mint leaves*

2 scallions, thinly sliced

2 large red radishes, chopped

½ cup (4 ounces/100 g) heirloom or cherry tomatoes, halved or quartered

1 mini Persian cucumber, halved lengthwise and sliced into ¼-inch-thick half moons

1 large head romaine lettuce (10 to 12 ounces/280 to 340 g),* chopped

1 cup (145 g) strawberries,* hulled and chopped

1 cup (60 g) salted pita chips

*INSTEAD OF . . .

Pomegranate molasses, use good-quality, thick balsamic vinegar

Sumac, use the zest of 1 lemon

Mint, use any tender-stem herbs, like basil, cilantro, or parsley

Romaine lettuce, use other crisp greens

Strawberries, use any other ripe, in-season fruit, like pomegranate, papaya, mango, grapes, peaches, or persimmon

A Levantine classic, fattoush is a truly craveable salad. It's refreshing and tangy thanks to a combination of three tart elements: pomegranate molasses, sumac, and lemon juice. It's traditionally made with freshly fried pita scraps, but I use packaged pita chips to keep things fast and easy. Another atypical addition: strawberries (or any ripe in-season fruit I have on hand) for a sweet contrast to the tangy dressing. It's very riff-friendly, so use this ingredient list as a guideline and substitute whatever crunchy veg, herbs, and fruit you're trying to use up. And, if you're not a fruit-in-salad person, you can skip the strawberries and be left with a fairly traditional fattoush.

METHOD

To make the dressing: Combine the lemon juice, olive oil, pomegranate molasses, garlic, sumac, salt, and a few turns of the peppermill in a large bowl. Taste and adjust to your preference. If it's punchier than you prefer, add an extra tablespoon or so of olive oil.

To assemble: Tilt the bowl to coat the sides with the dressing. Add the mint, scallions, radishes, tomatoes, cucumber, lettuce, strawberries, and pita chips to the bowl. Toss to coat and serve immediately.

GRAPE AND FENNEL SALAD

Serves 6 to 8
1 hour

7 ounces (200 g) stale sourdough bread, torn into 1-inch pieces

⅓ cup (75 ml) plus 2 tablespoons olive oil, divided

½ teaspoon Diamond Crystal kosher salt, plus more for the croutons

Freshly cracked black pepper

¼ cup (60 ml) fresh lemon juice, from 1 to 2 lemons

1 tablespoon red wine vinegar*

1 tablespoon maple syrup

1 tablespoon Dijon mustard

10 ounces (280 g) spring mix lettuces*

1 medium (5-ounce/140 g) fennel bulb, very thinly sliced

1 small red onion, very thinly sliced

2 cups (300 g) red or green seedless grapes,* halved or quartered depending on size

2 ounces (55 g) white cheddar cheese,* shaved

7 pickled pepperoncini,* whole or very roughly chopped

2 ounces (55 g) beef salami,* thinly sliced, optional

*INSTEAD OF...

Red wine vinegar, use another tablespoon of Dijon mustard

Spring mix lettuces, use torn kale or radicchio

Grapes, use apples, pears, roasted sweet potato, or roasted squash

White cheddar, use Parmesan, Gorgonzola, or another type of blue cheese

Pickled pepperoncini, use pitted Castelvetrano or mixed marinated olives

Beef salami, use any salty cured meat

It took me way too long to hop aboard the fennel train. I was mildly traumatized by the overpoweringly fragrant bite of saunf mouth freshener, a South Asian fennel seed–based candy, and I mistakenly judged the fresh vegetable against the pungency of its dry seeds and assumed it would be just as strong. It's not. In fact, it's a pleasant addition to soups and salads, imparting a surprisingly (to literally just me) delicate anise flavor that works really well in savory applications.

Here, it graces a salad made with a punchy maple and mustard vinaigrette and a medley of ingredients I'll often gather together for a snack plate. This salad is much more wholesome than that, and if you absolutely need meat for it to feel like a full meal, salami or a different salty, cured meat would be a welcome addition. I'll also switch up the leafy green and fruit I use depending on what's available and in season. Kale and apples are a favorite alternative of mine in the fall (massage the de-ribbed kale well with half of the dressing before assembling the salad).

This recipe does serve quite a few people; if you're making a salad this elaborate and flavorful, I feel like it should, but it can easily be scaled down if you're serving a more modest number.

And as with any dressing recipe, if you know you like a lot, double it. To be honest, it's so good, I'd double it regardless just to have it on hand in the fridge.

METHOD

Preheat the oven to 400°F (205°C).

Put the torn bread on a baking sheet and drizzle with 2 tablespoons of the olive oil. Season with an even sprinkle of salt and pepper and toss to coat. Arrange on a single layer on the sheet. Bake until golden and crisp, 8 to 10 minutes.

Meanwhile, in a large jar with a lid or a medium bowl with a whisk, combine the remaining ⅓ cup (75 ml) olive oil, the lemon juice, vinegar, maple syrup, mustard, salt, and lots of pepper. Shake or mix until well combined.

Arrange half the spring mix on a large platter in an even layer or in a large bowl. Top with half of the fennel, red onion, grapes, cheese, pepperoncini, and salami, if using. Repeat with the remaining spring mix, fennel, red onion, grapes, cheese, pepperoncini, and salami. This process helps ensure even distribution of the toppings when mixing later. Top with the croutons and drizzle with the dressing. Toss to combine and serve immediately.

START SMALL 53

GYOZA WITH GARLICKY LABNEH AND CHILI BUTTER

Serves 4 to 6
30 minutes

FOR THE GARLICKY LABNEH
1 cup (240 ml) labneh*
2 garlic cloves, finely grated
1 teaspoon Diamond Crystal kosher salt, plus more as needed

FOR ASSEMBLY
2 tablespoons pine nuts*
2 tablespoons olive oil, divided
24 store-bought or homemade beef, chicken, or vegetable gyoza

FOR THE CHILI BUTTER AND ASSEMBLY
¼ cup (½ stick/55 g) unsalted butter*
1 teaspoon Aleppo chili flakes*
½ teaspoon ground cumin
¼ teaspoon smoked paprika*
¼ teaspoon Diamond Crystal kosher salt
1 bunch Tuscan kale,* ribs and stems removed, leaves torn
2 tablespoons torn mint leaves*

*INSTEAD OF . . .
Labneh, use plain whole-milk Greek yogurt
Pine nuts, use chopped walnuts
Unsalted butter, use ¼ cup (60 ml) olive oil
Aleppo chili flakes, use an additional ¾ teaspoon paprika plus ¼ teaspoon cayenne pepper
Smoked paprika, use regular paprika
Kale, use Swiss chard, collard greens, or spinach
Mint, use dill

At one of my favorite restaurants in the world, Dubai's Orfali Bros, Syrian chef and restaurateur Mohammad Orfali reimagines the classic Levantine dish shish barak (beef dumplings in spiced yogurt sauce) as wagyu dumplings served over seasoned yogurt and topped with a spicy oil rendered from sujuk sausage.

Inspired by his riff, I created a version of my own using a similar treatment, turning store-bought gyoza into a simple and spectacular weeknight-friendly dish. I kept the garlicky labneh, added greens to make this feel like a complete dinner, and opted for melted butter infused with mild chili flakes, smoked paprika, and cumin to add a rich, flavorful finish.

While I typically think of gyoza as an appetizer, this dish can stand on its own as a main course as well. Just adjust the serving size to account for about eight dumplings per person.

METHOD

To make the garlicky labneh: Combine the labneh, garlic, salt, and 1 tablespoon water in a small bowl. Spread the mixture onto a platter and set aside.

Toast the pine nuts in a large dry skillet over medium heat, tossing occasionally, until golden brown, about 3 minutes. Transfer to a small bowl and leave to cool.

In the same skillet, heat 1 tablespoon of the olive oil. Working in two batches, cook 12 gyoza at a time in a single layer, undisturbed, until golden underneath, about 2 minutes. Pour 3 tablespoons water into the skillet, quickly cover, and steam until the gyoza are cooked through and deep golden brown on the bottom, about 3 minutes. Transfer the gyoza to the reserved platter with the labneh mixture. Repeat with the remaining 1 tablespoon olive oil and 12 gyoza, and an additional 3 tablespoons water.

To make the chili butter: Reduce the heat to low and melt the butter in the same skillet. Add the chili flakes, cumin, paprika, and salt and cook, swirling the pan, until fragrant, about 30 seconds. Pour half of the chili butter into a small bowl and set aside.

Add the kale to the pan with the remaining chili butter. Season with a pinch of salt and 2 tablespoons water. Cook, stirring occasionally, until the kale is wilted, about 2 minutes. Top the gyoza with the wilted kale.

Spoon the reserved chili butter over the top and scatter with the toasted pine nuts and torn mint leaves. Serve immediately.

HERBY, GARLICKY PASTA SALAD

Serves 6
35 minutes

- 2 teaspoons Diamond Crystal kosher salt, plus more for boiling the pasta
- 2 cups (100 g) mixed herbs, ideally a combination of mint, dill, and parsley,* chopped
- ¼ cup (40 g) pitted kalamata or Castelvetrano olives, roughly chopped
- 2 cups (1 pint/290 g) cherry tomatoes, halved
- ⅔ cup (165 ml) extra virgin olive oil
- 8 garlic cloves, roughly chopped
- 2 tablespoons za'atar*
- 1 teaspoon red pepper flakes
- 1 pound (455 g) dry fusilli or rotini pasta*
- 3 tablespoons red wine vinegar
- 1 teaspoon honey,* plus more as needed
- 1 (7-ounce/200 g) block feta cheese, crumbled

*INSTEAD OF...
Herbs, use arugula
Za'atar, use 2 teaspoons dried oregano plus ½ teaspoon sesame seeds and ½ teaspoon sumac
Fusilli, use any other short pasta good for pasta salad
Honey, use maple syrup

One of the last vacations we took as a family of six (before my sisters got married) was to Greece, a trip I remember with the fondest nostalgia—partially for the free vacation, but mostly for the authentic Greek salad. I had never tasted something so simple and so delicious before. Culturally, I was accustomed to more elaborate dishes, so the idea that something had an ingredient list I could count on one hand and still be so delicious was foreign to me, an experience that exposed me to the world of quality ingredients and their importance in achieving a great final dish.

Borrowing from the ethos of a Greek salad, this pasta salad is similarly bright and simple and perfect for a sweltering summer day. Now, I wouldn't usually tamper with a concept so pure in its original form (a task rarely executed with success), but if there ever was a right way to interfere with the otherwise perfect Greek salad, this pasta salad is the one.

Instead of the traditional dried oregano that usually sits atop a whole block of feta, I opted for flavorful za'atar, a Palestinian herb blend featuring bible hyssop (akin to dried oregano), along with sumac, sesame seeds, and sometimes salt. Infusing the olive oil with garlic, and then using that hot oil to toast the spices and take the raw edge off the tomatoes, allows the flavors to come through strong enough to stand up to a hearty pasta. As with all simple, fresh dishes, be sure to use good-quality ingredients—because there aren't many, you really *will* be able to taste the difference.

P.S. If you put the pot of water to boil while you prepare everything else, this pasta salad will come together in the time it takes to cook the pasta.

METHOD

Set a large pot of salted water over high heat and bring to a boil.

Meanwhile, combine the herbs, olives, and tomatoes in a large heatproof bowl.

Combine the olive oil and garlic in a small pot or skillet. Set over medium heat and cook, swirling occasionally, until the garlic is golden around the edges. Add the za'atar and red pepper flakes and cook, swirling the pot, until fragrant, about 30 seconds. Remove from the heat and pour the hot oil over the herbs, olives, and tomatoes. Let stand undisturbed for 5 minutes to allow the oil to soften the tomatoes.

Meanwhile, cook the pasta according to the package directions to al dente, anywhere from 6 to 10 minutes for fusilli and 8 to 10 minutes for rotini, and drain.

Return to the tomatoes. Add the vinegar, honey, and salt and stir to combine. Use the back of the spoon to encourage some of the tomatoes to burst. Taste the dressing and adjust it to your preference. Depending on the quality of your tomatoes and the season, you may need to add another teaspoon of honey to balance the flavors.

Transfer the pasta to the dressing, toss to combine, and finish with the cheese.

Serve warm, cold, or at room temperature. Store leftovers in an airtight container for up to 2 days.

HOT AND SOUR TOMATOES

Serves 4
20 minutes

18 ounces (505 g) mixed heirloom tomatoes, larger ones thinly sliced, smaller ones halved

Flaky sea salt

1 large lime*

2 tablespoons capers, drained

2 tablespoons Chili Crisp, homemade (page 192) or store-bought

2 tablespoons extra virgin olive oil

Crusty bread, for serving

*INSTEAD OF...
Lime, use ½ large lemon

It was early June and I was dining at Early June, a quaint, walk-in-only restaurant in Paris's charming 10th arr. It was 8:30 p.m. but bright as day—the energy was just right. The restaurant was hosting a pop-up menu for Belly, a British restaurant, which was surprisingly flexible in accommodating my dietary restrictions, unlike my previous experiences with pop-ups. Our entire meal was perfect: from the spicy, juicy tomato and burrata appetizer (that inspired this) down to the strawberry granita we had for dessert. I think about that entire experience often, wishing I had eaten more, and more specifically wondering why we didn't order another one of their unreal tomato appetizers.

Considering the fleeting nature of pop-ups, I resorted to trying to make a version of my own to re-create that idyllic summer experience. Similarly spicy, bright, tangy, and salty, I decided I didn't miss the ball of burrata cheese it was originally served with (shocking, I know), but if the idea of it piques your interest, please do add it (an 8-ounce/225 g ball should do the trick).

METHOD

Arrange the tomatoes evenly on a platter, cut side up. Sprinkle generously with salt. Set aside for 5 to 10 minutes to allow the tomatoes to release some of their juices. Roll the lime on the countertop and zest it over the tomatoes. Halve and squeeze the lime juice over the top. Scatter the capers over the top and drizzle with the chili crisp and olive oil. Serve with crusty bread for dipping.

LEMONY CUCUMBER SALAD WITH SALTED YOGURT

Serves 2 to 4
20 minutes

- 1 cup (240 ml) plain whole-milk yogurt
- 1¾ teaspoons Diamond Crystal kosher salt, divided
- 1 lemon,* zested and juiced (about ¼ cup/60 ml juice)
- 1 green bird's-eye chili,* halved lengthwise
- 2 tablespoons extra virgin olive oil
- 4 mini cucumbers* (12 ounces/ 340 g), sliced into 1½-inch pieces
- 1 cup (145 g) cherry tomatoes, halved or quartered depending on the size
- ½ cup (55 g) sliced red onion

*INSTEAD OF...
Lemon, use lime
Bird's-eye chili, use jalapeño or lots of black pepper
Cucumbers, use another crunchy raw or roasted veg

A zesty combination of two necessary accompaniments to most of the food I grew up eating: kachumber and salted yogurt. Kachumber is an acidic side salad, usually made with vinegar or lemon juice, onions, tomatoes, sometimes cucumbers, and always chilis. And salted yogurt is, well, salted yogurt. Here they're served together as a crunchy, creamy, cool salad that's as good on its own as it is with biryani or roast chicken.

METHOD

In a small bowl, whisk the yogurt with 1 teaspoon of the salt. Spread the mixture over the bottom of a shallow platter.

In a medium bowl, combine the lemon zest and juice, chili, olive oil, and the remaining ¾ teaspoon salt. Add the cucumbers, tomatoes, and onion to the dressing and toss to coat. Spoon over the yogurt mixture and serve immediately.

ZA'ATAR AND MAPLE KETTLE CORN

Serves 4
10 minutes

4 teaspoons ghee*
½ cup (100 g) popcorn kernels
3 tablespoons pure maple syrup
2 teaspoons za'atar*
1 teaspoon Aleppo chili flakes*
1 teaspoon Diamond Crystal kosher salt

*INSTEAD OF...
Ghee, use vegetable oil
Za'atar, use a mix of 1 teaspoon oregano, ½ teaspoon sumac, and ½ teaspoon sesame seeds
Aleppo chili flakes, use Kashmiri red chili powder, urfa chili, silk chili, or ½ teaspoon red pepper flakes

When I was growing up, Friday night was family movie night, and I was always on popcorn duty. I'd stand in front of the microwave watching the paper bag unfold as it inflated, delighting in the sound of popping kernels, removing the bag and shaking it up to cool off, and pulling the corners to release the steam before dividing it between steel mixing bowls.

We were a split household, some preferring sweet-and-salty kettle corn and some die-hard salted butter fans. I sat in the latter camp until the night we ran out of butter popcorn packs. I skeptically grabbed a handful of kettle corn and surprisingly enjoyed it—sweet, salty popcorn reigned supreme.

This maple-za'atar kettle corn is that and more, featuring savory, herby za'atar; fruity, spicy Aleppo chili flakes; and maple syrup for an earthy sweetness. I like to pop the popcorn in ghee, which imparts a buttery flavor, without the burnable milk solids whole butter possesses. You can swap out the za'atar for another herb medley or spice blend, but it offers a tangy, herbal flavor that I absolutely adore.

This might not be as easy as microwave popcorn, but it's certainly more flavorful.

METHOD

Melt the ghee in a large, lightweight pot with a lid (something you'd feel comfortable lifting and shaking around easily) over medium-high heat. Make sure the entire bottom of the pan is coated in the ghee.

Add a few popcorn kernels. As soon as they begin to pop, add the remaining kernels, cover, and cook, vigorously shaking the pot over the heat to keep the kernels moving so they don't burn, until they begin to pop. Remove the lid and drizzle in the maple syrup. Cover the pot and continue to cook the popcorn, shaking the pot, until most of the kernels have popped and the rate of popping has significantly slowed (you should hear only an occasional pop), about 4 minutes. Don't worry if all the kernels don't pop.

Carefully transfer the popcorn to a large bowl and sprinkle the za'atar, chili flakes, and salt over the top. Toss the popcorn with a wooden spoon to coat.

Do-ahead: Kettle corn can be made 5 days ahead. Store in an airtight bag at room temperature.

PEPPERY POTATO PAKORAS

Serves 2 to 4
45 minutes

2 large russet potatoes (1 pound/455 g), peeled

1 small yellow onion, thinly sliced

1½ teaspoons Diamond Crystal kosher salt

Freshly cracked black pepper

½ cup (45 g) chickpea flour

1 teaspoon baking powder

Vegetable oil, for frying

Flaky sea salt

Sour cream,* for serving

Fresh chives,* chopped, for serving

Fried eggs, for serving, optional

Caviar, for serving, optional

*INSTEAD OF...

Sour cream, use creme fraîche or Greek yogurt

Chives, use dill

Our customary Saturday breakfast spread always featured a big bowl of deep-fried, cubed russet potatoes, tossed with salt and tons of cracked black pepper, known as mari wara batata (Gujarati for "potatoes with pepper"). So tasty served alongside fried eggs, toast, and Ashraf's Tomato Saag (page 94), no matter how many potatoes my mom employed to cook up that dish, it was never enough. As a big fan of this combo, for my peppery potato pakoras, I highlighted the flavors of that appetizing breakfast dish but borrowed on the method of pakoras and the visual of a latke.

If you ask me, South Asian pakoras are a sleeper hit in the world of fritters, and the use of chickpea flour and the natural juices from whatever veg you're pakora-ing as the binder is a genius technique. No need to over-obsess over removing all the moisture from the potato and then introduce a binder in the form of eggs. Here, some of the starchy potato juice hydrates the chickpea flour just enough to allow everything to hold together. In the spirit of traditional vegetable pakora and latkes, a little onion joins the mix, adding a savory sweetness that's familiar to the world of breakfast potatoes.

Thanks to the natural starch in potatoes, baking powder, and chickpea flour, you'll be left with pakoras that have surprisingly crispy, crunchy, craggy edges. Serve with eggs for a brunchy vibe or with caviar for a fancy little snack.

METHOD

Cover a cutting board with a tea towel and, using a box grater, grate the potatoes over it, holding the potatoes vertically adjacent to the grater as much as possible, so the strands of potato are long. Gather the ends of the tea towel and squeeze the potatoes tightly over the sink to expel excess moisture. No need to overdo it here—one good squeeze is enough. Transfer the shredded potatoes to a bowl along with the onion, kosher salt, and lots of pepper. Add the chickpea flour and baking powder and stir to combine. The potato mixture should hold together when squeezed—if it doesn't, let it stand for 5 minutes and mix again.

Meanwhile, pour oil into a large cast-iron pan to come about ¼ inch up the sides and heat over medium heat. Once shimmering, use a large ice-cream scoop or a ⅓-cup (75 ml) measuring cup to portion out the potato mixture. Working in batches of 3 or 4, drop each portion into the oil and use the back of the scoop or a spatula to press the mixture into a patty with lots of scraggly edges. Cook, flipping halfway through, until deep golden brown and crispy around the edges, 4 to 6 minutes per side. Transfer to a paper towel–lined plate and sprinkle with flaky salt. Repeat with the remaining mixture.

Finish with sour cream and chives, and serve with eggs and caviar, if using.

Rumina's KEBABS AND COCONUT CHUTNEY

Makes about 35
1 hour 30 minutes

FOR THE COCONUT CHUTNEY

1 cup (180 g) grated frozen coconut, preferably Goya brand

½ cup (15 g) fresh cilantro, tender stems and leaves

4 green bird's-eye chilis, stems removed

1 teaspoon Diamond Crystal kosher salt, plus more as needed

1 cup (240 ml) warm water, plus more as needed

2½ tablespoons fresh lemon juice (from 1 to 2 lemons), plus more as needed

FOR THE KEBABS

1 pound (455 g) Italian bread (about 2½ loaves)

1 tablespoon Diamond Crystal kosher salt

2 green bird's-eye chilis, stems removed

1 large egg

1 tablespoon finely grated ginger

1 tablespoon minced garlic

1 teaspoon ground coriander

½ teaspoon ground turmeric

½ teaspoon ground cumin

½ teaspoon garam masala

½ teaspoon red chili powder, plus more depending on spice tolerance

½ small yellow onion, finely chopped

⅓ cup (15 g) chopped fresh cilantro

1½ pounds (680 g) lean ground beef (90:10 lean-to-fat ratio)

Vegetable oil, for deep-frying

"Rumi's kebabs!" are words I began hearing surprisingly often after getting married, and as soon as I had one, I understood why. Crispy, crunchy, and surprisingly light, these kebabs really are something special.

Every year, halfway through the month of Ramadan, Rumina Aunty sends over a round, clear plastic plate lined with kebabs with a small tub of pale green coconut chutney sitting neatly in the center. They almost never last longer than a few hours. And if they do, they reheat beautifully, retaining their crispy crunchy exterior.

Rumina Khalfan is my husband's aunt by marriage. She's known to be resilient, intelligent, and light-hearted. Even before I had the pleasure of experiencing her company, I had the joy of eating her food. She's an intentional cook, and one of the few "foodies" in my husband's family. While learning to make her kebabs, a recipe she's perfected over the years based on her mother's method, we talked about restaurants, purses, family dynamics, generational shifts, and the importance of women's education (my favorite things to chat about).

Her kebabs are a rendition of the original, famously crispy deep-fried kebabs at K Tea Shop in Dar es Salaam, Tanzania.

METHOD

To make the coconut chutney: Combine the coconut, cilantro, chilis, salt, warm water, and lemon juice in a blender or food processor and blend until combined. You may need up to an additional ¼ cup (60 ml) water to help the blender along. Taste for salt and lemon juice and adjust to your preference. Transfer to a small bowl, cover, and refrigerate until ready to serve.

To make the kebabs: Roughly tear the bread into 3-inch segments and place in a large bowl. Cover with water and let soak for at least 10 minutes, until the bread is completely hydrated and the ends have softened. Drain the water and squeeze out as much excess water as you can using your hands. Transfer to a fine-mesh sieve set over a bowl and let sit for at least 10 minutes to drain further excess water.

Meanwhile, combine the salt and chilis in a mortar and pestle and crush them together to break down the chilis. Transfer the mixture to a large bowl and add the egg, ginger, garlic, coriander, turmeric, cumin, garam masala, red chili powder, onion, and cilantro and mix to combine. Add the ground beef and use your hands or a rubber spatula to combine. Add the drained, soaked bread and mix again until evenly distributed and very well combined.

Pour vegetable oil into a large, high-sided skillet or karahi over medium heat to come 2 to 3 inches up the sides. Heat until warmed through (325 to 350°F/165 to 175°C). Meanwhile, divide the meat mixture into 2-ounce (55 g) portions (about 2 heaping tablespoons) and roll into balls. Fry, working in batches without overcrowding the skillet and flipping halfway through, until deeply browned in color on both sides, 13 to 18 minutes. Using a slotted spoon, transfer the kebabs to a paper towel–lined plate to drain any excess oil.

Serve immediately with the coconut chutney.

Store any leftover fried kebabs in a resealable bag in the fridge for up to 1 week or in the freezer for up to 3 months. Reheat in the oven at 325°F (165°C) until warmed through and crisp. Store any leftover chutney in an airtight container in the fridge for up to 1 week or in the freezer for up to 3 months. Thaw frozen chutney in the refrigerator overnight.

SALTY LITTLE HEARTS

Makes 40 hearts
30 minutes

2 (9-ounce/490 g) sheets frozen puff pastry
2 tablespoons unsalted butter
Flaky sea salt

My husband, Mikhail, and I are two Virgos with very similar interests and mindsets, but unfortunately very different breakfast habits: I am an avid breakfast lover, while he rests his laurels on a simple cup of morning coffee or tea.

Even after many attempts to seduce him with my morning-meal wiles, he simply will not divert from his breakfast-less ways. On the weekends, however, he always reaches for a plastic package of Khari biscuits, a flaky, crispy South Asian snack with Iranian roots (and the inspiration for this recipe), to have with his morning cup of sweet chai.

Whenever my mom and grandmother had leftover puff pastry from making Chicken Pot Pie (page 90), they'd slice it up into bars, sprinkle over some salt, and bake them into a semi-homemade Khari biscuit. These are similar to those, but instead take the cutesy shape of palmiers, another popular pastry.

For me, these are not a breakfast replacement, but rather a teatime snack. But Mikhail would beg to differ. We agree to disagree on this, to the dismay of my salty little heart.

METHOD

Set the puff pastry on the counter to thaw until pliable, about 25 minutes.

Meanwhile, arrange the oven racks in the upper and lower thirds of the oven and preheat to 400°F (205°C). Line 2 baking sheets with parchment paper.

Melt the butter in the microwave in 15-second increments.

When the puff pastry can be easily unrolled, working with one sheet at a time, transfer to a cutting board. Discard the paper sheets between the puff pastry sections and use a rolling pin to even out the creases. Brush a thin layer of melted butter over the entire sheet. Sprinkle gently with salt.

Fold the edges of the puff pastry toward the center so they go halfway to the middle. Brush the now-exposed dry puff pastry with butter and sprinkle with salt. Fold again so the two folds meet exactly at the middle of the dough. Brush the now-exposed dry puff pastry with butter and sprinkle with salt. Fold one half over the other half to resemble a closed book. This will result in 6 layers. While still lying flat on the cutting board, cut into 20 to 24 pieces, ¼ to ½ inch thick. Transfer, cut side up, to the parchment-lined baking sheet, leaving about ½ inch between the sides of each cookie.

Repeat with the other sheet of puff pastry.

Bake until browned and crisp, 18 to 22 minutes, swapping the baking sheet positions in the oven halfway through. Don't worry if the hearts touch on the baking sheet as they expand—they won't stick together.

Let cool completely on the baking sheet. Transfer to an airtight container or zip-top bag and store at room temperature for up to 10 days.

SAMOSAS TWO WAYS

Makes about 25 samosas of each variety
3 hours

FOR THE BEEF FILLING

1 pound (455 g) lean ground beef (90:10 lean-to-fat ratio)

1½ teaspoons Diamond Crystal kosher salt

Freshly cracked black pepper

3 large garlic cloves, finely grated

1-inch piece ginger, finely grated

1 tablespoon garam masala

1 medium yellow onion, finely diced

¼ cup (10 g) finely chopped fresh cilantro

FOR THE POTATO FILLING

2 large russet potatoes, peeled

2 teaspoons vegetable oil

3 fresh curry leaves

1 green bird's-eye chili,* finely chopped

2 garlic cloves, finely grated

½ teaspoon cumin seeds

¼ teaspoon ground turmeric

¼ teaspoon Kashmiri red chili powder

¼ teaspoon garam masala

1 tablespoon fresh lemon juice (from about ½ lemon), plus more as needed

2 tablespoons chopped fresh cilantro leaves and tender stems, optional

Diamond Crystal kosher salt

(continued)

When I hear the term "labor of love," I think of samosas. They are a crisp, satisfying, stuffed and deep-fried South Asian pastry. Often enjoyed as a snack or appetizer, they have main character energy, outshining anything they sit beside.

I have vivid memories of my mom and other women in our family sitting together around the kitchen table, folding samosas for hours in preparation for our month of fasting, Ramadan. They'd usually assemble them in bulk, dividing up the loot to take home and freeze to have on hand during the coming weeks.

The folding technique takes some practice, but once you get the hang of it, it's like riding a bike.

I offer recipes for the two most common fillings: an oniony ground beef one and a spiced potato one. Most people prefer the ground beef variety, but I've come to really enjoy the vegetarian version. Try both.

METHOD

To make the beef filling: Put the ground beef in a large nonstick skillet and place over medium heat. Add the salt, lots of pepper, the garlic, and ginger and brown the beef, breaking it up thoroughly with a wooden spoon, about 10 minutes. Drain any fat (the meat should be dry) and remove from the heat. Add the garam masala, onions, and cilantro to the pot and mix to combine. Set the beef mixture aside to cool off for 15 to 20 minutes.

To make the potato filling: Bring a large pot of water to a boil. Add the potatoes and cook until fork-tender, about 20 minutes. Drain the water and let cool until easy to handle. Finely dice the boiled potatoes and transfer to a large bowl.

Heat the vegetable oil in a small pot with a lid over medium heat. Once shimmering, add the curry leaves, swirl the pot, cover, and cook until fragrant. Remove the lid and add the chili, garlic, cumin seeds, turmeric, Kashmiri red chili powder, and garam masala. Stir and cook until fragrant, about 1 minute. Transfer the mixture to the bowl with the potatoes. Add the lemon juice and cilantro leaves, if using, and season with salt. Stir to combine and distribute the seasonings. Taste for salt and lemon juice and adjust to your preference. Keep in mind that the flavor will be slightly milder after frying.

Note that both fillings can be made up to 2 days ahead.

To assemble the samosas, first make the glue that will seal the samosas by combining the flour and 3½ tablespoons water in a small bowl until smooth.

Trim 1 spring roll pastry block into a 6 × 7-inch rectangle using a sharp knife. Cut in half lengthwise to make two 3 × 7-inch blocks. You can discard any excess pastry or save it to fry up into little crunchy bits for snacking on. Cover with a damp (not wet) kitchen towel or paper towel to prevent the pastry from drying out.

To fold a samosa, peel 2 layers of pastry off the block. Make sure to re-cover the block with the damp towel before continuing.

Lay the rectangle sheets directly on top of each other on a cutting board. Take the bottom left corner of the pastry and bring it up

START SMALL 71

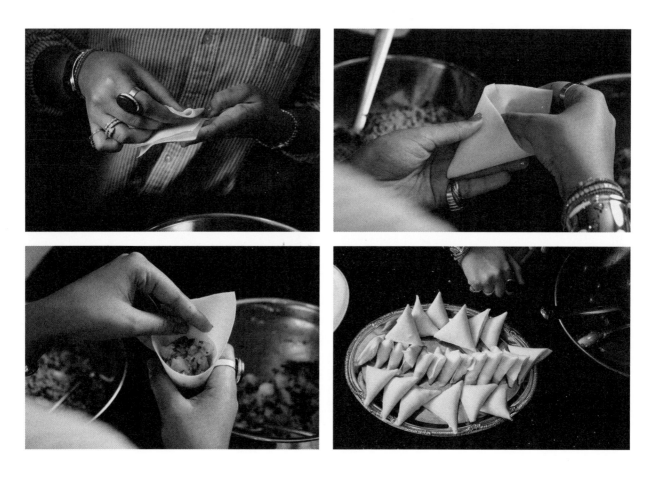

72 THIRD CULTURE COOKING

FOR ASSEMBLY AND FRYING:

¼ cup (30 g) all-purpose flour

2 (12-ounce/340 g) packages spring roll pastry, preferably KIMBO brand

Vegetable oil, for frying

Green Chutney (page 196) and ketchup, for serving, optional

*INSTEAD OF...

Bird's-eye chili, use jalapeño or ¼ teaspoon cayenne pepper

1½ inches below the upper right corner. Bring the now-bottom right corner up to the top left corner to make a triangle-shaped pocket. Fill the pocket with about 2 tablespoons of the filling, pressing down gently to compress. Using a pastry brush, spread a thin layer of the glue on the flap and seal diagonally to make a triangle. Make sure the corners are tight and no filling is exposed. Use more glue as needed to make a clean triangle—sometimes it's helpful to seal it horizontally just above the filling to keep things contained while you get the hang of the folding motion. Repeat with the remaining filling.

Pour vegetable oil in a large, high-sided skillet to come 3 inches up the sides and heat over medium-high heat until an instant-read thermometer registers 325°F (165°C). Working in batches of about 6 samosas, cook samosas until crisp and golden, flipping halfway through, about 2 to 3 minutes per side. Use a slotted spoon to transfer the samosas to a wire rack set inside a rimmed baking sheet and let drain. Alternatively, transfer to a paper towel–lined plate. If you saved the excess pastry from earlier, deep-fry the scraps until golden brown, about 1 minute, then transfer to a paper towel–lined plate.

Serve the samosas immediately with green chutney and ketchup, if desired.

To freeze, lay uncooked samosas flat in a large container topped with a layer of parchment paper to stack another layer on top. Repeat as needed. The samosas can be fried from frozen by adding 1 to 2 minutes to the cooking time.

SHAWARMA-SPICED CARROTS

Serves 4 to 6
40 minutes

FOR THE CARROTS
½ teaspoon ground cinnamon*
½ teaspoon ground coriander*
½ teaspoon ground cumin*
½ teaspoon ground turmeric*
½ teaspoon sweet paprika*
¼ teaspoon freshly cracked black pepper*
⅛ teaspoon ground cardamom*
⅛ teaspoon ground cloves*
2 garlic cloves, finely grated
2 teaspoons Diamond Crystal kosher salt
¼ cup (60 ml) olive oil
1½ pounds (680 g) medium carrots,* trimmed, halved lengthwise

FOR THE HERB SALAD AND ASSEMBLY:
2 tablespoons fresh lemon juice, plus more as needed
1 tablespoon extra-virgin olive oil, divided
1 teaspoon Diamond Crystal kosher salt, divided
1 small red onion, thinly sliced
7 Medjool dates, pitted, roughly chopped
2 jalapeños, seeds removed, roughly chopped
1 cup (30 to 50 g) roughly chopped tender herbs (such as cilantro, dill, or parsley)
1 cup (240 ml) labneh*

*INSTEAD OF...
Individual spices, use 1 tablespoon store-bought shawarma spice blend
Carrots, use chopped parsnips or sweet potatoes (add about 10 minutes to the roast time)
Labneh, use plain whole-milk Greek yogurt

A winner from the Ramadan story I worked on for *Bon Appétit* back in 2022 (Date and Dark Chocolate Cookies, page 230, are also from this story), this veggie side dish works well for a multitude of reasons. The shawarma spice blend in combination with the sweet, crisp-tender carrots is surprisingly delightful, and the firm but succulent texture from the high-heat roast keeps this from feeling like glorified baby food. The juicy herb salad on top is my favorite part, made with sweet dates, a medley of herbs, sharp red onion, some chilis, and a bit of lemon juice for brightness. It is the perfect texture and flavor pairing for the earthy, spiced carrots that sit atop creamy labneh.

The spices in the ingredient list may seem overwhelming, but trust the blend. Combined, they lend a unique and important flavor that truly delivers on that shawarma-like taste. Of course, if homemade seasoning isn't your thing, an equal amount of prepackaged shawarma spice blend will do the trick, too.

METHOD
To roast the carrots: Place a rack in the middle of the oven and preheat to 450°F (230°C).

Put the cinnamon, coriander, cumin, turmeric, paprika, pepper, cardamom, cloves, garlic, salt, and olive oil in a small bowl and stir to combine.

Toss the carrots with the spice mixture on a large rimmed baking sheet until evenly coated. Transfer to the oven and roast until the carrots are crisp-tender and deeply browned, 15 to 20 minutes. Remove the pan from the oven and let it cool.

To make the herb salad and assemble: Whisk the lemon juice, olive oil, and ½ teaspoon of the salt in a medium bowl. Add the red onion, dates, jalapeños, and herbs and toss to coat. Taste the salad and add more lemon juice if needed.

Stir the labneh and remaining ½ teaspoon salt in a small bowl.

To serve, spread the labneh on a platter, scatter the carrots over it, and top with the salad.

SUMMER ON A PLATE

Serves 4 to 6
30 minutes

1 mini seedless watermelon, rind removed and cut into 1- to 2-inch pieces

1 small ripe cantaloupe, rind removed and cut into 1- to 2-inch pieces

1 cup (145 g) heirloom cherry tomatoes, left whole, halved, and/or quartered, depending on the size

1 large lemon*

Flaky sea salt

1 (7-ounce/198 g) package feta cheese*

1 teaspoon Aleppo chili flakes*

½ cup (20 g) fresh basil*

High-quality extra virgin olive oil

*INSTEAD OF . . .
Lemon, use 2 limes
Feta, use another soft cheese, like goat cheese or blue cheese
Aleppo chili flakes, use another mild chili flake, like Urfa or gochugaru
Basil, use mint or dill

While in no way revolutionary, the makings of this salad are a result of a summertime farmers market binge. Featuring almost all the best of summer produce (no stone fruit, but if it's calling you, please add it) in a singular salad, it's sweet, salty, and simple and ideal for a refreshing midday lunch or as a barbecue side dish.

All the fruit can be cut ahead of time and stored in airtight containers in the fridge until ready for assembly. To keep things easy, breezy, and in true summertime fashion, the dressing is really more of a finish, featuring a combination of a bright floral chili pepper, lemon juice, olive oil, and salt.

METHOD

Arrange the watermelon and cantaloupe on a large platter. Scatter on the tomatoes. Zest the lemon directly over the platter, then halve and squeeze the juice over your hand to catch any seeds. Sprinkle with salt and let stand for a few minutes.

Meanwhile, tear any large basil leaves and roughly crumble the feta. Top the fruit with cheese and sprinkle with the chili flakes and basil leaves. Finish with a generous drizzle of olive oil.

Do-ahead: Cut the fruit and store in airtight containers in the refrigerator for up to 2 days.

START SMALL 77

RED, HOT TANDOORI WINGS

Serves 4 to 6
1 hour 15 minutes

3 pounds (1.3 kg) chicken wings, flats and drumettes separated, patted dry

1 tablespoon baking powder*

1 tablespoon Diamond Crystal kosher salt, plus more as needed

1 lime, plus wedges, for serving

3 tablespoons Frank's RedHot Original Hot Sauce*

1 tablespoon honey

3 garlic cloves, finely grated

6 tablespoons (85 g) unsalted butter

1 tablespoon tandoori masala, preferably Spicewalla*

Warmed garlic naan, for serving, optional

½ cup (23 g) fresh mint and cilantro leaves*

White sauce (page 203) or salted yogurt, for serving, optional

*INSTEAD OF...

Baking powder, use ½ teaspoon baking soda mixed with the salt before seasoning

Frank's hot sauce, use another loose hot sauce

Spicewalla tandoori masala, use another available brand

Cilantro and mint, use another tender herb combo

These crowd-pleasing spicy wings feature two iconic spicy seasonings: aromatic tandoori masala spice blend and traditional Louisiana-style hot sauce for a nod to classic Buffalo wings, with a little flair.

If you're new to the magical world of tandoori masala, the market varies widely—some are spicier than others, and some include salt while others don't, so be sure to taste your tandoori powder to check and adjust the hot sauce and season accordingly.

When it comes to chicken wings, transforming the texture of the skin is everything, and when it comes to cooking the wings, it's all in the technique. Baking powder (a combination of baking soda and cornstarch) helps to absorb excess moisture on the skin's surface and speeds up the browning process, ensuring the browned and crisp skin we all love, but without the frying. Baking the wings on a rack and turning them often helps with even browning and preventing stickage, but if I'm honest, I often don't bother and it's fine.

Sometimes I like to serve these over garlic naan to absorb all the extra sauce from the wings, with white sauce or salted yogurt on the side to tame the heat.

METHOD

Place a rack in the upper third of the oven and preheat to 450°F (230°C). Line a rimmed baking sheet with foil and set a wire rack inside it.

Place the chicken wings in a large bowl. Sprinkle with the baking powder and salt and toss to coat. Transfer to the prepared baking sheet, evenly spaced.

Roast the wings, turning halfway through, until lightly browned, 30 to 40 minutes, depending on the size of your wings.

Switch the oven to broil.

Turn the wings again and broil until charred in spots and crisp, 6 to 10 minutes, turning halfway through. Remove from the oven and let cool slightly.

To make the sauce, slice 1 lime in half and squeeze its juice into a large bowl. Stir in the hot sauce and honey. Reserve the remaining ½ lime for dressing the herbs.

Cook the garlic and butter in a small skillet over medium heat, stirring occasionally, until the butter is melted and the garlic is fragrant, about 2 minutes. Add the tandoori masala and cook, stirring, until fragrant, about 30 seconds. Add the spice mixture to the large bowl and whisk vigorously to emulsify. Taste and add more salt if needed. Transfer the cooked wings to the sauce and toss to coat. Let stand for a minute or two to allow the sauce to really cling to the wings. Transfer the wings to a platter lined with garlic naan, if using, and spoon over any remaining sauce.

Place the herbs in a small bowl. Squeeze the juice of the reserved lime over the top and season with salt. Toss to coat.

Scatter the herb salad over the wings and serve immediately with white sauce or salted yogurt, for dipping, if using.

TARKA OLIVES

Serves 4 to 6
25 minutes

6 ounces (170 g) Castelvetrano olives,* pitted or unpitted, drained and dried
½ cup (120 ml) olive oil
1 teaspoon black mustard seeds*
2 dried red chilis*
3 garlic cloves, thinly sliced
5 fresh curry leaves, optional
1 lemon, zested in wide strips
Freshly cracked black pepper
1 (7-ounce/200 g) block feta cheese,* cut or broken into ½-inch pieces
Crusty bread, for serving

*INSTEAD OF . . .

Castelvetrano olives, use another variety

Mustard seeds, use cumin or coriander seeds

Dried chilis, use 1 fresh whole chili or ½ teaspoon red pepper flakes

Feta cheese, use Gouda, cheddar, Parmesan, pecorino, blue cheese, or another cheese

For someone like me who loves a pickle-y, briny thing, olives are the perfect snack. So, when spicy marinated olives are on the menu, I'm ordering them. Unlike typical spicy olives, this recipe imparts flavor through a tarka, a popular South Asian cooking technique where whole spices are bloomed in oil, infusing the oil and extracting their flavors.

Here, a slightly unique tarka made with lemon zest, garlic, and chili, among other spices, gets poured over the most buttery of olives, Castelvetranos, before cubed feta is introduced to the mix. Serve with crusty bread for dipping and store any leftovers in the fridge for unexpected company or easy snacking.

METHOD

Put the olives in a medium bowl. Set aside.

Heat the olive oil in a small saucepan over medium heat. Once the oil is shimmering, add the mustard seeds, red chilis, garlic, curry leaves, and lemon zest. Cover and cook until the mustard seeds have stopped popping and the garlic is toasted, 2 to 3 minutes.

Immediately pour the tarka over the olives, season with black pepper, and let stand until warm to the touch, about 10 minutes. Add the cheese and toss to coat. Transfer to a serving plate or bowl. Finish with more black pepper and salt. Serve with crusty bread for dipping.

The olives can be stored in an airtight container for up to 5 days.

TGIF
ARTICHOKE DIP

Serves 4 to 6
1 hour

My favorite fun fact about my mom is that she notoriously has four filled-to-the-brim freezers at her house—a place I imagine she got to from trying to feed a family of six-plus regularly. In the largest of our basement freezers, sitting right next to the Stouffer's Fettuccini Alfredo and Ellio's pizza stacks, were bright red boxes of TGI Friday's Spinach and Artichoke Cheese Dip—a favorite for family movie night. A simple corner tear of the plastic surface, five-ish minutes in the microwave, and I was in metaphorical heaven.

My nostalgic re-creation of this dip is just as creamy and cheesy, and while I used to avoid the artichokes, they've become my favorite part of the dish. Tortilla chips are classically my serving vehicle of choice, but with age, I've come to love the contrast radish, endive, and pear offer to help offset the richness of this dip. So many creamy, fatty, cheesy elements may seem like overkill, but each does a very different thing, helping to create the perfect body, flavor, and mouthfeel.

10 ounces (280 g) frozen chopped spinach

1 (8-ounce/225 g) block cream cheese, at room temperature

¾ cup (180 ml) mayonnaise

1 cup (240 ml) sour cream

3 garlic cloves, finely grated

½ teaspoon red pepper flakes

1 (14-ounce/397 g) can or jar quartered artichoke hearts,* drained, roughly chopped

3 cups (12 ounces/330 g) shredded mozzarella cheese

1 cup (3 ounces/100 g) finely grated Parmesan cheese,* divided

¾ teaspoon Diamond Crystal kosher salt, plus more as needed

Freshly cracked black pepper

½ cup (40 g) panko breadcrumbs

1 tablespoon olive oil

Tortilla chips, radish, pear, cucumber, and/or endive, for serving

*INSTEAD OF...

Artichoke hearts, use canned white beans

Parmesan cheese, use white cheddar or pecorino romano cheese

METHOD

Preheat the oven to 350°F (175°C).

Put the frozen spinach in a large, microwave-safe bowl. Microwave in 1-minute increments until thawed, about 3 minutes. Don't discard any of the water.

In the same bowl, combine the cream cheese, mayonnaise, sour cream, garlic, red pepper flakes, artichokes, mozzarella cheese, ¾ cup (2¼ ounces/65 g) of the Parmesan cheese, the salt, and lots of pepper. Taste and adjust the seasoning to your preference. Transfer to an oven-safe medium casserole dish or 9-inch or so cast-iron skillet. Spread into an even layer.

Combine the remaining ¼ cup (¾ ounce/35 g) Parmesan cheese, the breadcrumbs, and olive oil in a small bowl. Sprinkle the mixture over the surface.

Bake until the dip is warmed through and the panko-Parmesan crust is starting to turn golden brown, 40 to 45 minutes. Switch the oven to broil and broil on high to evenly brown the surface, about 3 minutes. Remove from the oven and serve immediately with tortilla chips, radish, pear, cucumber, and/or endive for dipping. Be careful—the dish will be very hot.

FILL UP

(86—185)

The main meal

ACHAAR, EGG, AND CHEESE

Serves 2
10 minutes

2 large English muffins,* split
3 large eggs
1 tablespoon milk
1 tablespoon olive oil
Diamond Crystal kosher salt
Freshly cracked black pepper
2 slices American cheese*
2 tablespoons achaar,* divided, plus more to your preference

*INSTEAD OF...

English muffins, use 4 slices of bread

American cheese, use pepper Jack, cheddar, Gruyère, or another melting cheese

Achaar, use pickled chilis or chili paste, such as Calabrian chili paste, or Shortcut Lemon Achaar (page 202)

Bodegas are one of the best things about living in New York, and the bacon, egg, and cheese sandwich craze is one I've always had FOMO over (I don't eat pork). While still delicious, my order of egg and cheese on a roll is far less exciting than the version I make at home: achaar, egg, and cheese. Reminiscent of the breakfast sandwiches I grew up with, from McDonald's and Dunkin' Donuts specifically, these soft-cooked scrambled eggs are paired with creamy American cheese on a warmed English muffin.

Growing up in a household where chili pickles basically had a permanent spot on the dining table, the breakfast spread was no different, making achaar the perfect nostalgic addition. My preference, AKI Chilli and Ginger Pickle, offers a sharp acidity that offsets the fatty eggs and cheese, while adding a bit of spice.

Whisking in a splash of milk to the eggs before adding them to the pan helps achieve a fluffy egg patty that's got enough structure to hold up to being stacked but isn't overcooked—a tried-and-true technique courtesy of my mom. And while my original preference was classic white sandwich bread, it's evolved into the more ideal English muffin, but almost any sandwich-friendly bread you have on hand will do.

METHOD

In a toaster or under the broiler, toast the English muffin halves until light golden and warmed through.

Crack the eggs into a small bowl, add the milk, and whisk until completely combined.

Heat the olive oil in a small nonstick skillet with a lid over medium-high heat. Pour in the egg mixture and season the surface with a sprinkling of salt and pepper. Once the edges appear almost set, about 30 seconds, stir using long strokes to keep the egg curds large. Push the eggs to the center and divide the mixture into two masses, stacking if needed to form egg patties small enough to fit on the English muffin. Reduce the heat to low and place a cheese slice over each egg. Cover with the lid and let the cheese melt completely, 30 seconds to 1 minute.

Transfer an egg patty to each bottom muffin and top with 1 tablespoon of the achaar. Close to assemble. Serve immediately.

AN ICONIC CHICKEN POT PIE

Serves 4 to 6
1 hour 30 minutes

It's not lost on me that a chicken pot pie is not what you'd expect from an immigrant grandmother who's otherwise an authority on cooking spice-forward Khoja food. But my grandmother's chicken pot pie is *iconic*, and this adaptation of her specialty dish hits the spot every time. In addition to the traditional ingredients you can expect from a chicken pot pie, the secret weapon here is the American cheese. Sure, you can opt for another melty variety, but the sodium citrate found in American cheese is unmatched, lending creaminess a cheese without it won't be able to offer. To keep it fast and light on the dishes, I use quick-cooking-but-still-juicy chicken tenders instead of whole chicken shredded off the bone and reach for an oven-safe cast-iron skillet to make this a one-pan meal. When it comes to laying the puff pastry, the looser the better and easier (there's just something about those imperfect crispy edges and folds). And remember to serve with a good dousing of hot sauce.

If the idea of seasoning with salt and pepper alone scares you (I get it), feel free to add dried or fresh herbs (thyme, bay leaf, oregano, tarragon) or play with different spice blends (curry powder, garam masala, Cajun seasoning) to suit your taste.

1 pound (455 g) chicken tenders,* patted dry

2 teaspoons Diamond Crystal kosher salt, divided, plus more as needed

2 tablespoons olive oil, divided

1 tablespoon unsalted butter*

1 medium yellow onion,* thinly sliced

1 medium russet potato, cut into ½-inch cubes

1 (10-ounce/284 g) bag frozen mixed vegetables

2 garlic cloves, minced

Freshly cracked black pepper

2 tablespoons all-purpose flour

2 ounces (55 g) American cheese, finely chopped (3 Kraft Singles, torn into small pieces)

¼ cup (13 g) finely chopped fresh parsley

1 sheet puff pastry, thawed

1 large egg, beaten

Flaky sea salt

Cholula hot sauce,* for serving

*INSTEAD OF...

Chicken tenders, use chicken breast or boneless, skinless chicken thighs

Unsalted butter, use salted butter

Yellow onion, use 3 medium shallots

Cholula hot sauce, use Frank's RedHot or Homemade Hot Sauce (page 197)

METHOD

Heat a 10- or 11-inch cast-iron skillet or other deep oven-safe skillet over medium heat.

Season the chicken tenders with ½ teaspoon of the kosher salt.

Add 1 tablespoon of the olive oil to the heated skillet and place the chicken tenders in an even layer. Cook, flipping halfway through, until cooked through and golden brown on both sides, about 10 minutes. Transfer to a cutting board to rest.

Deglaze the skillet with ¼ cup (60 ml) water, scraping up any browned bits with a wooden spoon. Add the remaining 1 tablespoon olive oil and the butter and stir to melt the butter. Add the onions and potato, season with 1 teaspoon of the remaining salt, and cook until the onion has softened and started to reduce in volume, 4 to 6 minutes. Add the frozen vegetables and garlic and stir to combine. Season with the remaining ½ teaspoon salt and lots (I mean it) of pepper. Cook until the frozen vegetables are heated through, another 4 to 6 minutes.

Meanwhile, whisk the flour and 1 cup (240 ml) water in a small bowl to dissolve the flour. Chop the cooled chicken into ¾-inch pieces or shred with two forks.

Reduce the heat to medium-low and pour in the flour mixture. Stir, bring it to a gentle simmer, and cook until thickened, 2 to 3 minutes. If the mixture seizes or becomes too thick at this stage, your pan is likely too hot, and you'll need to stir in more water ¼ cup (60 ml) at a time. Aim for a texture slightly saucier than how you'd like to eat it when all is said and done. Turn off the burner and arrange the cheese over the top in an even layer. Stir well until the cheese has completely melted and the sauce is no longer translucent. Add the chicken and parsley and stir to combine. Taste for salt and pepper and adjust to your preference. Spread the mixture into an even layer and let stand to cool until the skillet is warm to the touch (this ensures the puff pastry gets a good rise in the oven), about 20 minutes.

Meanwhile, place an oven rack in the center of the oven and preheat to 400°F (205°C).

Transfer the thawed puff pastry to a cutting board and use a glass or rolling pin to flatten the creases, if any. Make sure the puff pastry is large enough to cover the pan—don't worry about cutting it to shape (unless you want to). Make four 2-inch cuts in the pastry to vent. Transfer it over the skillet and encourage it to sink into the pan and make contact with the filling. Tuck any overhang along the edges. I usually leave the corners as is. Brush the surface with the beaten egg and sprinkle with flaky salt. If the filling is coming up very high on the sides and you're worried about spillage, place the entire skillet on a baking sheet.

Transfer to the oven and bake for 30 to 35 minutes, until the pastry is golden brown and cooked through. Let stand for 5 to 10 minutes. Serve with hot sauce.

ARROGANT TOMATO TOAST

Serves 1 or 2
15 minutes

3 tablespoons extra-virgin olive oil, plus more for drizzling*
1½ teaspoons za'atar*
2 thick slices sourdough bread*
4 tablespoons labneh*
4 thick-cut heirloom or beefsteak tomato slices*
Flaky sea salt*
Freshly cracked black pepper*

*INSTEAD OF...

Olive oil, use ghee
Za'atar, use ¾ teaspoon curry powder or another ground spice blend
Sourdough, use naan or pita
Labneh, use cream cheese, mayo, or crème fraîche
Heirloom or beefsteak tomatoes, use a handful of cherry tomatoes, halved
Flaky sea salt, use kosher salt
Black pepper, use red pepper flakes

The humble tomato sandwich is the simplest summer pleasure. All you need are ripe tomatoes, a creamy spread, lots of salt, and good bread. This take, however, isn't so humble, thanks to the crispy fried sourdough that sizzles in an infused aromatic oil.

The combinations and varieties to play with within this formula are endless, which is why nearly every ingredient has a swap. Don't like labneh? Try mayo. Don't like mayo? Try cream cheese. Don't like cream cheese? Try crème fraîche. In this version, I use za'atar to infuse the oil with lots of flavor, while relying on labneh for the creamy spread element (a classic combination). Another combination worth fawning over is a Madras curry powder–infused oil with Kewpie mayo.

Using in-season tomatoes is of course ideal, but it isn't summer all year round here in New York, so when the colder months roll around and I find myself craving a tomato toast, halved cherry tomatoes from the grocery store do the trick. Regardless of seasonality, remember, tomatoes love salt, so don't skimp on it.

METHOD

Heat a medium skillet over medium heat. Add the olive oil and let it warm through. Add the za'atar and swirl the pan to evenly disperse it in the oil. Add the bread and fry until golden brown, 2 to 3 minutes per side. Transfer to a plate.

Spread 2 heaping tablespoons of labneh over 1 side of each fried bread slice. Top each with 2 slices of tomato and season generously with salt.

Finish with pepper and drizzle with any remaining za'atar oil from the pan. Finish with even more olive oil.

Ashraf's
TOMATO SAAG

Serves 6 to 8 as a main or 8 to 10 as a side dish
1 hour 45 minutes

½ cup (120 ml) any neutral oil

3 medium yellow onions (1 pound/455 g), quartered lengthwise and thinly sliced (4 cups/440 g sliced)

3 garlic cloves, finely grated (or 2 teaspoons garlic paste)

15 Roma tomatoes (4 pounds/ 1.8 kg), finely chopped (about 8 cups)

2 teaspoons Diamond Crystal kosher salt

2 teaspoons ground coriander

2 teaspoons ground cumin

1½ teaspoons red chili powder or Kashmiri red chili powder

½ teaspoon ground turmeric

Fried eggs, for serving, optional

Warm crusty bread, for serving

One of my earliest tactile memories of food is the feeling of my pruning fingers as I finely chopped my way through fifteen-plus pounds of Roma tomatoes to help make this tomato saag (*tameta nu shaak* in Gujarati) for a family breakfast.

My grandmother Ashraf is known for her elaborate yet seemingly effortless cooking style, and, in many ways, this dish personifies her. Cooking is her love language, and she's the type to spend her Friday evenings finely chopping up pounds and pounds of hand-selected tomatoes from a South Asian farmers market (if Patel Brothers is considered a farmers market) and wake up the next morning to slow-cook them into a tomato curry to feed her entire extended family (thankfully, she taught me how to make this for a mere eight people). Bear in mind, this was just one of the many dishes making up her brunch spread, which included omelets, homemade achaars, French toast, and fresh rotis.

I call my grandmother Nani Ma, which translates to "little mother" from Gujarati to English, and that's exactly what she is. Nani Ma lived in our house for a lot of my childhood, and when she didn't, I'd spend weeks with her in the kitchen at her home in Los Angeles. She's always been incredibly particular and very independent, much like myself (we're proudly the two Virgos in the fam), and over the years she's taught me so much about cooking and the kitchen.

Of those lessons, most notable are the etiquette of feeding those you love (and to never stop asking if you can continue to feed them more food, even after they're full) and the traditional cooking methods and techniques I care so much about preserving, like rolling roti and folding samosas.

Like all of Ashraf's recipes, tomato saag scales very well. Just keep in mind, the more tomatoes, the longer the cook time. Look to color and viscosity to get an understanding of doneness.

METHOD

Heat the oil in a medium pot over medium heat. Once warm and shimmering, add the onions and cook, stirring occasionally, until deep golden brown and reduced in volume, 17 to 20 minutes. Add the garlic and stir to coat in the oil. Once fragrant, add the tomatoes and stir to combine. Add the salt, coriander, cumin, chili powder, and turmeric and stir to combine. Bring to a boil, cover, and cook, stirring often, until the tomatoes have broken down and released their water, about 25 minutes. Reduce the heat to medium-low, maintain a simmer, and continue to cook, stirring often, until the tomatoes have deepened and color, completely softened, and most of their liquid has evaporated, 40 to 50 minutes.

Remove from the heat and serve with fried eggs, if using, and crusty bread for dipping.

BLACK BEAN SMASHED BURGERS

Serves 4
1 hour

½ cup (120 ml) mayonnaise

2 tablespoons adobo sauce from a can of chipotle peppers in adobo*, and 2 of the chipotle peppers, chopped*

2 tablespoons vegetable oil, divided, plus more as needed

1 medium red onion, finely chopped

1½ teaspoons Diamond Crystal kosher salt, divided, plus more for sprinkling

3 garlic cloves, finely chopped

1 teaspoon ground cumin

½ teaspoon ground coriander

8 ounces (225 g) pepper Jack cheese,* divided

1 (15-ounce/425 g) can black beans, drained and rinsed

1 large egg, beaten

½ cup (60 g) plain breadcrumbs*

4 brioche buns,* split

Butter, at room temperature, for the buns

Shredded iceberg lettuce, sliced red onion, and sliced heirloom or beefsteak tomato, for serving

*INSTEAD OF...

Adobo sauce, use sriracha or other hot sauce

Chipotles, use jalapeños

Pepper Jack cheese, use any other good melting cheese

Plain breadcrumbs, use panko breadcrumbs

Brioche buns, use plain or seeded burger buns

I'd be lying if I said keeping a halal diet is easy—particularly at amusement parks, where turkey legs, hot dogs, and burgers are the most common options. Enter: veggie burgers. I've eaten my fair share, and not all are created equal. As far as vegetarian burgers go, I've always felt the black bean variety reigns supreme in terms of taste. The downside: its texture. Instead of the typically thick, borderline-gummy patty, my version borrows its technique from the smashburger, yielding thin, flavorful patties with lots of surface area and crispy edges. And because they're so thin, a double-patty burger doesn't feel overly indulgent. That said, if a single patty is more your style, feel free to adjust accordingly.

METHOD

Put the mayonnaise and adobo sauce in a small bowl and stir to combine. Chill the chipotle mayo until ready to serve.

Heat 1 tablespoon of the vegetable oil in a large cast-iron skillet over medium heat. Add the chopped red onion and sprinkle with ½ teaspoon of the salt. Cook, stirring often, until the onion begins to soften, about 4 minutes. Add the garlic and cook, stirring often, until softened, about 2 minutes. Add the cumin and coriander and cook, stirring, until the spices are fragrant, about 30 seconds. Remove from the heat and let cool for 5 to 10 minutes.

Meanwhile, cut 6 ounces (170 g) of the cheese from the block, slice it into 8 pieces, and set aside. Coarsely grate the remaining 2 ounces (55 g) cheese.

In a large bowl, coarsely mash the black beans with a fork. Add the grated cheese, egg, chipotles, breadcrumbs, and the remaining 1 teaspoon salt. Add the onion mixture from the pan (reserve the pan for later) and mix until the ingredients are evenly distributed.

Divide the bean mixture into 8 portions (about ¼ cup each) and roll into tight balls between your palms. Working in two batches and using fresh parchment paper for each patty, sandwich the balls between 2 sheets of parchment paper, spacing them 6 inches apart, and firmly smash with a meat mallet or a heavy skillet to create thin, 4-inch-diameter patties.

Butter the buns. Wipe out the reserved skillet and place over medium heat. Working in batches, toast the buns, cut side down, until golden brown and warmed through, about 2 minutes. Transfer to a baking sheet.

Add the remaining 1 tablespoon vegetable oil to the skillet and heat over medium-high heat. Working in batches of 3 or 4 and adding more oil if the skillet looks dry, cook the patties, undisturbed, until deeply browned underneath, about 3 minutes. Flip and cook until the edges begin to brown, about 2 minutes. Place a slice of reserved cheese on top of each patty, cover with a lid, and cook until the cheese is melted, about 1 minute. Transfer to the baking sheet with the buns.

Spread a generous amount of chipotle mayo on the cut sides of the buns. Build burgers with lettuce, 2 patties, sliced red onion, and tomato. Sprinkle the tomato with salt, then close with the top side of the buns.

B-L-D TOMATOES AND EGGS

Serves 4 to 6
30 minutes

3 tablespoons olive oil*

6 scallions,* thinly sliced, white and light green parts separated from dark green parts

6 garlic cloves, minced

2½ teaspoons Diamond Crystal kosher salt, divided

1 teaspoon ground cumin

2 teaspoons smoked paprika*

1 teaspoon Aleppo chili flakes*

1 (28-ounce/800 g) can whole peeled tomatoes

4 large eggs

Feta cheese, crumbled, for serving

Cooked jasmine rice or crusty bread, for serving

*INSTEAD OF...

Olive oil, use vegetable oil

Scallions, use 1 medium yellow or red onion

Smoked paprika, use regular paprika

Aleppo chili flakes, use red pepper flakes or Kashmiri red chili powder

Stewed tomatoes served alongside eggs is a breakfast I grew up eating often (see Ashraf's Tomato Saag, page 94). This recipe calls upon the same pairing but can be enjoyed for any meal: breakfast, lunch, or dinner. Inspired by the flavors of North African and Palestinian shakshuka, the function of Chinese stir-fried tomatoes and eggs, and the method of Mediterranean menemen, these breakfast-lunch-dinner tomatoes and eggs are the ultimate multipurpose meal.

Good-quality whole peeled tomatoes will be easier to break down in the pan with a wooden spoon, so if you can't get your hands on a can of the good stuff, transfer the tomatoes to a bowl and crush them with your hands.

METHOD

Heat a medium nonstick or stainless-steel skillet over medium heat. Add the olive oil and heat until shimmering. Add the white and light green parts of the scallions, the garlic, and 1 teaspoon of the salt and cook, stirring often, until softened and beginning to brown around the edges, 3 to 5 minutes. Add the cumin, paprika, and chili flakes and stir to toast the spices. Once fragrant, add the tomatoes and 1 teaspoon of the remaining salt. Stir and use a wooden spoon to break down the tomatoes to your desired consistency (I prefer a few larger pieces of tomato). Add ½ cup (120 ml) water and stir to combine. Bring to a simmer and cook until thickened and the flavors have come together, 6 to 9 minutes.

Meanwhile, in a medium bowl, whisk the eggs with the remaining ½ teaspoon salt until completely combined. Let stand while the tomato sauce is simmering.

Once the tomato sauce has thickened, reduce the heat to low and pour in the beaten egg in as even a layer as possible. Cover and cook until eggs appear set, 3 to 4 minutes. Remove from the heat and gently stir from the outside in, being careful not to overmix. The eggs should appear ribbony and gently set. Finish with the crumbled cheese and scallion greens.

Serve over rice or with crusty bread.

CALABRIAN CHILI CHICKEN WITH CAPER RAITA

Serves 4
1 hour 30 minutes

- 4 to 6 bone-in, skin-on chicken thighs (2 pounds/910 g)*
- 4¼ teaspoons Diamond Crystal kosher salt, divided
- ¾ cup (180 ml) plain whole-milk yogurt
- 2 tablespoons Calabrian chili paste*
- 5 garlic cloves, finely grated
- 1 tablespoon finely grated ginger (about 2 inches)
- 2 pounds (910 g) sweet potatoes,* cut into 2-inch pieces
- 2 tablespoons olive oil, plus more for drizzling
- 2 teaspoons ground cumin
- 3 mini Persian cucumbers, divided
- 2 tablespoons fresh lemon juice
- 1 to 2 ounces (30 to 55 g) feta cheese
- 1 tablespoon capers*
- 2 teaspoons caper brine*
- Freshly cracked black pepper

*INSTEAD OF...
Chicken thighs, use drumsticks
Calabrian chili paste, use another concentrated chili paste
Sweet potatoes, use delicata squash
Capers, use olives
Caper brine, use lemon juice or olive brine

Yogurt marination is a tried-and-true South Asian technique for succulent and juicy chicken. The acidic quality of yogurt helps to tenderize and relax the proteins in chicken (and other meats, too, for that matter), making it the perfect vehicle to carry bold flavors.

The yogurt-marinated chicken dishes I grew up on featured a myriad of spices along with garlic and ginger paste. This recipe borrows on that idea, but instead of opening up every spice jar in the cabinet, I reach for one of my favorite, easy-to-find condiments: Calabrian chili paste. To complement the chilis, sweet potatoes, cooling caper raita, and quick pickled cucumbers serve as the perfect accompaniments.

METHOD

To make the roasted chicken and sweet potatoes: Pat the chicken dry with paper towels. Remove any excess skin and fat. Put it in a bowl or zip-top bag and rub 2 teaspoons of the salt all over. Add ¼ cup (60 ml) of the yogurt, the chili paste, garlic, and ginger and toss to coat. Cover or seal the bag and marinate in the refrigerator for at least 15 minutes or up to overnight.

Preheat the oven to 425°F (220°C).

Put the sweet potatoes on a baking sheet and drizzle with the olive oil. Sprinkle with 2 teaspoons salt and the cumin and toss to coat. Arrange the chicken so that it is sitting on top of the sweet potatoes, placing larger pieces toward the edges and smaller pieces toward the center.

Bake until the chicken is cooked through and the skin is browned, 45 to 50 minutes.

While the chicken is in the oven, make the quick-pickled cucumbers and caper raita. Thinly slice 2 of the cucumbers and put them in a bowl. Add the lemon juice and remaining ¼ teaspoon salt and toss. Set aside.

Using a fork, mash the cheese with the capers in a small bowl. Finely chop the remaining cucumber. Add the remaining ½ cup (120 ml) yogurt, the caper brine, and the remaining cucumber and stir well to combine. Taste and season with salt as needed. Drizzle with olive oil and finish with black pepper. Chill until ready to serve.

Transfer the sweet potatoes to a serving platter, top with the quick-pickled cucumbers, nestle the chicken over the top, and serve the caper raita alongside.

CARTHAGE MUST BE DESTROYED

Serves 1
25 minutes

1 small heirloom or beefsteak tomato,* sliced
½ avocado, sliced
Flaky sea salt
Freshly cracked black pepper
Lemon wedges,* for serving
Roughly chopped fresh basil, dill, chives, and/or parsley, for serving
Sliced crusty sourdough bread, for serving
2 large eggs
1 tablespoon milk
½ teaspoon Calabrian chili paste,* or more depending on heat tolerance
1 tablespoon grated Parmesan cheese,* plus more for serving
1 tablespoon unsalted butter*
Diamond Crystal kosher salt
Extra virgin olive oil, for drizzling

*INSTEAD OF...

Heirloom or beefsteak tomato, use a handful of cherry tomatoes
Lemon wedges, use lime wedges
Calabrian chili paste, use chili oil or sriracha
Parmesan cheese, use cheddar or pecorino romano
Unsalted butter, use salted butter

I lived in Bushwick, Brooklyn (now referred to as East Williamsburg), back in 2018, and two restaurants defined my time there: Carthage Must Be Destroyed and Roberta's. Roberta's is still around today, and I highly recommend you visit (and order the Famous Original with honey, well done), but Carthage closed down in 2023. Each time I stepped into that millennial pink Australian café, I knew I'd leave happy. The restaurant was spacious and airy with lots of light, the cappuccinos were solid, and the food was so fresh and simple I could die. This was my first extraordinarily devastating restaurant closure, and I find myself remaking my go-to order there often.

I'm indecisive when offered two options. I'll likely want both (see Slightly Salty Mango Lassi, page 261, and Pasta Day Pasta, page 137). Choosing between the scrambled egg options at Carthage left me with that same feeling. In this version of their signature Not-So-Scrambled Eggs, I combined both their topping offerings—Parm and chili—for the cheesy, spicy scrambled eggs of my dreams, served alongside sourdough, herbs, avocado, and tomato, just like theirs was.

METHOD

Arrange the tomato and avocado slices on a platter or large plate. Season with flaky salt and lots of pepper. Squeeze the lemon over the avocado and roughly scatter the herbs on top, reserving some to top the eggs. Arrange the bread alongside.

Heat a small nonstick skillet over medium-low heat. Meanwhile, combine the eggs, milk, chili paste, and cheese in a small bowl and whisk with a fork to combine. Add the butter to the skillet and, once melted, pour in the egg mixture. Season with kosher salt and scramble gently in large strokes until the eggs are just set. Transfer to the platter and sprinkle with more cheese and the remaining herbs. Finish with a drizzle of olive oil.

Serve immediately and build bites combining all the elements for the most ideal eating experience.

CHICKEN KITCHRI

Serves 4
1 hour 15 minutes

Savory porridge is an extremely familiar concept to me. One was kitchri and kadhi, a lentil and rice–based porridge served with a spiced yogurt sauce. When I first tried Korean dakjuk (similar to Chinese congee), a rice porridge made with chicken, it immediately reminded me of the kitchri my mom used to make. Similarly comforting and cozy, the chicken in it made it feel hearty and filling in a haleem-like way (see Shenaz's Chicken Haleem, page 152). Inspired by those flavors, this chicken kitchri is a little bolder in taste than both the dakjuk and the kitchri I grew up with.

The flavor builds fast, but in stages. It starts with rendering the chicken fat from some bone-in thighs. Then onions join in and cook in the residual chicken fat until softened before the spice medley and garlic gets toasted. Add rice, lentils, and water and cook until everything is tender and silky.

I like to serve the kitchri with chilis and black pepper for a fresh, spicy bite, and to add textural contrast, and because I can't resist a good crunchy topping, I like to remove the chicken skins and bake them to a crisp, but that's entirely optional. If you're not up for it, just discard the chicken skins before returning the chicken to the pot to stew with the rice and lentils.

1½ pounds (680 g) bone-in, skin-on chicken thighs (4 to 6)*

2½ teaspoons Diamond Crystal kosher salt, divided

2 tablespoons olive oil*

1 medium yellow onion,* thinly sliced

½ cup (95 g) red split lentils*

½ cup (90 g) basmati rice*

3 garlic cloves, finely grated

½ teaspoon ground turmeric

1 teaspoon ground cumin

½ teaspoon Kashmiri red chili powder

6 cups (1.4 L) water*

½ cup (120 ml) plain whole-milk yogurt*

1 to 2 green bird's-eye chilis,* thinly sliced, for serving

Freshly cracked black pepper, for serving

*INSTEAD OF...

Chicken thighs, use any other bone-in, skin-on cut

Olive oil, use ghee or a neutral oil

Yellow onion, use red onion or 2 large shallots

Red split lentils, use any other quick-cooking lentil variety, or an equal quantity of rice

Basmati rice, use jasmine rice

Water, use broth (chicken, beef, or vegetable)

Plain yogurt, use Greek yogurt or labneh

Bird's-eye chilis, use tender herbs such as cilantro, mint, or dill

METHOD

Preheat the oven to 425°F (220°C). Line a baking sheet with foil.

Season the chicken thighs with ½ teaspoon of the salt.

Heat a large pot over medium heat. Add the olive oil and swirl to coat. Arrange the chicken thighs, skin side down, in a single layer and cook until golden brown, about 5 minutes. Flip and brown the other side (don't worry about it being cooked through at this stage). Remove the chicken from the pan and set aside.

Add the onion to the pot, stir to coat in the fat, and cook, mixing occasionally, until softened and browned around the edges, 5 to 8 minutes.

Meanwhile, rinse the lentils and rice under cold water until the water runs mostly clear. Remove the skins from the chicken thighs and transfer them to the lined baking sheet. Bake the chicken skins until golden brown and crisp, 12 to 15 minutes.

Add the garlic, turmeric, cumin, and chili powder to the onions and stir until fragrant and the spices are toasted, 30 to 60 seconds. Return the skinned chicken to the pot, along with the rinsed lentils and rice and 1½ teaspoons of the remaining salt. Stir to coat the lentils and chicken in the spices. Cover with the water, increase the heat to high, and bring to a boil. Reduce the heat to medium-low and simmer until the chicken is cooked through, 20 to 25 minutes. Remove the chicken from the pot and rest until it's cool enough to handle. Shred the chicken from its bones and transfer the shredded chicken back into the rice mixture. Continue to cook the rice mixture, stirring occasionally, until the rice has split and the mixture is porridge-like in texture, another 20 to 25 minutes.

Meanwhile, combine the yogurt with the remaining ½ teaspoon salt in a small bowl and stir vigorously with a fork until smooth and viscous.

To serve, divide the kitchri among bowls and top with a generous dollop of yogurt. Finish with green chilis and black pepper and crumble the crispy chicken skin over the top.

CUMIN FRIED RICE

Serves 2 to 4
40 minutes

3 tablespoons soy sauce, plus more as needed

2 tablespoons oyster sauce*

½ teaspoon sugar

2 teaspoons cumin seeds*

1 (10-ounce/285 g) New York strip steak or similar well-marbled, fatty steak, thinly sliced*

1 teaspoon Diamond Crystal kosher salt

Freshly cracked black pepper

2 tablespoons unsalted butter, divided

5 scallions, white and light green parts thinly sliced, dark green parts cut into 1-inch batons, divided

5 garlic cloves, minced

2-inch piece ginger, minced

5 cups (600 g) day-old cooked white rice

1 tablespoon toasted sesame oil

Crispy fried eggs, for serving

Sriracha, for serving

Pickled Kachumber (page 198) or pickled onions, for serving

*INSTEAD OF...

Oyster sauce, use 1 tablespoon soy sauce plus 1 teaspoon sugar and omit the ½ teaspoon sugar

Cumin seeds, use 1 teaspoon ground cumin

Steak, use thinly sliced chicken

Cumin, meat, and carbs work exceptionally well together (see Spicy Lamb and Cumin Noodles, page 156, and Rishma's Pilau, page 143), and this dish is no exception. This simple, satisfying meal comes together pretty quickly considering just how much flavor it packs in thanks to the cumin-y stir-fry sauce and all the alliums. While I consider this dish to be ideal with juicy, sliced strip steak, any very thinly sliced cut of tender beef or chicken will work.

METHOD

Stir the soy sauce, oyster sauce, and sugar together in a small bowl.

Crush the cumin seeds in a mortar and pestle until coarsely ground.

Heat a high-sided, nonstick skillet or wok over high heat. Add the steak in an even layer and season with salt and pepper. Cook, undisturbed, until crisp and browned on the underside, about 2 minutes. Stir and then transfer to a plate, leaving as much rendered fat behind in the skillet as possible.

Add 1 tablespoon of the butter, the white and light green parts of the scallions, the garlic, and ginger to the wok and stir-fry until fragrant and beginning to brown around the edges, about 1 minute. Add the cumin seeds and season well with pepper. Add the rice, the remaining 1 tablespoon butter, and the reserved soy sauce mixture to the skillet. Toss the rice to coat in the sauce. Press the rice firmly into the skillet, making sure it makes contact with the skillet, and top with the reserved steak and remaining dark green parts of onion. Cook, undisturbed, until the beef is warmed through and rice is slightly crisp on the underside, about 2 minutes. You'll know the rice has crisped when you hear dry popping sounds. Drizzle with the sesame oil and toss once again.

Serve with crispy fried eggs, sriracha, pickled kachumber, and more black pepper and soy sauce, if desired.

FILL UP 107

Farzana's BIRYANI

Serves 6 to 8
3 hours 30 minutes, plus marinating

FOR THE MEAT MARINADE

¾ teaspoon Iranian saffron threads

2 pounds (910 g) goat or beef, excess fat trimmed, cut into 1½ to 2-inch cubes

2 tablespoons Green Chutney (page 196)*

¼ cup (60 ml) plain whole-milk yogurt

½ teaspoon ground turmeric

1 teaspoon ground cumin

1 teaspoon garam masala

1½ teaspoons table salt*

2 small Roma tomatoes (7 ounces/200 g), grated

3 tablespoons flourless fried onions, preferably Lal Tadka brand

1 tablespoons olive oil

FOR THE MASALA AND POTATOES

2 cups (360 g) good-quality basmati rice

1 tablespoon olive oil

½ cinnamon stick

2 green cardamom pods

3 whole cloves

3 whole black peppercorns

1 (14-ounce/400 g) can crushed tomatoes

2 teaspoons saffron salt*

¾ cup (50 g) flourless fried onions, preferably Lal Tadka brand, divided

Vegetable oil, for frying

2 large russet potatoes,* halved lengthwise and cut into thirds

---

Farzana's constant open kitchen has provided so much respite for me over the years. Whenever I need a place to find comfort, she's there for me, feeding me with an open heart along the way.

Farzana Khalfan is my sister-in-law, married to my husband's eldest brother. She is always in the kitchen with her family, which in so many ways reminds me of my own: mom, dad, four kids who are seemingly always hungry, so much extended family around, and even more snacks. Seeing her with the family she's created makes me nostalgic for the old days of mine. She even cooks like my mom does, in abundance and with a true caring, nurturing attitude. So put together and on the ball, she's the furthest thing from lazy, and inspiring in so many ways.

Khoja biryani is typically a celebratory dish, reserved for Eid, birthdays, and weddings. It's a little more moist than other biryani varieties and is absolutely my favorite kind. It takes a bit of time and quite a few ingredients, but the result is nuanced yet bold. The yogurt-marinated beef braises for hours in a spiced, saffron-forward tomato and onion sauce (aka masala) with fried potatoes (that she sometimes air fries as a shortcut) and lots of aromatic basmati rice. It's a dish I'm always craving and Farzana is somehow always making. Keeping with her can-do attitude, it makes sense she'd make this dish casually, and I can't thank her enough for it.

METHOD

To make the meat marinade: Crush the saffron threads in a mortar and pestle until almost powdery.

Put the goat, crushed saffron, green chutney, yogurt, turmeric, cumin, garam masala, salt, tomato, fried onions, and olive oil in a medium bowl. Stir, preferably by hand, to coat the meat and distribute the marinade evenly. Cover and marinate for 2 hours at room temperature or in the fridge overnight or up to 48 hours.

Put the rice in a medium bowl and agitate it under running water to release the excess starch. Continue rinsing until the water runs near clear. Cover with water and set aside for at least 30 minutes or up to 4 hours.

Preheat the oven to 350°F (175°C).

To prepare the masala, put the oil, cinnamon, cardamom, cloves, and peppercorns in a large oven-safe pot with a lid over medium heat. Toast until fragrant, about 1 to 2 minutes. Add the crushed tomatoes and saffron salt and cook, stirring often, until thickened slightly, 3 to 5 minutes. Add ½ cup (37 g) of the fried onions and the marinated meat and stir to combine. Cover and cook for 5 to 7 minutes, until the mixture is simmering and begins to cook through. Add 1 cup (240 ml) water, cover, and transfer the pot to the oven. Cook undisturbed for 1 hour. Remove the pot to stir, then return it to the oven and continue to cook until the meat is tender, 60 to 90 minutes. The mixture will have deepened in color and thickened considerably.

Meanwhile, cook the rice using the pasta method: Bring a large pot of salted water to a boil over medium heat. Once boiling, drain the

½ teaspoon Iranian saffron, crushed and bloomed in 1 tablespoon water

FOR THE KACHUMBER

1 small yellow or red onion, thinly sliced

1 small carrot, grated on the large holes of a box grater

1 mini Persian cucumber, diced

1 serrano chili, thinly sliced

⅓ cup cilantro leaves, roughly chopped

⅛ teaspoon red chili powder

¼ teaspoon Diamond Crystal Kosher Salt

3 tablespoons white vinegar

FOR THE RAITA

1½ cups plain whole-milk yogurt (not Greek)

1 mini persian cucumber, shredded on the large holes of a box grater

½ teaspoon Diamond Crystal Kosher Salt, plus more as needed

1 small red onion, finely diced

½ teaspoon ground cumin

½ serrano chili, thinly sliced

⅓ cup cilantro leaves, finely chopped

*INSTEAD OF . . .

Green chutney, use a mix of ¼ cup (10 g) chopped fresh cilantro, 1 green bird's-eye chili, 2 garlic cloves, 1 tablespoon lemon juice, and a pinch of salt

Table salt, use 1 tablespoon Diamond Crystal kosher salt

Saffron salt, use ½ teaspoon saffron threads plus 2 teaspoons Diamond Crystal kosher salt crushed together in a mortar and pestle

Russet potatoes, use 6 medium Yukon Gold potatoes, halved

soaked rice, add it to the pot, and cook until tender with a bite, 6 to 10 minutes. Drain in a colander and set aside.

Next, fry the potatoes. Add vegetable oil to come 3 inches up the sides of a large pot or high-sided skillet and heat over medium heat. Once the oil is shimmering (300 to 325°F/150 to 165°C), add the potatoes, working in batches if needed, and fry until golden brown and cooked through, 15 to 17 minutes. Use a paring knife to check for doneness. Using a slotted spoon, transfer the potatoes to a paper towel–lined plate.

Returning to the meat, add the fried potatoes to the pot and stir to combine. If needed, add more water ¼ cup (60 ml) at a time to form a tight but saucy consistency. Cover with one-third of the cooked rice spread into an even layer. Cover and return to the oven to cook for another 10 to 15 minutes to allow the flavors to come together.

Meanwhile, add the remaining rice to an oven-safe serving dish. Drizzle the saffron water over it and gently toss the rice, making sure not to overmix; some of the grains should be stained and some should not be. Sprinkle with the remaining ¼ cup (19 g) fried onions and cover the dish with foil. Transfer to the oven and heat until warmed through, about 10 minutes.

Meanwhile, prepare the kachumber and raita. For the kachumber, add the onion, carrot, cucumber, serrano chili, cilantro, chili powder, salt, and vinegar to a medium bowl. Toss to coat everything in the vinegar and break up the onions. Chill until ready to serve. For the raita, add the yogurt, cucumber, salt, red onion, cumin, serrano chili, and cilantro to a small bowl. Mix to thoroughly combine. Taste for salt and adjust seasoning to your preference. Chill until ready to serve.

Remove the serving dish and pot from the oven and use a serving spoon to transfer the meat and rice mixture over the saffron rice.

Serve immediately with kachumber and/or raita.

FISH FILLET

Makes 4 sandwiches
50 minutes

McDonald's was the fast-food joint that defined my childhood. Between the borderline-too-convenient five-minute drive from my childhood home in New Jersey and the limited pescatarian-friendly options that could accommodate our halal diet at most fast-food spots when I was growing up, the Filet-O-Fish from McDonald's was always a trusty option. Over the years, I really grew to love it. There was something so idyllic about the crisp fish patty, generous dollop of creamy tartar sauce, and salty melted American cheese sandwiched between a fluffy steamed bun.

I don't find myself at McDonald's nearly as much anymore, but I am still in love with a good fish sandwich. This one features all those same components, just tailored exactly to my liking. That means a tender, moist haddock fillet battered and fried until crisp, tons of punchy tartar sauce with lots of pickles and dill (and a little sugar to balance it all), and the same melty American cheese and fluffy brioche bun, for nostalgia's sake.

Feel free to use this breading-and-frying technique for everything. I originally developed it for crispy fried olives back in 2021, but it works well to create a shatteringly crisp coating on just about anything. And if you have extra pieces of fish, trim them into sticks, coat them, and fry them up to make extra fish fingers.

FOR THE CRISPY FISH

- 4 (6-ounce/170 g) boneless, skinless haddock fillets
- 1 teaspoon Diamond Crystal kosher salt, plus more for the fish
- ½ cup (60 g) all-purpose flour
- ½ cup (60 g) cornstarch
- 1 teaspoon baking powder
- 2 cups (160 g) panko breadcrumbs

FOR THE TARTAR SAUCE

- ⅔ cup (140 ml) mayonnaise
- 1 tablespoon whole-grain mustard*
- 2 tablespoons finely chopped fresh dill*
- 1 dill pickle spear,* finely chopped (about 2 tablespoons)
- ½ teaspoon sugar
- Freshly cracked black pepper

FOR FRYING AND ASSEMBLY

- Vegetable oil, for frying
- 4 slices American cheese
- 2 tablespoons unsalted butter
- 4 brioche buns, halved

*INSTEAD OF...

Whole-grain mustard, use Dijon mustard

Dill, use parsley or chives

Pickles, use 1 tablespoon capers

METHOD

To prep the fish: Trim the haddock fillets to a similar size to your buns. Sprinkle salt all over the fish and let stand for 5 to 10 minutes. Keep any extra fish to batter and fry as fish sticks.

Meanwhile, make the tartar sauce: Combine the mayonnaise, mustard, dill, pickle, sugar, and a few cracks of pepper in a small bowl. Chill until you're ready to assemble.

Fill a high-sided skillet halfway up with vegetable oil or a Dutch oven with 1 inch of oil. Heat over medium heat until the oil reaches about 350°F (175°C). If you don't have a thermometer, you can check by dropping a breadcrumb in the skillet. It should sink first, then quickly rise.

To prepare the wet batter: Whisk together the flour, cornstarch, baking powder, ½ teaspoon of the salt, and ½ cup (120 ml) water in a medium bowl. The batter should be similar to pancake batter in texture (you may need an extra tablespoon or so of water to achieve this). In another medium bowl, combine the panko and remaining ½ teaspoon salt and use your fingers to distribute the salt while breaking down some of the panko between your fingertips, creating a finer texture.

Return to the fish and pat dry with paper towels. Transfer the fillets to the wet batter, move them around to coat on all sides, then move them into the breadcrumbs and turn to coat, pressing down to make sure the coating is well adhered.

Gently lay the coated fish into the oil and cook, flipping halfway through using a fish spatula, until the fish is golden brown on both sides, 3 to 5 minutes. Transfer the fish to a paper towel–lined plate and place a slice of cheese on top of each piece while the fish is hot.

Melt 1 tablespoon of the butter in a large skillet over medium heat. Place 4 bun halves cut side down onto the skillet, swirling them in the pan to make sure they're making contact with the skillet, and toast until golden and warmed through, about 1 minute per side. Repeat with the remaining 1 tablespoon butter and 4 bun halves.

To assemble, spread a generous spoonful of tartar sauce over the bottom buns, top with a piece of fish, add more tartar sauce, if desired, and cover with the top buns. Serve immediately.

FRENCH ONION RAMEN

Serves 4 to 6
1 hour 30 minutes

¼ cup (½ stick/55 g) unsalted butter

1 tablespoon olive oil

2 large yellow onions (2 pounds/905 g), very thinly sliced on a mandoline

1 teaspoon Diamond Crystal kosher salt, plus more as needed

¼ teaspoon sugar, optional

¼ cup (60 g) white miso paste

4 ounces (115 g) shiitake mushrooms, sliced

1 teaspoon freshly cracked black pepper, plus more for finishing

2 tablespoons rice vinegar*

8 cups (1 L) good-quality beef broth*

8 to 10 thyme sprigs

12 ounces (340 g) dried wheat noodles, such as ramen

Toasted sesame oil, for serving

2 heads baby bok choy, halved lengthwise

Soft-boiled eggs, for serving, optional

Finely grated Parmesan cheese, for serving

*INSTEAD OF...

Rice vinegar, use a splash of sherry vinegar or red wine vinegar

Beef broth, use chicken broth or good vegetarian broth

The idea of cheesy ramen is not novel, and after watching endless TikTok videos featuring the same, I was reminded of another familiar cheesy brothy soup: French onion. This combination of two iconic comforting dishes—ramen and French onion soup—is all about the broth; it's caramelized-onion-forward with lots of miso and mushrooms to add umami and depth.

As always, starting with a good broth will dramatically improve the flavor of this dish, so I'll usually use homemade beef broth or, in a pinch, beef bouillon cubes to ensure a deep, savory flavor, but a good vegetarian broth, like mushroom, will work well here, too. Still, if a bargain broth is all you have to work with, increasing the miso and and adding a bit of soy sauce to taste will fortify the broth flavor and impart the extra umami that we're after.

METHOD

Heat the butter and olive oil in a large, heavy-bottomed pot over medium heat. Once the butter foams, add the onions, salt, and sugar, if using. (Sugar helps to jump-start the caramelization process.) Stir to coat the onions in the fat and cook, stirring every so often, until the onions are deeply browned, 50 to 60 minutes.

Add the miso, mushrooms, and pepper to the caramelized onions and stir to break up the miso and encourage it to coat the onions. Cook, stirring often, until the miso is fragrant, about 2 minutes. Add the vinegar and broth to deglaze the pot and scrape up any browned bits. Add the thyme, stir, and bring to a boil. Reduce the heat to low and simmer gently until the flavors come together and the broth has thickened slightly, 17 to 20 minutes.

Meanwhile, bring a medium pot of water to a boil. Add the ramen and cook according to the package directions, then drain and divide it among bowls. Drizzle with toasted sesame oil. (If you're serving yours with soft-boiled eggs, add them to the water before draining and cook at a gentle boil over medium heat for 6½ to 8 minutes, depending on your desired level of doneness.)

Just before serving, add the bok choy to the broth and cook until crisp-tender, 3 to 5 minutes. Remove the thyme from the broth and discard it. Taste and season the broth with more salt as needed. Divide the broth among bowls, laying the bok choy over the noodles. Drizzle with more sesame oil and serve with soft-boiled eggs, lots of cheese, and more pepper.

SUPER-SAVORY CHICKEN NOODLE SOUP

Serves 4 to 6
45 minutes

1 pound (455 g) skin-on, bone-in chicken thighs*
Diamond Crystal kosher salt
1 tablespoon olive oil
1 (2-inch) piece ginger, peeled and cut into matchsticks
6 garlic cloves, thinly sliced
1 bunch scallions,* white and pale green parts thinly sliced, dark green parts thinly sliced, divided
1 tablespoon curry powder, preferably Madras style
Freshly cracked black pepper
4 cups (960 ml) chicken broth
3 medium carrots,* sliced ¼ inch thick on a diagonal
6 to 8 ounces (170 to 225 g) fresh wheat noodles, such as yakisoba or ramen*
1 tablespoon fresh lime juice,* or more as needed
Lime wedges, for serving

*INSTEAD OF...
Chicken thighs, use an equal amount of bone-in skin-on breast or legs
Scallions, use 1 medium yellow onion
Carrots, use snap peas, broccoli, or any other veg you enjoy crisp-tender
Wheat noodles, use 6 ounces (170 g) dried ramen noodles
Lime juice, use lemon juice

These noodles are inspired by my childhood delight, Maggi's Masala 2-Minute Noodles. Here, a heavy hand of aromatic curry powder and ginger create an instantaneous depth similar to what Maggi's glorious foil packet achieves. The spice blend, along with a few alliums, lends lots of flavor while keeping things speedy, especially if you're working with a good prepared broth. Skin-on, bone-in chicken thighs also provide maximum opportunity for extracting flavor into the broth, while lime juice adds just enough brightness to offset the deep savoriness of the curry powder.

To keep things easy and in just one pot, and stay true to the thick, almost starchy quality of Maggi Masala Noodles, I cook the noodles directly in the broth. If you prefer a brothier pot of noodle soup, feel free to reduce the amount of noodles, increase the amount of broth by 2 cups (480 ml), or cook the noodles in a separate pot of boiling water so they don't absorb any broth.

METHOD

Season the chicken thighs all over with salt and let sit at room temperature while you start the soup.

Heat the olive oil in a large saucepan over medium heat. Add the ginger, garlic, and white and pale green parts of the scallions and season with salt. Cook, stirring often, until the scallions are softened and beginning to brown around the edges, about 5 minutes. Add the curry powder, season generously with pepper, and stir to coat.

Pour in the chicken broth and 3 cups (720 ml) water and bring to a boil. Add the chicken, reduce the heat to medium-low, and simmer until the thighs are cooked through, 18 to 22 minutes. Using tongs, transfer the chicken to a plate and let cool slightly.

Add the carrots to the broth and cook for 3 minutes. Add the noodles and dark green scallion parts. Cook, stirring occasionally, until the noodles are just tender. Remove from the heat and stir in the lime juice. Taste and add more salt and/or lime juice if needed.

Remove the skin from the chicken thighs and shred the meat with 2 forks or your hands; discard the skin and bones.

Divide the soup among bowls and top with the chicken. Season with pepper and serve with lime wedges for squeezing over.

GOCHUJANG SESAME NOODLES

Serves 4
30 minutes

8 to 10 ounces (225 to 280 g) fresh or dried wheat noodles, such as lo mein, udon, or ramen*

Diamond Crystal kosher salt

¼ cup (70 g) gochujang

3 tablespoons soy sauce

2 tablespoons light brown sugar*

2 tablespoons tahini

2 teaspoons toasted sesame oil

2 tablespoons vegetable oil

1 bunch broccoli rabe,* roughly chopped

4 garlic cloves, finely chopped

Freshly cracked black pepper

Toasted sesame seeds, for serving

Handful of torn fresh basil leaves, plus sprigs for serving

Lime wedges, for serving

*INSTEAD OF...

Fresh or dried wheat noodles, use spaghetti or another long-noodle variety, cooked according to package directions (just don't use anything too flimsy)

Light brown sugar, use granulated sugar

Broccoli rabe, use any leafy green, such as kale, Swiss chard, bok choy, or arugula

This fast noodle dish relies on some heavy-hitting pantry and fridge staples to carry the weight of a *real* thirty-minute dinner. The fiery orange sauce that coats the noodles is made with Korean red pepper paste—called gochujang—earthy tahini, and soy sauce to tame its heat. I prefer using lo mein and bitter, leafy broccoli rabe, but any noodle variety and leafy green you have on hand will do just fine. The basil might seem like a surprising addition, but its peppery quality works really well to reinforce the heat from the gochujang.

METHOD

Cook the noodles in a large pot of boiling salted water according to the package directions. Drain and rinse under cool running water. Set aside.

Whisk the gochujang, soy sauce, brown sugar, tahini, sesame oil, and 2 tablespoons water in a small bowl to combine. Set the sauce aside.

Heat the vegetable oil in a wok or large nonstick skillet over medium-high heat. Add the broccoli rabe and garlic and season with salt and lots of pepper. Cook, tossing often, until the broccoli rabe stems are crisp-tender and the leaves have wilted, about 2 minutes. Add the reserved sauce and cook, stirring often, until thickened slightly, about 2 minutes. Add the noodles and torn basil leaves and toss gently until the sauce clings to the noodles, about 1 minute.

Divide the noodles among bowls and top with sesame seeds and basil sprigs. Serve with lime wedges for squeezing over.

GREEN EGGS
AND HUMMUS

Serves 4 to 6
45 minutes

Through much time spent traveling in the Middle East, I've become accustomed to Arabic-style breakfasts. Usually served with lots of different herbs, olives, dips (including hummus), vegetables, and eggs, they're elaborate yet simple. I think of this recipe similarly: the herby, za'atar-spiced frittata is visually striking yet comes together fairly quickly, and serving it alongside a lemony radish salad and creamy hummus makes it feel much more involved than it actually is.

The frittata—a gift that keeps on giving—is one of my favorite things to make. Frittatas keep for days and reheat beautifully. If you're in a real time crunch, you can skip sauteing the herbs and greens, but the color might not be as vibrant and the frittata may have a little extra moisture. Neither outcome is the end of the world; it'll still be delicious.

Don't be intimidated by the concept of a general mix of greens and herbs—this is the perfect recipe to use up what you have in the fridge and experience the glorious flexibility of this frittata.

120   THIRD CULTURE COOKING

FOR THE FRITTATA

- 2 tablespoons olive oil, divided
- 2 cups (3½ to 4¼ ounces/90 to 120 g) mixed baby kale leaves, dill, chives, or parsley,* roughly chopped
- 1½ teaspoons plus a pinch Diamond Crystal kosher salt
- ½ cup (120 ml) heavy cream
- 1 garlic clove, peeled
- 10 large eggs
- 1 tablespoon za'atar*
- Freshly cracked black pepper

FOR THE SALAD AND ASSEMBLY

- 3 small red radishes, thinly sliced
- ¼ cup (35 g) cherry tomatoes, halved
- ¼ cup (40 g) pitted Castelvetrano or Kalamata olives, roughly chopped, optional
- 1 cup (50 to 75 g) leafy greens or herbs
- Diamond Crystal kosher salt
- Lemon wedges, for squeezing and serving
- Hummus,* for serving
- Olive oil, for drizzling
- Freshly cracked black pepper

*INSTEAD OF...

- Mixed kale, dill, chives, and parsley, use other greens and tender herbs
- Za'atar, use a mix of 2 teaspoons dried thyme, ½ teaspoon sesame seeds, and ½ teaspoon sumac
- Hummus, use labneh or fava bean dip

METHOD

To make the frittata: Preheat the oven to 350°F (175°C).

Heat 1 tablespoon of the olive oil in a 10-inch oven-safe nonstick skillet over medium heat. Add the greens and herbs and season with a pinch of salt. Cook, stirring often, until they've wilted and reduced in volume, about 3 minutes. Transfer them to a blender or food processor; reserve the skillet. Add the heavy cream and garlic to the cooked greens and blend until a paste forms. Add the eggs, the remaining 1½ teaspoons salt, the za'atar, and black pepper to taste and blend until just combined. (Alternatively, transfer the greens mixture to a large bowl, add the eggs, 1½ teaspoons salt, the za'atar, and black pepper to taste and whisk with a fork to combine.)

Pour the remaining 1 tablespoon olive oil into the reserved skillet and heat over medium-high heat. Swirl the pan so the bottom is coated in the oil. Pour in the egg mixture and leave to cook undisturbed until set around the edges, about 3 minutes. Transfer to the oven and cook until just set and slightly jiggly in the center, 12 to 16 minutes. If a custardy texture is not your preference, leave it in the oven until completely set in the center, an additional 2 to 4 minutes.

Carefully remove the pan from the oven. Let rest for 5 to 10 minutes, then slide onto a platter or cutting board.

Meanwhile, make the salad: Combine the radishes, tomatoes, olives, and leafy greens or herbs in a small bowl and add a pinch of salt and a squeeze of lemon.

To serve: Transfer the frittata to a cutting board and slice into wedges. Serve over a swoosh of hummus, top with the radish salad, and finish with a drizzle of olive oil and a grinding of pepper.

Store leftover frittata in an airtight container in the refrigerator for 3 to 5 days. Reheat in the microwave in 30-second increments or in the oven at 350°F (175°C) until warmed through.

Gully's
GAJJAR CHICKEN

Serves 10 to 12
3 hours

FOR THE CHICKEN

7 pounds (3.2 kg) skinless chicken pieces, cut into 4-inch pieces

¼ cup (60 g) garlic paste or finely grated garlic

¼ cup (60 g) ginger paste or finely grated ginger

1 (50 gram) Shan Chicken Tikka seasoning mix packet

FOR THE GAJJAR MASALA

¾ cup plus 1½ teaspoons (100 g) paprika

¼ cup (25 g) Indian red chili powder

2 tablespoons plus 2 teaspoons ground cumin

2 tablespoons plus 2 teaspoons ground coriander

1 teaspoon citric acid, plus more as needed

1½ teaspoons table salt, plus more as needed

1 cup (240 ml) vegetable oil

1 (28-ounce/794 g) can tomato sauce

French fries or rice, for serving

To my mother, all of her aunts are her second mothers. Gulzar "Gully" Ebrahim is my maternal grandmother's youngest sister, and she and my mom have the kind of aunt-niece relationship so many yearn for. Gully Masi (*masi* is maternal aunt in Gujarati) has a generous, loving spirit, and that translates to the way she feeds those around her. Despite coming from a family of incredible cooks, Gully Masi was the only one bold enough to take her talents to the community forefront and was catered for many years, informing my idea of traditional Khoja food almost entirely.

Gully Masi has looked after me and fed me my entire life, even stepping in as my mom from time to time. One of Gully Masi's most iconic dishes (there are *so* many) is her Gajjar chicken, also called Natasha's chicken or chicken poussin, a take on an East African specialty, made with bone-in grilled or roasted chicken, generously spiced and served with fries.

The secret is in the homemade Gajjar masala, made with lots of bloomed paprika and chili powder and some tomato sauce to add body and turn it into a sauce. With this many ground spices, expect the sauce to have a somewhat grainy texture—that's how it's meant to be, and it's truly delicious. Citric acid is one of my all-time favorite ingredients (although I don't call for it in my own recipes very often because it's not easily accessible), and its lemony presence in this dish is what makes it so addictive, in my opinion.

In true Gully Masi fashion, this recipe feeds a crowd, but it can be halved for similar results. Because of the high yield, she recommends using a deep foil tray to catch all the delicious chicken drippings that flavor the Gajjar sauce. If you're halving the recipe, a foil-lined rimmed baking sheet should do the trick.

METHOD

To marinate the chicken: Make 2 deep scores in the flesh of each piece of chicken (stopping just shy of the bone) with a sharp knife and transfer the chicken pieces to a large bowl. Add the garlic paste, ginger paste, and chicken tikka seasoning mix to the bowl and mix together to coat the chicken well. Cover and let marinate in the refrigerator overnight or on the counter for 20 minutes.

While the chicken is marinating, make the Gajjar masala mixture: Put the paprika, red chili powder, cumin, coriander, citric acid, and salt in a medium bowl and mix to combine. Set aside.

Position an oven rack in the upper third and preheat to 350°F (175°C). Spray an extra-large, deep foil tray with cooking spray.

Transfer the marinated chicken to the prepared tray. Bake until just cooked through, 40 to 45 minutes. Remove from the oven and set near the stove.

Increase the oven temperature to 400°F (205°C).

To make the Gajjar sauce: Heat the vegetable oil in a very large pot over high heat. Once it's very hot and shimmering, remove from the heat and add reserved masala mixture. Stir to toast the spices and combine, then immediately add the tomato sauce and stir again to combine. Taste for salt and citric acid and adjust to your preference.

Transfer half of the baked chicken and any resulting juices to the pot. Stir to combine, ensuring each piece is well coated in the sauce. Using tongs, return the chicken to the baking tray. Add the remaining chicken to the pot and toss again. Transfer the chicken and any remaining sauce to the baking tray. This process ensures that each piece is very well coated in the sauce.

Return the baking tray to the oven and bake for 15 to 20 minutes, until the chicken and sauce are warmed through and the flavors have come together.

Serve the chicken alongside lots of fries or rice with the remaining Gajjar sauce for dipping.

HALAL CART
SALAD

Serves 4 to 6
1 hour

New York City's halal cart has become a genre of its own. Adel's Famous Halal Food, on 49th Street and 6th Avenue, is my favorite halal food cart in the city. Their chicken and rice platter features a generous portion of seasoned rice, topped with marinated chopped chicken, salad, grilled pita, hot sauce, and *a lot* of white sauce. As with many things (apart from my career), TikTok has ruined it for me, and a trip to Adel's now includes a one-hour or more wait time. To satisfy the craving on a whim, I've taken the halal cart's ethos and transformed it into a weeknight-friendly salad dinner. The key takeaway here is that broiling chicken is magic, and in less than twenty short minutes, the chicken thighs are browned on the outside and completely cooked through without any active labor or grease splatters. As for the salad, I'm not usually a massive fan of iceberg lettuce, but it really does shine when cut into big chunks—crisp, refreshing, and in true NYC cart style. Before serving, toss the chicken in a quick dressing made of bloomed warm spices and lemon juice that'll seep into the iceberg and permeate throughout the dish. If you like *a lot*, feel free to double it.

1½ pounds (680 g) boneless, skinless chicken thighs (4 to 6)*

¼ cup (60 ml) plus 1 tablespoon extra virgin olive oil, divided

2 teaspoons Diamond Crystal kosher salt, divided, plus more as needed

Freshly cracked black pepper

1 cup (240 ml) plain whole-milk yogurt

¼ cup (60 ml) mayonnaise

½ teaspoon sugar*

3 garlic cloves, finely grated, divided

4 tablespoons fresh lemon juice,* divided

1 small red onion, thinly sliced

1½ cups (220 g) cherry tomatoes, halved

½ teaspoon dried oregano*

½ teaspoon ground coriander*

½ teaspoon ground cumin*

½ teaspoon ground turmeric*

1 large head iceberg lettuce*

1 cup (60 g) salted pita chips,* crushed

Cholula or Valentina hot sauce, optional, for serving

*INSTEAD OF...

Chicken thighs, use any cut of boneless, skinless chicken

Sugar, use ¼ teaspoon honey or maple syrup

Lemon juice, use lime juice, red wine vinegar, or apple cider vinegar

Spices, use 2 teaspoons of a dry spice blend or za'atar

Iceberg lettuce, use 3 medium romaine hearts

Pita chips, use croutons

METHOD

Preheat the broiler to high. Line a baking sheet with foil.

Put the chicken thighs on the prepared baking sheet. Drizzle with 1 tablespoon of the olive oil, 1 teaspoon of the salt, and a few turns of pepper. Toss to coat. Arrange the chicken with the thinner side of each piece toward the middle of the sheet and broil for 16 to 18 minutes, until the chicken is browned, cooked through, and a thermometer inserted in the thickest part of the thigh registers 165°F (74°C). Transfer the chicken thighs to a cutting board and set aside to rest.

Meanwhile, make the salad dressing: Whisk together the yogurt, mayonnaise, sugar, 2 of the garlic cloves, 1 tablespoon of the lemon juice, and the remaining 1 teaspoon salt in a small bowl. Season with pepper.

Combine the red onion and cherry tomatoes in another small bowl. Season with a pinch of salt and toss to coat.

Once the chicken is cooled, chop or shred it. Heat the remaining 1 tablespoon olive oil in a small saucepan over medium heat. Add the oregano, coriander, cumin, and turmeric and cook until fragrant, about 30 seconds. Transfer to a medium bowl and whisk in the remaining garlic clove and remaining 3 tablespoons lemon juice. Add the chopped chicken, toss to coat, and taste for salt. Adjust to your preference; usually an additional ½ teaspoon is needed.

To serve, cut the head of lettuce into 6 wedges, then cut each wedge into 3 pieces. Pour three-quarters of the creamy dressing onto a platter and top with the lettuce and reserved chicken and any resting juices from the chicken, then the tomato-onion mixture and pita chips. Drizzle with the remaining dressing and some hot sauce, if using, and season generously with pepper.

KOOBIDEH MEATBALLS with MINTY YOGURT

Serves 4 to 6
1 hour

¼ teaspoon saffron threads, optional

1 tablespoon hot water, optional

2 medium yellow onions, peeled, divided

1 egg, beaten

2½ teaspoons Diamond Crystal kosher salt, divided

½ teaspoon sumac

⅛ teaspoon ground turmeric

½ cup (50 g) plain breadcrumbs*

2 pints (580 g) cherry tomatoes

2 tablespoons olive oil, plus more for serving

1 pound (455 g) ground beef (85:15 lean-to-fat ratio),* at room temperature

⅔ cup (75 ml) plain whole-milk yogurt*

2 sprigs mint,* leaves finely chopped, plus more torn whole leaves, for serving

Freshly cracked black pepper

2 tablespoons salted butter, melted

Cooked basmati rice, for serving

*INSTEAD OF...

Plain breadcrumbs, use panko breadcrumbs, crushed to a finer texture between your fingertips

Ground beef, use ground turkey or ground chicken (the texture may be slightly less tender)

Whole-milk yogurt, use Greek yogurt plus 1 to 2 tablespoons water

Mint, use dill

Koobideh is a flavorful, bouncy, grilled Persian kebab usually served alongside grilled tomatoes and onions, rice, and a simple yogurt sauce. Between the traditional shaping and grilling of the kebabs, making koobideh is quite an involved process. It's certainly not something you can't do, just something I couldn't do on a weeknight, which is usually when I'm craving this comforting meal. In actuality, kebabs aren't all that different from meatballs, and by flavoring the panade (a French technique for hydrating bread often used in Italian meatballs), I get a soft, tender meatball reminiscent of koobideh.

Part of koobideh's savory flavor comes from juiced grated onion. The grating part doesn't bother me—in fact, it's easier than chopping one up (use a cold one to minimize tears), but wringing out the onion juice feels like a nonstarter for ordinary Tuesday night cooking. So, instead of draining it, I swapped it in for the milk that's usually called for in a panade. The saffron water also imparts a koobideh-like flavor, but I've made it without saffron in a pinch and the meatballs were still very flavorful. Roasting them alongside onions and tomatoes means a fairly inactive cook time, resulting in a built-in side to enjoy with the rice, mimicking the original serving pairings.

If you find yourself on Long Island, Ravagh Persian Grill makes some of the best koobideh (and khoresh gheymeh, a beef and yellow pea stew) I've ever had. They have locations in the city, too, but the location in Roslyn Heights will always have a special place in my heart.

METHOD

Place a rack in the top third of the oven and preheat to 425°F (220°C). Set it on convection, if possible.

If using the saffron, crush it to a powder in a mortar and pestle. Add the hot water or an ice cube to the mortar and stir to bloom the saffron. Set aside.

Grate 1 of the onions on the large holes of a box grater into a medium bowl. Add the egg, 1½ teaspoons of the salt, the sumac, turmeric, and saffron water, if using. Mix to combine. Add the breadcrumbs, mix to combine, and set aside to hydrate. This will ensure the meatballs stay tender.

Meanwhile, cut the remaining onion into quarters and break it up into petals (2 or 3 layers of onion is good) and transfer to a baking sheet. Add the cherry tomatoes to the baking sheet and drizzle with the olive oil. Season with ½ teaspoon of the remaining salt and toss to coat, making sure any excess oil is evenly distributed on the bottom of the baking sheet.

Return to the onion mixture. By now the breadcrumbs should be soft and hydrated; you can check for this with your fingers. You shouldn't feel any grittiness when you squeeze the paste between your fingertips. Add the ground beef and use your hands to completely incorporate.

Using a ¼-cup (60 ml) measuring cup, divide the mixture into 12 to 14 portions (about 2 ounces/55 g each) and roll each portion between your hands into balls. Transfer the raw meatballs to the baking sheet and roll them around in the remaining oil. Bake for 18 to 20 minutes, until browned all over. Switch the oven to broil and broil on high for 3 to 5 minutes, until the tomatoes and onions are charred.

Meanwhile, combine the yogurt, mint, pepper to taste, and the remaining ½ teaspoon salt in a small bowl.

Brush the meatballs with butter. Serve the meatballs over rice and top with the roasted tomatoes, some charred onion, and a dollop of mint yogurt. Finish with more pepper, torn mint leaves, and a drizzle of olive oil.

LAST-MINUTE TAHDIG

Serves 2
20 minutes

⅓ cup (75 ml) plain whole-milk yogurt

¼ teaspoon ground turmeric

1 teaspoon Diamond Crystal kosher salt

4 cups (450 to 500 g) cold cooked basmati rice, divided

2 tablespoons butter (salted or unsalted)

2 tablespoons dried cranberries,* optional

*INSTEAD OF...

Dried cranberries, use chopped dried cherries or raisins

There's always some leftover rice lingering in my fridge. And when I don't have a plan for it, this is it.

Inspired by tahdig, a crispy Persian rice, while not as crunchy as its namesake, this fast and simple dish is perfect for a weeknight whim. Combining some of the rice with a spiced yogurt seasons it, keeps it an even layer, and helps to slow the browning process so the rice heats through evenly before it crisps up in the butter. I've also always been a fan of zereshk polo (Persian rice with barberries), so to mimic that tart, sweet pop of flavor, I use dried cranberries.

I usually eat this with jammy eggs or leftover protein, salted yogurt, and green chutney or herbs to make it a meal. Not bad for twenty minutes and some boring old rice.

METHOD

Combine the yogurt, turmeric, and salt in a large bowl. Mix to combine with a rubber spatula. Add half of the rice and gently fold to coat each grain in the yogurt, being careful not to break the grains.

Before proceeding, check that you have a dish, platter, or cutting board that is larger than an 8-inch nonstick skillet that you can flip the rice onto. Heat the skillet over medium heat and add the butter. Once the butter has melted, swirl to coat the bottom and sides of the pan.

Add the yogurt rice in an even layer and press down to ensure the grains are making contact with the skillet. Sprinkle with the dried cranberries, if using, in an even layer and top with the remaining rice. Press down with the back of a spoon to help fuse the two layers together. Using the blunt end of a spoon, make holes in the rice cake to allow steam to escape to ensure a crispy rice layer.

Cook until the rice on the surface is warmed through to a quick touch and you can see browning around the edges, 8 to 10 minutes. You can also listen to hear the sound change from a constant "hiss" to a "crackle-pop."

Turn off the heat and place a large plate upside-down over the skillet. Carefully, in a swift motion, flip the tahdig onto the plate.

Serve with eggs and/or leftover protein, salted yogurt, and green chutney.

LEMONY, HERBY SHRIMPIES

Serves 2 to 4
45 minutes

5 garlic cloves, divided

1½ pounds (680 g) large shrimp,* peeled and deveined

5 tablespoons olive oil, divided

1 teaspoon Diamond Crystal kosher salt

1 lemon, divided

2 green bird's-eye chilis*

½ preserved lemon (about 40 g),* seeded and finely chopped

¾ cup (180 ml) chicken broth*

¼ cup (½ stick/55 g) unsalted butter

1 loosely packed cup (40 to 50 g) mixed herbs, such as parsley, mint, cilantro, dill, and/or chives, finely chopped

Crusty bread, cooked white rice, or pasta, for serving

*INSTEAD OF...

Shrimp, use chicken, white fish, salmon, or thinly sliced steak, adjusting the cook time accordingly

Bird's-eye chilis, use 1 teaspoon red pepper flakes or 1 jalapeño or serrano chili

Preserved lemon, use 2 tablespoons chopped capers, olives, or cherry peppers

Chicken broth, use vegetable broth or beef broth

Shrimp scampi was my sister's go-to Red Lobster order, and this dish is shrimp scampi adjacent: just a little funkier and spicier thanks to the preserved lemon, the nontraditional herb combo, and the bird's-eye chilis (inspired by the flavors of green chutney).

Using a mix of fresh and preserved lemons really drives home the lemoniness and adds that tastes-like-it-took-hours depth (the reason I love preserved lemon so much in general). And, of course, there's plenty of punchy pan sauce for dipping with crusty bread, tossing with pasta, or just slurping up with a spoon.

METHOD

Finely grate 3 of the garlic cloves and thinly slice 2 of them.

Combine the shrimp, finely grated garlic, 2 tablespoons of the olive oil, and the salt in a medium bowl. Toss to coat the shrimp and set aside to marinate for 5 to 10 minutes. I would do this first thing and then begin to prepare the rest of the ingredients.

Meanwhile, slice the lemon in half, thinly slice one half, and juice the other half. You should have about 2 tablespoons fresh lemon juice.

Heat a large, high-sided skillet over medium heat. Add 2 tablespoons of the remaining olive oil and add the shrimp in an even layer; don't worry if the pan is crowded. Cook, undisturbed, until the shrimp tails have turned pink, about 1½ minutes. Flip and cook on the other side until mostly cooked through, another minute or so. Using a slotted spoon, transfer the shrimp to a platter, leaving behind as much oil as possible.

Add the remaining 1 tablespoon olive oil to the skillet, along with the sliced garlic, chilis, and preserved lemon and stir to toast the garlic, 1 to 2 minutes. Once the garlic has browned in spots and is beginning to stick to the pan, deglaze with the chicken broth and stir to scrape up any browned bits. Stir in the lemon juice and cook until slightly reduced, about 2 minutes. Add the butter and lemon slices and keep stirring to emulsify the butter into the sauce. Return the shrimp to the skillet, add the herbs, and toss to combine.

Transfer to a platter and serve with crusty bread or rice, or toss with pasta.

FILL UP 131

NOT SO NORMA PASTA

Serves 4 to 6
1 hour

⅓ cup (75 ml) plus 2 tablespoons olive oil, divided

1 large eggplant (455 g), cut into 1-inch cubes

3 teaspoons Diamond Crystal kosher salt, divided, plus more as needed

6 garlic cloves, finely grated, divided

2 teaspoons ground cumin

2 teaspoons ground coriander

½ teaspoon red pepper flakes

3 tablespoons double-concentrated tomato paste

1 (28-ounce/794 g) can whole peeled tomatoes*

1 pound (455 g) rigatoni pasta*

1 cup (240 ml) plain whole-milk yogurt

3 tablespoons finely chopped fresh mint,* plus leaves for serving

*INSTEAD OF...

Whole peeled tomatoes, use canned crushed tomatoes

Rigatoni, use another large pasta shape

Mint, use dill

I have a deep love for both Italian food and Afghan food. And while they are not all that similar, they meet in this spectacular, satisfying vegetarian pasta that tastes like it took hours to make.

This dish is partly inspired by pasta alla Norma, a coastal Italian specialty made with eggplant and chilis, and partly inspired by mantu, Afghan filled dumplings served with a fragrant spiced tomato sauce and yogurt. The yogurt to finish might throw you, but just trust me, something magical happens on your palate when that tangy, garlicky yogurt combines with rich, spiced tomato sauce.

P.S. Some of my favorite Afghan food is made at Sami's Kabab House in Queens. If you're in the area, definitely pay it a visit.

METHOD

Heat ⅓ cup (75 ml) of the olive oil in a large heavy-bottom skillet over medium heat. Add the eggplant and 1 teaspoon of the salt and cook, stirring occasionally, until the eggplant is softened and golden brown, 8 to 10 minutes. Transfer to a bowl.

Bring a large pot of salted water to a boil.

Heat the remaining 2 tablespoons olive oil in the skillet. Add two-thirds of the garlic (4 cloves), the cumin, coriander, and red pepper flakes. Cook to toast the spices, 15 to 30 seconds. Add the tomato paste and cook, stirring often, until darker in color, about 3 minutes. Add the canned tomatoes, ½ cup (120 ml) water, and 1 teaspoon of the remaining salt. Crush the tomatoes using a wooden spoon until the sauce is smooth. Bring to a boil over high heat, then reduce the heat to medium and cook until the sauce comes together, about 20 minutes.

Meanwhile, drop the pasta in the boiling water and cook for 2 minutes less than al dente. While the pasta is boiling, make the yogurt sauce by combining the yogurt, the remaining 1 teaspoon salt, the mint, and remaining garlic (2 cloves). Set aside.

Returning to the tomato sauce, add the eggplant and continue to cook until the eggplant is tender and warmed through, about another 5 minutes.

Transfer the cooked pasta to the sauce along with a ladle of pasta water. Stir to coat and continue cooking until the pasta has cooked through, about 2 minutes.

Divide among bowls and serve with the mint yogurt and mint leaves.

ONE PAN(TRY) PASTA

Serves 4 to 6
25 minutes

1 pound (455 g) spaghetti*
2 tablespoons olive oil
1 tablespoon Diamond Crystal kosher salt
6 garlic cloves, thinly sliced
¼ cup (30 g) capers*
1 tablespoon Calabrian chili paste*
1 cup (100 g) finely grated Parmesan cheese,* divided
½ cup (25 g) finely chopped fresh parsley,* divided, optional
Lemon wedges, for serving, optional

*INSTEAD OF...

Spaghetti, use bucatini (increase the water as needed)
Capers, use finely chopped briny olives or preserved lemon
Calabrian chili paste, use 2 teaspoons red pepper flakes
Parmesan cheese, use pecorino or grana padano
Parsley, use chives

I still remember the anxiety that ensued the first time I made Martha Stewart's one-pan pasta. Everything seemed so wrong, but the result was almost too good to believe. How could twenty minutes be enough to have a full-blown pasta dinner that was actually good? Well, it is, and I've been using that technique for my lazy one-pot pasta dinners ever since. There are endless combinations of ingredients, but this one happens to be my favorite. It relies heavily on pantry staples and requires very minimal cutting board time (no onions, yay!).

METHOD

Combine the spaghetti, olive oil, salt, garlic, capers, chili paste, and 6 cups (1.4 L) water in a large pot and bring to a boil over high heat. Cook, stirring often, until the pasta is cooked through and the water has reduced into a smooth sauce, 9 to 11 minutes. If the contents of the pot begin to look dry, add more water, ¼ cup (60 ml) at a time as needed, to form a smooth sauce.

Remove the pot from the heat, add most of the parsley, if using, and cheese, and stir until the sauce is thick and glossy. Transfer to a large bowl and top with remaining parsley, if using, and cheese. Serve with lemon wedges for squeezing over, if desired.

PASTA DAY PASTA

Serves 4
45 minutes

1 teaspoon Diamond Crystal kosher salt, plus more for boiling the pasta

¼ cup (60 ml) olive oil

5 garlic cloves, smashed

¼ cup (10 g) loosely packed fresh basil leaves, plus more for serving (optional)

¾ teaspoon red pepper flakes,* plus more for serving (optional)

1 (28-ounce/794 g) can good-quality whole peeled tomatoes*

1 pound (455 g) spaghetti, penne, or rigatoni*

2 tablespoons good-quality salted butter, plus more for serving

Grated Parmesan cheese,* for serving

*INSTEAD OF...

Red pepper flakes, use fresh chilis, Aleppo chili flakes, or black pepper

Whole peeled tomatoes, use crushed tomatoes

Spaghetti or rigatoni, use any long or tube pasta

Parmesan cheese, use another Italian cheese, like burrata, pecorino romano, or ricotta salata

For most people, Friday is the best day of the week. Growing up, this was true for a couple reasons. Yes, it meant the end of the school week, but it was also the best day for school lunches: pasta day.

Picture massive foil trays stacked and filled with penne (a sight for sore eyes) prepared two ways: with red sauce or with butter. Each Friday, I'd get on line, grab my white paper plate, and wait in agony over making the decision between the two. The truth is, I wanted half of each. I'd tried my luck a few times, but they never obliged. So, I did what any soon-to-be recipe developer would do: I asked for an extra butter packet for my slice of Italian loaf and headed to the table ready to stir it into my pasta. I've been partial to a buttery red sauce ever since.

Silkier than a classic marinara, this pasta day pasta features a full-bodied but clean red sauce. The key to achieving that unique, lusciously rich *umph* is simply using a great salted butter (nostalgically, for me, like the kind you'd use on bread).

METHOD

Bring a large pot of water to a boil and salt it.

Meanwhile, heat the olive oil in a large heavy-bottomed pot or large high-sided skillet over medium heat. Add the garlic and cook until fragrant and browned around the edges, about 3 minutes. Add the basil and red pepper flakes, if using, and cook until the basil is wilted, 30 seconds to 1 minute. Add the tomatoes with their juices and the salt and crush the tomatoes using the back of a wooden spoon until they are broken down. Finally, add ½ cup (120 ml) water and bring the mixture to a simmer. Cook, stirring occasionally, until the sauce thickens and the flavors come together, 18 to 23 minutes.

When the sauce is cooked halfway through, drop the pasta into the boiling water and cook for 2 to 3 minutes less than the package directions, or until nearly al dente. Transfer the cooked pasta directly from the pot into the sauce along with ½ cup (120 ml) pasta water and the butter. Reduce the heat to low and toss vigorously to coat the pasta in the sauce, gradually adding more pasta water as needed to form a silky sauce. Taste for salt and adjust to your preference.

Serve with a pat of butter and top with cheese, basil leaves, and more red pepper flakes, if desired.

RED CURRY ORZOTTO with MUSHROOMS and PEAS

Serves 4
1 hour

3 tablespoons olive oil,* divided

6 ounces (170 g) shiitake mushrooms,* tough stems torn out, caps sliced into strips

½ teaspoon plus a pinch Diamond Crystal kosher salt

1 large shallot,* finely diced

1-inch piece ginger, finely diced

3 garlic cloves, finely diced

¼ cup (4 ounces/115 g) red curry paste*

1 cup (175 g) orzo pasta

1 (13.5-ounce/398 ml) can full-fat coconut milk

1 cup (170 g) frozen peas

2 teaspoons fish sauce,* plus more as needed

1½ teaspoons sugar,* plus more as needed

Lime wedges, for serving

*INSTEAD OF...

Olive oil, use ghee or a neutral oil

Shiitake mushrooms, use portobello, oyster, or baby bella mushrooms

Shallot, use 1 small yellow or red onion, or 5 scallions, white and light green parts, thinly sliced

Red curry paste, use green curry paste

Fish sauce, use 2 anchovy fillets, added along with the curry paste

Granulated sugar, use brown sugar, honey, or maple syrup

Lime, use lemon

Italian risotto is really something special, and while even the classic version is easier to make than it sounds, this version, made with orzo pasta instead of rice, is pretty much effortless. Creamy and comforting, this cross between red curry and a classic mushroom and pea risotto is super flavorful and happens in one pot. It starts with hard searing some mushrooms, then building the base of a flavorful red curry by sauteing lots of aromatics. The orzo cooks until creamy in the curry and frozen peas get warmed through for serving.

The secret to using store-bought red curry paste and transforming it into something that tastes restaurant-worthy is the addition of salty, umami fish sauce and some sugar and lime to balance out the intense, savory spiciness of it all.

If you're looking for a bit more protein, cooking off some chicken or shrimp in some oil before building the curry (either before or after the mushrooms) is definitely an option. Just make sure to season it with kosher salt, check that it's cooked through, set it aside, and reintroduce it when you add the peas.

METHOD

Heat a medium saucepan over medium heat. Add 2 tablespoons of the olive oil and heat until shimmering. Add the mushrooms and cook, stirring occasionally, until browned and beginning to stick to the bottom of the pot, 7 to 10 minutes. Season with a pinch of salt and stir. Remove the mushrooms from the pot and set aside for later.

Add the remaining 1 tablespoon olive oil to the pot, then add the shallot, ginger, garlic, and the remaining ½ teaspoon salt. Stir to combine and cook, stirring occasionally, until the vegetables are softened, aromatic, and beginning to brown around the edges and stick to the pot, 5 to 7 minutes. Add the red curry paste and orzo and stir to coat the orzo in the paste. Toast until fragrant, 2 to 3 minutes. Add the coconut milk and 2 cups (480 ml) water, increase the heat to high, and bring to a boil. Reduce the heat to medium and cook, stirring occasionally, until the orzo is mostly cooked through, about 8 minutes.

Return the mushrooms to the orzo, add the peas, fish sauce, and sugar, and stir to combine. Cook until the orzo is fully cooked and the mushrooms and peas are warmed through, another 1 to 2 minutes. Taste and adjust the seasoning with additional fish sauce for salty savoriness and sugar for sweetness.

Divide among bowls and serve with lime wedges for squeezing over top.

FILL UP

Riffat's
KUKU PAKA

Serves 6
1 hour 30 minutes

(continued)

Riffat Khalfan, my mother-in-law, is a community leader I've admired from afar for most of my life. She's a vision of elegance and strength and inspires many women she meets. While she might not care for food in the romanticized way that I do (unless we're talking about butter), we do bond over a shared admiration for discipline, faith, a good deal, and clothes, of course.

Kuku paka, a coconut milk–based chicken curry, is an East African classic, and every family does it a little differently. Some serve it with rice exclusively, some with mandazi (a slightly sweet yeasted doughnut), and some with crusty bread or naan. I'll never forget the first time I tried hers. I was newly engaged to my now-husband and had begun attending Friday dinner, their weekly family meal, hosted at his parents' house. While they usually do a potluck-style affair, this time my mother-in-law cooked for us all. At only nineteen years old, I was naturally anxious for the occasion—new family, new traditions, new dynamics to learn and understand. But one bite of her kuku paka and a metaphorical shoulder drop occurred in my brain.

This kuku paka isn't like the more heavily spiced version I grew up with. It's simpler, cleaner, and you taste each element distinctly. It's undeniably different from what I knew while maintaining its nostalgic and comforting essence. I didn't know it at the time, but this dish would come to symbolize much for me regarding the path my life was about to take—different from what I was used to but very good nonetheless.

- 2 or 3 tablespoons olive oil, as needed
- 4 Roma tomatoes, halved lengthwise
- 1 medium yellow onion, roughly chopped
- 1 teaspoon garlic powder
- 1½ teaspoons ground turmeric, divided
- 1½ pounds (680 g) boneless, skinless chicken breast, cut into 3-inch pieces
- 2 pounds (910 g) bone-in, skinless chicken thighs, cut in half if large
- 2 teaspoons Diamond Crystal kosher salt, plus more as needed
- 2 (13.5-ounce/398 ml) cans full-fat coconut milk, preferably Chaokoh brand
- ½ cup (120 ml) warm water
- 1 cup (240 ml) unsweetened oat milk
- 2 tablespoons fresh lemon juice, or to taste
- Basmati rice, naan, or mandazi, for serving

METHOD

Heat 2 tablespoons of the olive oil in a large skillet over medium-high heat. Add the tomatoes, cut side down, and cook undisturbed until browned on the underside, 5 to 8 minutes. Transfer the tomatoes to a large bowl. If the skillet looks dry, add another 1 tablespoon olive oil. Add the onion and sear, stirring occasionally, until charred in spots, another 5 to 8 minutes. Transfer to the same bowl and let stand until warm. To the bowl, add the garlic powder, 1 teaspoon of the turmeric, the chicken breast and thighs, and 2 teaspoons of the salt. Stir to combine and leave to marinate on the counter for 10 minutes, or in the refrigerator up to overnight.

Preheat the oven to 400°F (205°C).

Divide the chicken between two baking sheets or 9 × 13-inch baking dishes (the chicken and tomatoes will release liquid, so be sure to use something with a rim). Cover with foil and bake until the chicken is just cooked through, 25 to 30 minutes. Remove the foil, switch the oven to broil, and broil on high until the chicken is charred in spots, 3 to 6 minutes.

Meanwhile, make the coconut sauce: Combine the coconut milk, remaining ½ teaspoon turmeric, and warm water in a large pot. Bring to a boil over medium heat, then reduce the heat and simmer until the turmeric intensifies in color and the mixture thickens, 5 to 10 minutes.

Move the cooked chicken onto a plate. Using tongs, transfer the onion and tomato pieces to the pot with the coconut milk and pour in any juices from cooking the chicken. Using an immersion blender, blend until smooth. Return the pot to the stove, add the chicken pieces and oat milk to the coconut sauce, and bring to a boil over medium-high heat. Lower the heat and simmer until the chicken is warmed through and the sauce thickens slightly, 5 to 10 minutes. Remove from the heat, stir in the lemon juice, and taste for salt. Adjust to your preference, up to another 2 teaspoons salt.

Serve with basmati rice, naan, or mandazi.

Rishma's PILAU

Serves 6 to 8
3 hours 45 minutes, plus rice soaking time

FOR THE BROTH

1 pound (455 g) goat meat, cut into 2-inch pieces

1 pound (455 g) beef stew meat, cut into 2-inch pieces

1 tablespoon finely grated ginger (about a 2-inch piece)

1 tablespoon finely grated garlic (3 to 4 cloves)

1 tablespoon Diamond Crystal kosher salt

FOR THE PILAU

2½ cups (450 g) uncooked basmati rice

½ cup (120 ml) neutral oil

3 medium yellow onions, quartered and very thinly sliced

4¾ cups (1.1 L) broth from above, divided, plus more as needed

1 tablespoon finely grated garlic (3 to 4 cloves)

⅓ cup (32 g) cumin seeds

6 cloves

8 green cardamom pods

1 cinnamon stick, broken into pieces

7 whole black peppercorns

3 medium russet potatoes, peeled, halved, and cut into quarters

3 green bird's-eye chilis

1 Roma tomato, diced

1 tablespoon plus 1 teaspoon Diamond Crystal kosher salt

Cooked meat from above

(continued)

Three words: Death. Row. Meal.

It's crazy to think I feel this way about this dish today, considering my father's preference for it was the worst thing about my food life for a good part of my childhood. Like most kids, I loved saucy food more often than not, and for better or worse, pilau is not that. It's a meaty rice pilaf of sorts made with an aromatic broth, lots of cumin, and near-disintegrated jammy onions.

Rishma is my dear mother and obviously a big part of the reason I am who I am today. She is incredibly generous and nurturing in the most unique way: in the cuddles-and-let's-chat kind of way, but also in the you-need-an-investment-account-for-your-future kind of way. I admire that about her so much. She's never neatly fit into a box or stereotype and has always been fiercely, almost intimidatingly, independent in the kindest way, and thankfully she raised me to be the same. Not unlike our candid mother-daughter relationship, it's a dish I continue to grow fonder of and appreciate with age.

At any request, even via a same-day text, my mom will make this dish for me. While *technically* made the same way in every Khoja household, Rishma's pilau is better, in every sense of the word: The rice is tender, the potatoes hold their shape in the dish but melt in your mouth, and the meat just falls apart. Its excellence comes from her hand specifically—measuring the ingredients and cook time with love and experience.

I've watched and sometimes helped her make this dish, but our time spent together to record and share it in this book was truly special. She walked me through it in my own home kitchen, making sure I had all the tools I needed to be able to make it again without fail. Starting from the very beginning, showing me that good goat meat from the halal butcher means asking for meat from the back legs and requesting some bone-in pieces but still a decent amount of meat, that making the meat broth without a pressure cooker (at my request) takes time, and sharing that I absolutely should drink some of the broth as a treat, seasoning a mug of it with lemon and salt to my taste.

She approached teaching me this recipe in a way I can only dream of teaching my readers a recipe, with precision, intention, and warmth. In the kitchen and in life, Rishma (I call her that on occasion, to her dismay) will always be my role model.

METHOD

To make the broth: Combine the goat, beef, ginger, garlic, salt, and 12 cups (2.8 L) water in a large pot. Bring to a boil over high heat and cook uncovered for 30 minutes, or until it has reduced by about one-third. Reduce the heat to medium-low and maintain a simmer. Cover and cook until the broth has reduced by roughly another third and the meat is fork-tender, 1 hour 15 minutes to 1 hour 45 minutes. You should be left with the cooked meat and 5 to 6 cups (1.2 to 1.4 L) of broth. If too much water has cooked off, top up with water to make at least 4¾ cups (1.1 L) of liquid.

Meanwhile, to make the pilau: Put the rice in a large bowl and cover with water. Agitate the rice with your fingertips to release the starches.

FOR THE KACHUMBER AND
SALTED YOGURT

1 small yellow onion,* thinly sliced

Juice of 1 lemon*

2 green bird's-eye chilis or 1 jalapeño, seeds removed if desired, sliced

¼ cup (35 g) cherry tomatoes, halved, optional

1 teaspoon Diamond Crystal kosher salt, divided

¾ cup (180 ml) plain whole-milk yogurt

Lemony Cucumber Salad (page 60), for serving, optional

Wash and drain the rice until the water runs mostly clear. Let it soak in fresh water for at least 1 hour or up to 6 hours.

Meanwhile, make the kachumber: Combine the onion, lemon juice, chilis, tomatoes, and ½ teaspoon of the salt in a small bowl. Toss with a fork to combine, coaxing the onion rings apart. Let the kachumber sit at room temperature for at least 5 minutes, then chill until ready to serve.

Whisk the yogurt and the remaining ½ teaspoon salt in another small bowl. Taste and adjust to your preference. Chill until ready to serve.

Heat the neutral oil in a large nonstick pot with a lid over medium heat. Add the onions and cook, stirring often, until very softened and nicely browned, 23 to 26 minutes. If needed, deglaze with ¼ cup (60 ml) broth to prevent burning and cook until evaporated. Add the garlic, cumin seeds, cloves, cardamom, cinnamon, and peppercorns and stir to coat the onions and toast the spices. Add another ½ cup (120 ml) broth to deglaze and stop the spices from burning. Add the potatoes, chilis, tomato, and salt to the pot, cover, and cook, mixing every 5 minutes, until the tomato has broken down and the potatoes are about halfway cooked through, 10 to 15 minutes. Add 3½ cups (830 ml) broth, increase the heat to high, and bring it to a boil.

Drain the soaked rice.

Add the rice and cooked meat to the pot and stir. Return to a boil, then immediately cover and reduce the heat to low. Cook for 10 minutes and then stir. If the rice appears dry already, add an additional ½ cup (120 ml) broth. Cook for another 10 to 15 minutes undisturbed, until the rice is tender and all the broth is absorbed. Remove from the heat and let it stand, covered, for another 10 minutes. Remove the lid and fluff the rice with a fork.

Serve with the salted yogurt and kachumber or lemony cucumber salad.

ROASTED EGGPLANT SANDWICH

Serves 2 to 4
1 hour

1 medium (680 g) globe eggplant*

¼ cup (60 ml) plus 1 tablespoon olive oil, divided

1½ teaspoons ground cumin

2½ teaspoons Diamond Crystal kosher salt, divided

1 teaspoon sumac

2 tablespoons fresh lemon juice

2 teaspoons honey*

1 small red onion,* very thinly sliced

½ cup (25 g) roughly chopped parsley*

¼ cup (35 g) cherry tomatoes, quartered, optional

2 soft demi baguettes,* halved lengthwise

1 cup (250 g) hummus, preferably Cedar's

Pomegranate molasses,* for serving

*INSTEAD OF...

Eggplant, use bell peppers or squash (reduce the amount of oil used)

Honey, use maple syrup

Red onion, use yellow onion

Parsley, use cilantro or mint

Demi baguettes, use 1 long baguette, 4 ciabatta rolls, or 4 angel pitas

Pomegranate molasses, use balsamic glaze or very-good-quality thick balsamic vinegar

During Ramadan, for the many long drives to our mosque in Woodside, Queens, my sister, Fatema, would make a very simple pita wrap as a to-go, travel-friendly iftar. I can still picture her today: rushing around the kitchen trying to make enough wraps for all of us, she'd quickly swipe hummus on either side of a warmed pita pocket and fill it with romaine lettuce and sliced red peppers and red onions, wrap it in foil, and place a small plastic container filled with balsamic vinaigrette alongside it in a brown paper bag. That simple sandwich was ideal in so many ways and hit on every texture a good sandwich should; it just wasn't all that filling.

This version stays true to those juicy, crunchy yet soft textural elements but relies on spiced, roasted eggplant to add body and bulk. The crisp herb salad made with onions and tomatoes replaces the lettuce, peppers, and onions, and the sumac and pomegranate molasses dressing adds a deep, savory-sweet element that makes this sandwich so irresistible you won't even notice it's vegetarian (vegan even, if you swap the honey for maple syrup).

If you don't like eggplant, roasted bell peppers and squash would work just as well—you won't need quite as much oil for roasting. Eggplant really loves it and needs it to get to a tender, juicy place when roasted.

The one thing this sandwich isn't is spicy. So, if you absolutely need the heat, consider adding fresh chilis to the herb salad or roasting some whole or halved jalapeños alongside the eggplant.

METHOD

Place a rack in the center of the oven and preheat to 400°F (205°C). Line a baking sheet with parchment paper.

Trim the stem of the eggplant and slice it lengthwise into ½-inch-thick slabs (not rounds). Cut each slab in half lengthwise and transfer to the prepared baking sheet.

Combine ¼ cup (60 ml) of the olive oil and the cumin in a small bowl. Brush the cumin oil over the eggplant slices with a pastry brush and sprinkle the exposed side with ¾ teaspoon of the salt. Flip and repeat with the remaining cumin oil and another ¾ teaspoon salt. If your eggplant is on the larger side and you run out of cumin oil, don't worry. As long as one side is coated, you'll be good—just make sure to salt both sides. Transfer to the oven and roast until tender and beginning to brown, 28 to 33 minutes.

Meanwhile, whisk together the remaining 1 teaspoon salt, the sumac, lemon juice, remaining 1 tablespoon olive oil, and honey in a small bowl with a fork. Add the onion, parsley, and tomatoes, if using, and toss to combine, using the fork to help break up the rings of onion. Cover with plastic wrap and chill for at least 10 minutes, or until ready to serve.

Toast the baguette halves until just warmed through.

Spread ¼ cup (60 g) hummus on each side of the bread. Layer half of the roasted eggplant slices (5 or 6 slices) on the bottom piece and drizzle with pomegranate molasses. Cover with half the onion mixture and close the sandwich. Repeat with the remaining baguette, hummus, eggplant, molasses, and salad. Cut each sandwich crosswise and serve.

SAMOSA-SPICED BURGERS

Serves 4
45 minutes

2 teaspoons Diamond Crystal kosher salt, divided
1 teaspoon garam masala*
Freshly cracked black pepper
1 pound (455 g) ground beef (80:20 lean-to-fat ratio)
1 small garlic clove, peeled
1 green bird's-eye chili,* seeds removed
¼ cup (10 g) loosely packed fresh mint leaves*
¼ cup (10 g) packed fresh cilantro leaves*
1 tablespoon fresh lemon juice*
¼ cup (60 ml) mayonnaise
2 tablespoons canola oil, divided
1 medium yellow onion,* very thinly sliced
4 slices (3 to 4 ounces/84 to 112 g) pepper Jack cheese*
4 potato buns,* split

*INSTEAD OF...

Garam masala, use another savory spice blend or aromatic single ground spice, like cumin
Bird's-eye chili, use ½ jalapeño with seeds
Mint, use more cilantro
Cilantro, use more mint or other tender herb, like dill or parsley
Lemon juice, use lime juice
Yellow onion, use sweet or red onion
Pepper Jack cheese, use American or cheddar cheese
Potato buns, use sesame or brioche buns

I've already mentioned the star power samosas possess (see Samosas Two Ways, page 70), so translating those flavors into a main dish is a no-brainer. Here, garam masala and salt season classic smashburger patties before they get a quick sear in a very hot pan. The technique for this burger is borrowed from Oklahoma-style smashburgers, where very thinly sliced onions are adhered directly onto the burger balls, then frizzled in the beefy, fatty drippings from the meat.

The combination of that spiced, oniony patty with pepper Jack cheese and this burger sauce is what makes this burger truly craveable. When I say burger sauce, I really mean a mayo with green chutney energy thanks to crushed chilis, herbs, garlic, and lemon juice that get stirred in, perfect for cutting through the richness of the beef and cheese. I love potato buns for this because their slightly sweet quality helps balance the savoriness of the burger. If I were to use sesame or brioche buns, I'd probably add ¼ teaspoon sugar to the burger sauce to help tame the tang.

METHOD

Combine 1½ teaspoons of the salt, the garam masala, and lots of pepper in a small bowl.

Divide the ground beef into four 4-ounce (115 g) portions and roughly shape them into balls. Sprinkle the salt mixture all over.

For the burger sauce, combine the garlic, chili, and remaining ½ teaspoon salt in a mortar and pestle. Crush the garlic and chili until pastelike. Add the mint and cilantro and crush to form a rough paste. Stir in the lemon juice and transfer to a small bowl. Add the mayonnaise and stir to combine. Set aside until ready to assemble.

Heat a large, well-seasoned cast-iron skillet over high heat until very hot. Add 1 tablespoon of the canola oil and, working in batches of two, add the ground beef balls to the skillet. Working quickly, using a spatula or a burger press, press down to compress the meat into a ¼-inch-thick patty. Top with one-quarter of the thinly sliced onion and press it into the burger. Repeat with the other patty. Once nicely browned on the underside, 2 to 3 minutes, carefully flip the patties. Top with a slice of pepper Jack cheese and cover the cheese with the top bun, cut side down. Toast the bottom buns in the skillet alongside. Cook for another 3 to 4 minutes, until the cheese is melted, the top bun is warm, and the onions are browned. Once the bottom buns are golden brown, transfer them to a plate and spoon over a heaping tablespoon of the sauce. Transfer the patty and top bun onto the bottom bun. Repeat with the other patty.

Repeat the entire process with the remaining ground beef balls, onion, cheese, and burger buns.

FILL UP

SHAWARMA SALAD WRAP

Serves 4
1 hour

FOR THE CHICKEN

2 tablespoons fresh lemon juice
1 tablespoon double-concentrated tomato paste
2 tablespoons shawarma spice blend*
1 teaspoon Diamond Crystal kosher salt
Freshly cracked black pepper
3 tablespoons olive oil, divided
1 pound (455 g) chicken tenders*

FOR THE SALAD

½ cup (120 ml) mayonnaise
¼ cup (60 ml) fresh lemon juice
8 garlic cloves, finely grated
¼ cup (60 g) tahini
Diamond Crystal kosher salt
Freshly cracked black pepper
1 large head romaine lettuce,* chopped

FOR ASSEMBLY

4 sheets lavash bread*
8 to 12 pepperoncini,* stemmed and halved
1 cup (about 80 g) cooked French fries,* optional

*INSTEAD OF...

shawarma spice blend, use:
    1 teaspoon ground cinnamon
    1 teaspoon ground coriander
    1 teaspoon ground cumin
    1 teaspoon ground turmeric
    1 teaspoon sweet paprika
    ½ teaspoon freshly ground black pepper
    ¼ teaspoon ground cardamom
    ¼ teaspoon ground cloves

Growing up, I often visited Syria with my father. My favorite part of these trips was the day we'd go for shawarma at the very top of a hill somewhere in Damascus.

I was probably seven or eight years old when we stopped visiting, due to the political turmoil in the region, but Syrian shawarma will always be my favorite of the Levantine varieties—it's simple and perfectly balanced with aromatic, spiced chicken, toum (garlic spread), and tart Arabic pickles in a super-thin wheat wrap. I've succumbed to the notion that they're made best in Syria, but stateside, Al Shami Shawarma in Paterson, New Jersey, is the only place that has ever come close. So, when a trip to Jersey isn't in the cards, I make these shawarma salad wraps. They're a delightful cross between two beloved chicken wraps—a chicken Caesar salad wrap and the aforementioned shawarma. Instead of toum, I make a garlicky, lemony tahini dressing reminiscent of Caesar dressing. To replace the pickles, I use spicy, sour pickled pepperoncini for heat and acidity. The fries stuffed inside can be store-bought, leftover, or, if you've got the time, homemade, and are a starchy textural contrast that adds body and flavor. And, since I'm not at a point in my life where a vertical spit makes sense (maybe one day), juicy, pan-fried shawarma-spiced chicken will have to do the trick.

Shawarma spice blend is easy enough to find (either online or at a specialty foods grocer), but if you're heading to a standard grocery store, all the ingredients in the swaps will combine to create a similar flavor profile as the packaged blend.

METHOD

To marinate the chicken: Combine the lemon juice, tomato paste, shawarma spice blend, salt, plenty of pepper, and 2 tablespoons of the olive oil in a medium bowl or resealable bag. Whisk to combine, then add the chicken tenders. Toss to coat and marinate on the counter for 15 minutes to 1 hour or in the refrigerator for up to 3 hours.

While the chicken marinates, make the dressing: Combine the mayonnaise, lemon juice, garlic, and tahini in a large bowl. Whisk to combine, taste, and season with salt and lots of pepper. Depending on the brand of tahini, the dressing may seize. If it does, whisk in 1 tablespoon water. Reserve two-thirds of the dressing in a separate bowl and set aside. Add the lettuce to the remaining one-third of the dressing and let sit; don't toss until ready to assemble.

To cook the chicken: Heat the remaining 1 tablespoon olive oil in a large nonstick skillet over medium-high heat. Working in batches if needed, lay the chicken tenders in a single layer, making sure not to overcrowd the skillet, and cook until browned on all sides and cooked through, 4 to 6 minutes per side. Transfer to a cutting board and slice the chicken into ½-inch-thick pieces.

Toss the lettuce in the dressing.

To assemble: Heat the lavash in the skillet over medium heat, about 1 minute per side. If it comes folded, unwrap the bread into a single layer and spread over some of the reserved dressing. Add one-quarter of the dressed lettuce to the center, followed by one-quarter of the chicken, a

Chicken tenders, use an equal amount of any other boneless, skinless cut of chicken, cooked until a thermometer reaches 165°F (75°C) in the thickest part

Romaine lettuce, use iceberg or another crunchy leafy green

Lavash bread, use flour tortillas

Pepperoncini, use another briny pickle, like dill pickles, gherkins, pickled cherry peppers, or Arabic pickles

French fries, use potato chips or pita chips

few pepperoncini, and some french fries. Fold the sides in, roll tightly to secure, and repeat to make the remaining wraps. Serve any leftover dressing alongside the wraps or with fries.

Shenaz's
CHICKEN HALEEM

Serves 14 to 16 (32 cups)
8 hours, plus overnight soak

(continued)

Shenaz Chevel is the mother of my sister-in-law, Ferwa. I've known Shenaz Aunty for about ten years now, and as someone who's not easily forgotten in general, I still remember the first time I met her. It was before I even knew my husband, and it's interesting to think that she would soon become someone who would feed me so wholeheartedly.

I was traveling with my father from Casablanca to Marrakech on our way to a wedding, and our flight was indefinitely delayed. Someone had mentioned another wedding guest would be on our flight, and it was Shenaz Aunty. My dad and I are both too passive to make a fuss about delays, and when we all met at the boarding gate and expressed our dissatisfaction to each other, only Shenaz Aunty had the will to do something about it. I watched in amazement as she approached the flight desk, adamant that she be told what was going on and why. Long story short, the flight took off soon after, and I admired Shenaz's ability to recognize her power in the situation—she wasn't one to let life happen to her.

In the coming years, Shenaz would spend much time in the United States as she immigrated to North America, and during each visit to her daughter's home, she would gleefully make haleem for our entire extended family. A deeply savory, flavorful stew with Pakistani origins that she learned to make from her mother-in-law, this recipe is one I had been dying to learn.

While she taught me to make the haleem, we chatted about our lives: the complexity of living in a place and community like New York, her son's upcoming wedding, and the difficult adjustment so many women in our community face when they leave their whole life behind after marriage—a normalized reality in our cultural community.

This haleem is high on my list of all-time favorite meals. It's incredibly flavorful and freezes beautifully for cold, winter evenings when I want instantaneous comfort. Shenaz Aunty's recipe feeds a crowd, but halving the recipe won't compromise the flavor. Regardless, you'll need a few large pots to make this happen and a food mill to help process the wheat into a lush porridge. It takes quite a bit of time and should be split into two days as written to make things more manageable.

FOR THE WHEAT BASE

4⅔ cups (905 g) soft white wheat or soft white pearl wheat (2-pound/905 g bag)

¼ cup (60 ml) ghee

FOR THE CHICKEN MARINADE

4 pounds (1.8 kg) bone-in, skinless chicken, cut into 3-inch pieces (any mix of white and dark meat will work)

¼ cup (60 ml) white vinegar

¼ cup (80 g) finely grated garlic (about 12 cloves)

¼ cup (70 g) finely grated ginger (6-inch knob)

FOR THE MASALA

1 pouch (¼ cup/37 to 40 g) Shan brand haleem masala

3 tablespoons red chili powder

2 tablespoons red chili chutney,* optional

2 teaspoons ground turmeric

⅓ cup (30 g) coarsely ground coriander*

¼ cup (35 g) ground cumin

1 teaspoon garam masala

5 tablespoons (50 g) Diamond Crystal kosher salt

3 tablespoons crushed garlic (9 cloves/60 g)

2 tablespoons finely grated ginger (3-inch knob/35 g)

FOR THE CHICKEN CURRY

¾ cup (180 ml) vegetable oil

2 cups (135 g) flourless fried onions, preferably Lal Tadka brand

Masala from above

Marinated chicken from above

FOR ASSEMBLY AND GARNISH

1⅔ cups (115 g) flourless fried onions, plus more, preferably Lal Tadka brand

¼ cup (60 ml) ghee

⅔ cup (140 ml) vegetable oil

METHOD

THE DAY BEFORE

To prepare the wheat base, rinse the wheat in a bowl several times until the water is significantly less murky and the foaming has subsided, about 7 rinses. Transfer to a very large, oven-safe pot with a lid. Cover the washed wheat with water to at least 2 inches over the wheat, about 4 quarts (4 L) of water. Soak overnight at room temperature.

To marinate the chicken: Clean it thoroughly by removing any excess fat. Put the chicken in a large bowl and cover with water. Add the vinegar and soak the chicken for 10 minutes. Drain the vinegar water and quickly rinse the chicken pieces. Add the garlic and ginger to the chicken and toss to coat. Set aside until ready to use.

To make the masala spice blend: Combine the haleem masala, red chili powder, red chili chutney, if using, turmeric, coriander, cumin, garam masala, salt, garlic, and ginger in a bowl. Set aside until ready to use.

To make the chicken curry: Heat the vegetable oil in a large pot with a lid over medium-high heat. Add the fried onions and reduce the heat to medium. Stir to coat the onions in the oil, add the masala spice blend, and stir again. Use ¼ cup (60 ml) of water to rinse out the masala bowl and add it to the pot. Stir to combine the spices and onions, cover, and cook until the spices are toasted and fragrant, 1 to 2 minutes. Add the marinated chicken and any accumulated liquid from the bottom of the bowl and 4 cups (960 ml) of water to the pot. Stir, cover, and bring to a boil over medium-high heat. Reduce the heat to medium, cover, and simmer until the chicken is very well cooked, 45 to 55 minutes. Remove the curry from the heat and transfer the chicken and any bones to a plate to rest until cool to the touch, about 20 minutes. Using your fingers, shred the chicken into bite-sized pieces. Discard any cartilage and bones. Return the shredded chicken to the curry sauce and let stand until ready to use. If longer than 8 hours, cover and refrigerate, otherwise you can leave it on the counter overnight. You can also do this entire process the day of.

DAY OF

Return to the soaking wheat.

Add the ghee to the soaked wheat, cover, and bring to a boil over high heat. Reduce the heat to medium-low, cover, and simmer, stirring occasionally, for 2½ to 3 hours, until the wheat is very tender and can be crushed between your fingers easily, leaving behind just the dark brown husk. If the pot looks dry, add boiling water in 4-cup (960 ml) increments. The wheat should always be covered by ½ inch of water.

Set a food mill fitted with the medium-coarse disk over a large bowl. Preheat the oven to 350°F (175°C).

Once the wheat is cooked through, don't drain the water. While it's still hot, process most of the wheat through the food mill; it will take 4 to 6 rounds. Reserve about 4 cups of unmilled wheat. To help release any jammed husks while processing, turn the knob counterclockwise.

- ⅓ cup (70 ml) fresh lemon juice (from 2 to 3 lemons)
- ½ bunch mint, leaves only
- 4-inch piece ginger, peeled and cut into thin matchsticks
- 2 limes, cut into quarters, then halved
- Naan, for serving

*INSTEAD OF...

- Red chili chutney, use another 1 tablespoon red chili powder, or omit entirely if sensitive to spice
- Coarse-ground coriander, use the same amount of regular-ground coriander

Between processings, discard the husks to make it easier on the food mill. If things are ever feeling too dry, pour boiling water 2 tablespoons at a time into the mill to help process the wheat.

Transfer the milled wheat back to the pot with the unmilled portion. Add the chicken curry and stir to combine. The texture should be similar to a thin porridge. You may need to mix in an additional ½ to 1 cup (120 to 240 ml) water to achieve this texture.

To assemble: Return the pot to the stove over medium heat. Sprinkle the fried onions evenly over the surface. Meanwhile, heat the ghee and oil in a small pot over medium heat until hot, 1 to 2 minutes. Drizzle the hot oil mixture over the fried onions and immediately cover the pot with the lid. Let stand for 30 seconds to toast the onions, then uncover and stir to combine. Cover and transfer to the oven. Reduce the oven temperature to 250°F (120°C) and bake for 1 hour. Remove from the oven and stir in the lemon juice. Cover, transfer back to the oven, reduce the temperature to 200°F (95°C), and bake for another 1 hour.

Meanwhile, prepare the garnishes and accompaniments. Set aside for serving.

Remove the pot from the oven and transfer to a large serving bowl or serve directly from the pot. Top each serving with some mint, ginger, fried onions, and lime. Serve with naan for dipping.

Freeze leftover haleem in airtight containers for up to 6 months. Remove from the freezer and thaw on the counter or in the refrigerator overnight. The haleem will have congealed quite a bit. Transfer to a pot over medium-high heat, add about 1 cup (240 ml) water (plus more as needed) for every 2 to 3 cups (480 to 720 ml) of haleem, and bring to a simmer, stirring often, until the haleem is warmed through and has returned to its original texture.

SPICY LAMB AND CUMIN NOODLES

Serves 4 to 6
45 minutes

2 tablespoons cumin seeds*
½ cup (120 ml) olive oil
3 large shallots,* thinly sliced
Diamond Crystal kosher salt
2 tablespoons double-concentrated tomato paste
1 tablespoon smoked paprika*
1 teaspoon red pepper flakes*
1 pound (455 g) ground lamb
1 pound (455 g) pappardelle*
½ cup (25 g) roughly chopped fresh mint, plus more for serving

*INSTEAD OF...

Cumin seeds, use ground cumin

Shallots, use 1 medium red onion plus 3 garlic cloves, thinly sliced

Smoked paprika, use regular paprika

Red pepper flakes, use Kashmiri red chili powder or Aleppo chili flakes

Pappardelle, use another large pasta

While rich and meaty similar to a bolognese, these spicy lamb and cumin noodles aren't as saucy as a traditional meat sauce. The earthy, spiced oil made with frizzled shallots and caramelized tomato paste creates a deeply flavorful, slippery and silky coating for the wide pappardelle noodles. Another key note: the ground lamb and cumin. A flavor combination inspired by the classic Northern Chinese cumin lamb noodles, it's one I'm quite familiar with thanks to Rishma's Pilau (page 143). So, like bolognese and cumin lamb noodles, but actually not like bolognese and cumin lamb noodles at all.

METHOD

Coarsely grind the cumin seeds in a mortar and pestle; set aside.

Heat the olive oil in a large, high-sided skillet over medium-high heat. Add the shallots and season with salt. Cook, stirring occasionally, until the shallots have softened and are beginning to brown around the edges, 6 to 9 minutes. Add the tomato paste and stir to coat the shallots. Cook, stirring often, until the tomato paste has darkened in color, about 3 minutes. Add the smoked paprika, red pepper flakes, and ground cumin seeds. Stir and cook until the spices are fragrant, about 30 seconds. Add the ground lamb and break it up into small pieces with a wooden spoon. Season with salt. Continue to cook, stirring occasionally, until the lamb is cooked through, about 5 minutes. Reduce the heat to low and keep warm.

Meanwhile, cook the pappardelle in a large pot of generously salted boiling water until just al dente. Using tongs, transfer the pasta into the lamb mixture along with 1 cup (240 ml) of the pasta water and the mint. Cook over medium-low heat, tossing and adding more pasta water, if needed, to loosen the sauce until it coats the pasta, about 2 minutes. Taste and add more salt as needed.

Divide the pasta among bowls and finish with more mint.

SPICED CHICKPEA SOUP

Serves 4 to 6
45 minutes

2 tablespoons olive oil

1 large yellow onion, finely chopped

1 medium carrot (3 ounces/85 g), finely chopped

4 garlic cloves, finely chopped

1 teaspoon Diamond Crystal kosher salt, plus more as needed

2 tablespoons tomato paste*

1 teaspoon ground cumin

1 teaspoon smoked paprika*

1 teaspoon Aleppo chili flakes*

2 (15.5-ounce/439 g) cans chickpeas, drained and rinsed

8 cups (1.9 L) drinkable chicken broth*

Chili Crisp* (page 192), for serving

Lemon wedges,* for serving

*INSTEAD OF . . .

Tomato paste, use 4 chopped, ripe Roma tomatoes

Smoked paprika, use regular paprika

Aleppo chili flakes, use ½ teaspoon red pepper flakes

Chicken broth, use good-quality beef or vegetable broth, or chicken bouillon cubes

Chili crisp, use hot sauce of choice or similar store-bought variety

Lemon, use lime

My dad is forever partial to a stewy lentil situation. Be it a daal curry or a lentil soup, he finds comfort in these dishes, a nostalgic reminder of his college days studying in India. Because of this, I am no stranger to the applications and implications of embarking on the long journey to a hearty bowl of comforting, stewy lentils, and before this spiced chickpea soup came to mind, I'd usually opt for the nearest takeout option.

Inspired by the Lebanese and Turkish spiced lentil soups shorbat adas and mercimek corbasi respectively, I've found that using canned chickpeas results in a similar texture and body as lentils, while cutting the cook time in half (no soaking or cooking the legumes through). Delicately spiced like the inspiration, this version gets served with chili oil and lemon for a finishing boost of flavor, but if you know you like things bold, feel free to double the cumin and paprika.

If you don't keep chili oil on hand like I do, I'd strongly recommend making a simple spicy garlic oil for the top: Heat ⅓ cup (70 ml) olive oil with 3 finely chopped or thinly sliced garlic cloves over medium heat until the garlic is golden, about 3 minutes. Remove from the heat and stir in ½ teaspoon Aleppo chili flakes, ¼ teaspoon smoked paprika, and ¼ teaspoon dried mint, if you have it on hand.

METHOD

Heat the olive oil in a large pot over medium heat. Add the onion, carrots, garlic, and salt and cook until the onion is translucent and has softened, 6 to 8 minutes. Add the tomato paste, cumin, paprika, and chili flakes and stir to coat the onions in tomato paste and toast the spices. Cook until the tomato paste has darkened in color, about 3 minutes. Add the chickpeas and stir to combine. Smash the chickpeas well with a wooden spoon to release some of their starches. Add the chicken broth and stir. Increase the heat to high and bring to a boil. Cook for 10 to 15 minutes, until reduced by about one-quarter and the flavors have come together. Use an immersion blender to blend until smooth and season with more salt to taste. Alternatively, transfer to a blender and puree. Divide among bowls, top with chili crisp, and serve with lemon wedges.

SPICED SHORT RIBS AND POTATOES

Serves 6
4 to 5 hours

4 pounds (1.8 kg) English-style, bone-in beef short ribs, cut into 3-inch segments

4 teaspoons Diamond Crystal kosher salt, divided, plus more as needed

2 teaspoons freshly cracked black pepper

4 medium yellow onions,* thinly sliced

⅓ cup (90 g) double-concentrated tomato paste

6 garlic cloves, finely grated

2-inch piece ginger, finely grated

1 tablespoon plus 1 teaspoon ground coriander

2 teaspoons ground cumin

½ teaspoon ground turmeric

1 cinnamon stick*

1 teaspoon Kashmiri red chili powder*

1½ pounds (680 g) whole baby Yukon Gold potatoes, scrubbed clean if needed

¼ cup (10 g) fresh cilantro tender stems and leaves,* for serving

Basmati rice or crusty bread, for serving

Green bird's-eye chilis,* for serving

Lime wedges,* for serving

*INSTEAD OF...

Yellow onions, use red onions

Cinnamon stick, use ¼ teaspoon ground cinnamon

Kashmiri red chili powder, use ½ teaspoon red pepper flakes or ¼ teaspoon cayenne pepper

Cilantro, use parsley, mint, or dill

Bird's-eye chilis, use jalapeños or serranos

Lime wedges, use lemon wedges

Meat curry, a dish that frequented the dinner table growing up and ranks high on my list of classic Khoja comfort foods, is traditionally made with affordable stew beef cubes cooked until very tender and shreddy. Borrowing on an almost identical flavor profile, I opted for beefy, rich, bone-in short ribs for this cozy meal. It's visually a little more exciting and elevates that weeknight staple into something a little more "wow."

My favorite part of this dish is the whole baby Yukon Gold potatoes that braise alongside the meat for the entire cook time. Keeping them whole with their skin on means they retain their shape throughout the long cooking process but also become soft and fluffy in an otherworldly way without your having to do much.

I like to let the ribs braise in the oven (out of sight, out of mind), but you can continue to cook the meat on the stove over medium-low heat for 3½ to 4½ hours, until the meat is very tender. Remove the short ribs from the pot and boil the braising liquid to reach a saucy, gravy-like consistency.

METHOD

Season the short ribs all over with 2 teaspoons of the salt and the pepper. Heat a large, oven-safe Dutch oven with a lid over medium-high heat. Once warmed, working in batches, sear the short ribs in the dry pot until nicely browned on all sides, 6 to 8 minutes per batch. Transfer them to a plate between batches. Don't worry about adding additional oil for searing; the short ribs will render plenty of fat and release from the pan easily once browned. Add the onions to the rendered fat and cook, stirring often, until they are deeply browned and have reduced in volume significantly, 17 to 20 minutes.

Meanwhile, preheat the oven to 375°F (190°C).

Add the tomato paste, garlic, ginger, coriander, cumin, turmeric, cinnamon stick, and chili powder and stir to toast the spices and coat everything in the tomato paste, about 30 seconds. Add 6 cups (1.4 L) water and the remaining 2 teaspoons salt, then return the short ribs to the pot. Add the potatoes and stir gently. Cover, transfer to the oven, and bake for 3 to 4 hours, until the short ribs are tender and the sauce is gravy-like in viscosity. Taste for salt and adjust to your preference. Sprinkle with the cilantro and serve directly from the pot with basmati rice or crusty bread, chilis, and lime wedges.

STEAK SANDWICH WITH DATE CHUTNEY

Makes 2 (12-inch) sandwiches
Serves 4
50 minutes

2½ ounces (70 g) pitted Medjool dates (4 to 5), torn in half

⅓ cup (70 ml) boiling water

2 (10- to 12-ounce/280 to 340 g) New York strip steaks*

½ teaspoon plus a pinch of Diamond Crystal kosher salt, plus more for seasoning the steaks

¼ cup (60 ml) fresh lemon juice

1 garlic clove, finely grated

½ teaspoon Kashmiri red chili powder,* plus more depending on spice tolerance

2 tablespoons vegetable oil

1 large yellow onion,* thinly sliced

2 tablespoons unsalted butter, plus more as needed

2 (12-inch) soft baguettes,* halved horizontally, warmed

Kewpie mayonnaise, for serving

Flaky sea salt, for serving

2 cups (40 g) arugula*

*INSTEAD OF...

Strip steak, use rib eye or skirt steak

Kashmiri red chili powder, use ⅛ teaspoon cayenne pepper, or more to taste

Yellow onion, use red onion

Baguette, use ciabatta bread, kaiser roll, or another bread

Arugula, use mixed greens or escarole

One of the most popular East African barbecue dishes is mishkaki, small grilled pieces of tender marinated beef usually served alongside ambli, a loose, sweet, and tangy tamarind and date chutney. Borrowing on the flavors of that umami-forward combination, this steak sandwich features tender, seared strip steak and a date chutney with a similarly sweet and sour flavor profile to ambli.

The crisp-tender buttered onions in this recipe add texture and double down on the complex sweet and savory notes. I recommend using fresh, soft bread or toasting the bread until just warm for a more pleasant eating experience. Don't skimp on the peppery arugula and mayo for a truly indulgent experience.

METHOD

Lay the date halves in a small, shallow bowl in an even layer and cover with the boiling water. Soak for 10 to 15 minutes.

Meanwhile, pat the steaks dry with a paper towel and season them generously with kosher salt. Let them rest for 10 minutes.

Return to the soaked dates. Don't drain the water; use a fork to mash them into a paste. You can also do this in a food processor or with a mortar and pestle. Stir in ½ teaspoon of the salt, the lemon juice, garlic, and chili powder. Set aside or chill until ready to use.

Heat a large dry skillet, preferably cast-iron, over medium-high heat. Pat the steaks dry again (the salt will have drawn out more moisture) and rub each steak all over with 1 tablespoon of the vegetable oil. Cook the steaks, side by side and undisturbed, until a deep golden crust forms, 4 to 5 minutes. Turn the steaks over and cook until browned on the other side and an instant-read thermometer inserted into thickest part registers 120°F (49°C) for medium-rare, 3 to 5 minutes. Working with one steak at a time, using tongs, stand the steaks up on their side and cook until browned, about 1 minute. Repeat for the remaining edges. Transfer to a cutting board and reserve the skillet. Allow the steak to rest for at least 10 minutes.

Meanwhile, reduce the heat under the skillet to medium and add the onion, butter, and the remaining pinch of salt to the skillet. Toss to coat and cook, tossing occasionally and scraping up any browned bits on the bottom of the skillet, until the onion is browned and crisp-tender, 4 to 6 minutes. Set aside.

Return to the steak and slice it against the grain into ¼-inch-thick slices.

To assemble the sandwiches, squeeze mayonnaise on the inside of each warmed bread half. Divide the steak between the sandwiches, shingling it on a diagonal, and season with flaky salt. Top with the buttered onion and arugula. Divide the date chutney between the sandwiches, spreading it over the top pieces of bread, and close the sandwiches.

Cut the sandwiches into halves or quarters and serve.

FILL UP 165

Sukayna's OMELET

Serves 2 to 4
25 minutes

2 medium red onions, finely chopped
1 serrano chili,* finely chopped
1½ teaspoons garlic paste or finely grated garlic
1½ teaspoons ginger paste or finely grated ginger
1 teaspoon Himalayan pink salt
1 tablespoon sambal oelek*
5 large eggs
3 tablespoons vegetable oil
Buttered toast, for serving
Achaar, for serving

*INSTEAD OF...

Serrano chili, use 2 green bird's-eye chilis
Sambal oelek, use 1 teaspoon red chili powder

Both my dad's parents had passed away by the time he was twenty-five. His siblings are his everything, especially his younger brother, Abdul, and his wife, Sukayna, closest in age and proximity. As a result of losing his parents at a young age, my dad will take any opportunity to praise those who offered him support during his early life, the people who cared for him when his parents couldn't. Sukayna Chachi (Hindi for paternal uncle's wife) is one of those people. She always offers him a place in her home without a question asked or side eye in sight—a testament to her incredibly generous, kind-hearted, and compassionate nature. Though she is seemingly shy and reserved, she is one of the silliest, funniest people I know.

When I was growing up, our family would often stay over at my uncle's house, and the following morning my aunt would always prepare this dish for breakfast. And every time, without fail, my dad would remark, "This tastes just like Mummy's." I didn't think much of it then, but now I appreciate my aunt even more for creating a place where my dad could find a piece of a loved one long gone.

This simple spiced omelet is a common South Asian dish, sometimes called a masala omelet and made slightly differently from household to household. Hers is well-seasoned and heavy on the onion, lending a unique texture. My aunt would always serve this with achaar (spicy pickle), kaiser rolls, Country Crock butter, and chai. Anytime I make Sukayna's omelet now, I think of my late grandmother, knowing she had great taste despite never having known her.

METHOD

Combine the onions, chili, garlic paste, ginger paste, salt, sambal oelek, and eggs in a large bowl. Whisk well to combine.

Heat a 12-inch nonstick skillet over medium heat until warm. Add the vegetable oil, then pour in the egg mixture. Cook, undisturbed, until browned on the underside, 4 to 6 minutes. Working from the edge closest to you, fold in the omelet a few inches, then slide the whole omelet down toward you. Push any wet egg mixture from the exposed top of the omelet up into the now-empty edge of the pan. Continue this process, folding in the closest edge and pushing any wet egg out, until the entire omelet is rolled and the seam is on the underside. Slide onto a platter, slice into even sections, and serve with buttered toast, achaar, and chai.

SUNGOLD AND SAFFRON SPAGHETTI

Serves 4
1 hour

1 tablespoon Diamond Crystal kosher salt, plus more for boiling the pasta

½ cup (120 ml) olive oil, plus more for serving

1 large yellow onion, thinly sliced

¾ teaspoon saffron threads, preferably Iranian

6 garlic cloves

½-inch piece ginger, peeled

2 pints (550 g) sungold tomatoes*

Freshly cracked black pepper*

1 pound (455 g) spaghetti*

*INSTEAD OF...

Sungold tomatoes, use cherry tomatoes

Freshly cracked black pepper, use 1 teaspoon red pepper flakes

Spaghetti, use any other pasta shape

This idea hit me while learning to make Farzana's Biryani (page 108). As I watched my sister-in-law prepare the saffron-forward tomato and onion masala for the meat braise, I found myself wishing I had some spaghetti to twirl in that sauce.

In the coming days, I incorporated some of those flavors into my go-to basic summertime fresh tomato sauce. The result: an aromatic, bright, and simultaneously warming pasta dish. Saffron aside, the ingredients are quite simple and straightforward, and I consider this pasta an elevated basic of sorts—one that can make a Wednesday night feel like a Friday night.

I used sungolds for their sweet flavor and saturated yellow-orange hue, similar to the color of bloomed saffron, but good red cherry tomatoes will absolutely work.

METHOD

Bring a large pot of lightly salted water to a boil.

Heat the olive oil in a large, high-sided skillet or Dutch oven over medium heat. Add the onions and cook, stirring often, until completely softened and beginning to lightly brown around the edges, 10 to 12 minutes.

Meanwhile, combine the saffron and 1 tablespoon salt in a mortar and pestle and crush to form a powder. Add the garlic and ginger and smash together to create a paste.

Once the onion has cooked down, stir the saffron paste into the skillet and cook until fragrant. Add the tomatoes, cover, and cook until the tomatoes burst, 5 to 7 minutes. Season generously with pepper. Using a wooden spoon, gently press down on the tomatoes, encouraging any that haven't burst. Add ½ cup (120 ml) water and simmer for 12 to 15 minutes, until the sauce is thickened and any stubborn tomatoes have burst. If you prefer a smooth sauce, blend using an immersion blender or in a standing blender until smooth and transfer back to the skillet.

While the tomatoes simmer, cook the pasta according to the package directions 1 to 2 minutes less than al dente. Transfer to the sungold sauce along with ½ cup (120 ml) of the pasta water. Toss until the sauce clings to the pasta. Serve with more black pepper and a drizzle of good olive oil.

TANDOORI TACOS

Serves 4 to 6
1 hour 30 minutes

¼ cup (60 ml) plain whole-milk yogurt

1 tablespoon orange juice,* optional

1 tablespoon plus ½ teaspoon Diamond Crystal kosher salt, divided

1½ teaspoons garam masala

1 tablespoon Kashmiri red chili powder*

½ teaspoon ground turmeric

6 garlic cloves, finely grated

1-inch piece ginger, finely grated

1½ pounds (680 g) skirt steak,* cut into 4 (4- to 6-inch) segments

½ medium red onion,* finely chopped

1 cup (145 g) cherry tomatoes, halved or quartered

1 jalapeño,* thinly sliced

1 cup (40 g) roughly chopped fresh cilantro leaves and tender stems*

2 tablespoons fresh lime juice

2 tablespoons vegetable oil

Flaky sea salt

12 to 16 (5-inch) tortillas, for serving

Sour cream,* for serving

Lime wedges, for serving

*INSTEAD OF...

Orange juice, use ½ teaspoon sugar plus ½ teaspoon baking soda

Kashmiri red chili powder, use 2½ teaspoons paprika plus ½ teaspoon cayenne pepper

Skirt steak, use rib eye or sirloin

Red onion, use yellow onion

Jalapeño, use bird's-eye or serrano chili

Cilantro, use mint or dill

Sour cream, use crème fraîche or plain Greek yogurt

The term *tandoori* in South Asian cooking typically refers to yogurt-marinated protein cooked in a clay oven known as a tandoor. So, while this taco hasn't been anywhere near a tandoor, the yogurt-marinated skirt steak that sears hot and fast reminds me of that same concept.

The marinade draws inspiration from traditional tandoori chicken, with a mild, fruity heat from Kashmiri red chili powder and, of course, a yogurt base for tenderizing. The orange juice adds sweetness and serves as an additional meat tenderizer, a technique I borrowed from Mexican carne asada and Cuban mojo, dishes I came to know and love from my time at the *Bon Appétit* Test Kitchen (shout out to Inés Anguiano, who was always so mindful of my halal diet and made her unreal carne asada for me quite a few times). As ever, the salad ingredients are flexible—you can swap alliums and chili varieties with whatever you have on hand.

METHOD

To make the marinade: Combine the yogurt, orange juice, 1 tablespoon of the kosher salt, the garam masala, chili powder, turmeric, garlic, and ginger in a medium bowl. Add the steak and mix well to coat completely. Marinate the meat for at least 30 minutes or up to 4 hours at room temperature, or cover and refrigerate for up to 24 hours.

To assemble: Combine the onion, tomatoes, chili, cilantro, and lime juice in a small bowl. Chill until ready to serve. Add the remaining ½ teaspoon kosher salt just before serving.

Heat a large cast-iron or stainless-steel skillet over medium-high heat until very hot or smoking. Add 1 tablespoon of the vegetable oil and, working with 2 steak segments at a time, sear until deeply browned on both sides and cooked to your desired doneness, about 3 minutes per side for medium (140°F/60°C on a meat thermometer). Transfer to a cutting board, sprinkle with flaky salt, and let rest for 5 minutes. Repeat with the remaining 1 tablespoon vegetable oil and 2 steaks.

Meanwhile, warm the tortillas in a small nonstick skillet over medium heat for about 30 seconds per side. Transfer to a plate and cover with a tea towel to keep warm.

Return to the steak and thinly slice it against the grain and then crosswise into bite-sized pieces. Arrange the steak on the tortillas and top with some of the onion mixture and sour cream. Serve the tacos with lime wedges for squeezing over and the remaining onion mixture.

THAI-STYLE CRISPY SALMON AND RICE

Serves 4
1 hour

2 cups (360 g) jasmine rice*

5 tablespoons fresh lime juice, from 2 to 3 limes

¼ cup (60 ml) olive oil

3 tablespoons fish sauce

3 tablespoons packed light brown sugar*

1 to 2 green bird's-eye chilis,* halved lengthwise, plus more to taste, optional

Diamond Crystal kosher salt

4 (4-ounce/115 g) salmon fillets, skin on

1 pound mini cucumbers,* (about 5/455 g), sliced into ¼-inch-thick rounds

1 large shallot,* thinly sliced

1 cup (30 to 40 g) roughly chopped fresh cilantro, leaves and tender stems*

¼ cup (8 to 10 g) fresh Thai basil leaves,* roughly chopped

3 tablespoons roasted salted peanuts, roughly chopped

*INSTEAD OF...

Jasmine rice, use basmati rice, brown rice, or sushi rice

Light brown sugar, use dark brown sugar, maple syrup, or honey

Bird's-eye chilis, use jalapeño or serrano

Cucumbers, use another crunchy, raw veg

Shallot, use the equivalent of red onion plus a minced garlic clove

Cilantro, use another tender-stemmed herb

Thai basil, use Italian basil plus a few tarragon leaves to mimic the licorice-y quality of Thai basil

---

The skin on this salmon is so crispy and crunchy, it immediately reminds me of my favorite Thai dish: yum pla duk foo, a crispy fried whole fish served with a sweet, salty, and tangy green mango salad. My version is way less involved but satisfies that craving and mimics the interplay of flavors and textures well.

For a full dinner, I like to serve the fish and salad over a bed of rice to soak up all that extra dressing. Green mango isn't the easiest to find, so I doubled down on the crisp factor and opted for cucumber.

This technique for cooking salmon takes me by surprise every time I employ it, and it results in the crispiest salmon skin I've ever had, so don't be nervous. In my experience, the dry skillet method works every time, but if the idea of it makes you anxious and you don't feel like conquering your fears at dinnertime, I get it. Instead, I would recommend the following: Pat the salmon fillets dry with a paper towel and season the flesh side with salt. Heat enough olive oil to cover the bottom of a large stainless steel or nonstick pan and cook the salmon over medium heat, skin side down, in the oil, until mostly cooked through (6 to 7 minutes). Flip the salmon over and cook until just cooked through, another minute or two. Serve skin side up.

The salmon may seem austere, but between the fresh cucumber salad, the punchy dressing, and the texture of its crispy skin, there's plenty to chew on.

METHOD

Cook the rice according to the package directions.

To make the salad dressing: Put the lime juice, olive oil, fish sauce, brown sugar, and chilis, if using, in a jar and shake to combine. Taste the dressing for salt and spice and adjust to your preference with more salt as needed and/or another chili for more heat. Remove the chili at this point for a less intense heat (the dressing will continue to get spicier as the chili sits in it). The dressing can be made up to 2 days in advance. Transfer to an airtight container and chill.

Pat the salmon fillets dry with paper towels and season all over with salt. Arrange the fillets skin side down in a large, cold, dry cast-iron skillet. Place the skillet over medium heat and cook the salmon undisturbed until the skin is crisp and deeply browned and the flesh is opaque halfway up the sides, about 5 minutes. Turn the fillets over and cook until just opaque throughout, about 4 minutes. Stand the fillets on their sides and cook until lightly browned, about 30 seconds per side.

To make the salad: Combine the cucumbers, shallot, cilantro, basil, and most of the peanuts (reserving some to garnish) in a medium bowl. Set aside until just about to serve.

Just before serving, pour the dressing over the cucumber salad and toss to coat. Taste and season with salt to your preference.

To serve, arrange the salmon skin side up over the rice. Top with a heap of the cucumber salad and garnish with the remaining peanuts. Drizzle the remaining dressing on top.

A GREAT TUNA MELT

Serves 4
30 minutes

1 small red onion, finely chopped

1 medium celery stalk, finely chopped

½ cup (120 ml) Kewpie mayonnaise*

⅓ cup (17 g) finely chopped fresh dill*

1 tablespoon drained capers,* plus up to 1 tablespoon brine

1 tablespoon fresh lemon juice

1 (7-ounce/200 g) can oil-packed tuna* (filleted or chunked), drained

Freshly cracked black pepper

2 tablespoons butter, salted or unsalted, at room temperature

8 slices Pullman or sourdough bread

4 slices American cheese*

Dill pickles, for serving

Cape Cod Kettle Cooked Potato Chips, for serving

Frank's RedHot hot sauce, for serving

*INSTEAD OF...

Kewpie mayonnaise, use another type of mayonnaise

Dill, use parsley

Drained capers, use pickled jalapeños or pepperoncini

Oil-packed tuna, use tuna in water, very well drained

American cheese, use cheddar, Swiss, or pepper Jack cheese

A warm, toasty, cheesy tuna melt ranks high on my list of favorite sandwiches.

In my book, a good tuna melt must meet a few criteria: First, the cheese must be fully melted and oozy. Second, there must be an abundance of red onion and celery for crunch in every bite. Third, a pickle-y, briny element is necessary for both acidity and saltiness. And last but not least, there must be kettle chips alongside—ideally a dill pickle spear, too, but chips at the bare minimum. Dousing them with Frank's hot sauce is the way to go—just trust me on it. Enjoy this sandwich for lunch, dinner, or, my preference, as a midnight snack.

METHOD

In a medium bowl, combine the onion, celery, mayonnaise, dill, capers, and lemon juice. Mix in the drained tuna, breaking it up with a fork. Season generously with pepper. Taste for salt and add up to 1 tablespoon of brine as needed.

Spread butter over one side of the 8 bread slices, dividing it evenly. Turn the slices buttered side down. Put a slice of cheese on 4 slices of bread. Divide the tuna mixture evenly over the cheese. Close up the sandwiches with the remaining 4 bread slices, buttered side up.

Heat a large cast-iron skillet over medium heat. Working in batches if needed, place the sandwiches cheese side down in the skillet and cook, turning once and pressing down with a fish spatula to ensure good contact with skillet, until the bread is golden brown and crisp and the cheese is melted, about 4 minutes per side.

Transfer the sandwiches to a cutting board and slice in half. Serve with dill pickles and potato chips doused with hot sauce.

TORTELLINI EN PRESERVED LEMON BRODO

Serves 4
35 minutes

¼ cup (½ stick/55 g) unsalted butter
1 small preserved lemon, thinly sliced, seeds removed
3 garlic cloves, minced
8 cups (1.9 L) drinkable chicken broth
1¼ pounds (570 g) fresh cheese tortellini*
Freshly cracked black pepper, for serving
Grated Parmesan cheese, for serving
Lemon zest and juice, for serving

*INSTEAD OF...

Cheese tortellini, use another variety of tortellini, another small stuffed pasta, or frozen gyoza or wontons

Tortellini en brodo is a classic Italian comfort food featuring stuffed pasta swimming in a warm broth. It wasn't until a couple years ago that I tried a variation of it at Bonnie's in Brooklyn, New York, serving up wun tun en brodo featuring seafood-stuffed wontons in a citrus-Parm broth. In the months following my experience there, I thought about that cozy broth a lot. And when the Resy cards weren't in my favor one weeknight, I came up with this: a quick-fix dinner with fast flavor from savory chicken bouillon and punchy preserved lemon. The broth is the star here, and I'll often swap out the tortellini for frozen gyoza and add a sprinkle of spring onion.

Using a flavorful broth you'd be happy to drink is important when there are so few ingredients, and my-go to for broth in general is halal chicken bouillon cubes because they're an easy-to-source halal option and keep for quite some time in the pantry. The preserved lemon, browned butter, lemon, garlic, and Parmesan do some heavy lifting, but starting strong is always a good idea.

METHOD

Melt the butter in a large pot over medium heat. Lay the preserved lemon slices across the bottom in an even layer. Cook until the butter begins to smell nutty and starts to brown, 3 to 5 minutes. Add the garlic, stir to combine, and cook until fragrant and golden around the edges, another 2 minutes or so. Add the chicken broth and stir to combine. Increase the heat to high and bring to a boil. Add the tortellini and cook in the broth according to the package directions, usually 3 to 5 minutes. Divide the tortellini among bowls, pour over the broth, and serve with pepper, a heap of grated cheese, some lemon zest, and a squeeze of lemon.

TURKISH-ISH EGGS

Serves 4
30 minutes

6 large eggs

1½ cups (360 ml) labneh*

2 garlic cloves, grated

2 tablespoon finely chopped fresh dill,* plus sprigs for garnish

1 teaspoon plus a pinch of Diamond Crystal kosher salt

Flaky sea salt

2 tablespoons unsalted butter

1 teaspoon Aleppo chili flakes*

Lemon zest, for serving, optional

Crusty bread,* for serving

*INSTEAD OF...

Labneh, use Greek yogurt or skyr

Dill, use basil, cilantro, chives, or parsley

Aleppo chili flakes, use ½ teaspoon (or more to your preference) red pepper flakes plus ½ teaspoon smoked paprika

Crusty bread, use warmed pita or rice

If you've ever visited Turkey, or even been to a Turkish restaurant for breakfast for that matter, you've probably heard of çılbır. Pronounced "chl-br," it's an egg dish traditionally made with poached eggs, creamy strained yogurt, and a red pepper–spiced butter. I was skeptical of the combination before I tried it, but it really is more than the sum of its parts. Between the fatty elements of the jammy egg yolk and garlicky, spiced butter and the tangy, herby labneh, you're left with an indulgent and rich breakfast dish perfect for scooping up with crusty bread.

Because poaching multiple eggs at once is quite literally my worst nightmare, I've opted for some seven-minute boiled eggs, saving myself from stove-side babysitting. Keep in mind that the fats in the chili butter set quickly, so rewarm it just before serving.

This is a great prep-ahead dish to feed a group. The herby yogurt mixture, chili butter, and eggs can be made ahead and stored in the fridge.

Note: Older eggs are much easier to peel, so try to avoid using a fresh carton.

METHOD

Bring a medium pot of water to a gentle boil over medium-high heat. Add the eggs and boil for 6 to 8 minutes, depending on your desired level of doneness: 6 minutes for a runny yolk, 6½ minutes for a jammy yolk, 7 minutes for a set but moist yolk, and 8 minutes for a firm yolk.

Meanwhile, whisk together the labneh, garlic, dill, and 1 teaspoon of the kosher salt in a medium bowl, then spread the mixture over a platter.

Drain the water from the egg pot and run cold water over the eggs, letting the pot fill with cold water to cover the eggs. Let rest until they are just cool enough to handle, 30 seconds to 1 minute. Drain and reserve the pot. Peel and halve the eggs, then arrange them over the labneh mixture. Season the eggs with a sprinkle of flaky salt.

Just before serving, heat the butter in the reserved pot over medium heat until melted and beginning to bubble. Remove from the heat and add the chili flakes and the remaining pinch of kosher salt. Stir to combine and drizzle the chili butter over the eggs. Finish with flaky salt, lemon zest, if using, and dill sprigs. Serve with crusty bread for dipping.

Do-ahead: The chili butter can be made up to 2 days in advance; cover and chill. Reheat just before serving. The labneh mixture can be made up to 2 days in advance; cover and chill. Make the soft-boiled eggs up to 2 days in advance; do not peel. Before serving, peel the eggs and cover with very hot tap water to warm. Let stand for 2 minutes before draining the water.

UDON CARBONARA

Serves 4
30 minutes

3 large egg yolks, plus more (optional) for serving

4 ounces (115 g) pecorino romano cheese,* finely grated, divided

3 tablespoons olive oil

1 medium onion, very thinly sliced

Diamond Crystal kosher salt

3 (8-ounce/225 g) blocks frozen Sanuki udon noodles*

4 garlic cloves, thinly sliced

Freshly cracked black pepper*

1 teaspoon soy sauce*

*INSTEAD OF...

Pecorino romano, use Parmesan cheese

Udon noodles, use fettuccine, bucatini, or ramen noodles

Black pepper, use white pepper or red pepper flakes

Soy sauce, use white miso paste, tamari, oyster sauce, a mashed anchovy fillet, or fish sauce

The classic version of carbonara uses pork fat as a base for the creamy, rich sauce, lending tons of salty, meaty flavor that I, put simply, can't eat. Riffing off its basic formula, this version leans on onions and garlic to anchor the dish, while the combination of pecorino and soy sauce impart the umami of using meat. Using udon as the noodle here might feel a bit awkward, but trust me, the bouncy, chewy factor works. Behold: a culinary experiment gone right.

METHOD

Whisk the egg yolks and 3 ounces (85 g) of the grated cheese in a medium bowl to combine; set aside.

Heat the olive oil in a large skillet over medium-high heat. Add the onion and season with a pinch of salt. Cook, stirring occasionally, until the onion is softened and just beginning to brown around the edges, 7 to 9 minutes.

Meanwhile, cook the frozen udon noodles in a large pot of boiling salted water undisturbed for 20 seconds. Using tongs, gently release them from their caked state and continue to cook until tender, about 45 seconds more (but no longer than 1 minute). Drain the noodles, reserving 2 cups (480 ml) of the noodle cooking liquid.

Returning to the skillet, stir in the garlic and cook until fragrant and golden brown around the edges, about 3 minutes. Season generously with pepper (add more than you think; it can handle it) and stir to toast it in the oil. Add ½ cup (120 ml) of the noodle cooking liquid and the soy sauce and stir to combine, scraping up any browned bits stuck to the bottom of the pan. Reduce the heat to its lowest setting possible and add the noodles and reserved egg mixture. Pour 1 cup (240 ml) of the noodle cooking liquid over the egg mixture to gently temper, then toss vigorously with tongs, adding more pasta cooking liquid as needed, until the noodles are coated and a glossy, emulsified sauce forms.

Divide the noodles among shallow bowls, top with the remaining 1 ounce (30 g) cheese, and season with more pepper. Serve with additional egg yolk, if you like, for extra richness.

WALI YA MBOGA, SORTA

Serves 6 to 8
2 hours

FOR THE CHICKEN

3 tablespoons plain whole-milk yogurt

6 garlic cloves, finely grated, divided

1-inch piece ginger, finely grated

2½ teaspoons Diamond Crystal kosher salt

1 teaspoon Kashmiri red chili powder,* divided

1½ pounds (680 g) boneless, skinless chicken thighs, each thigh cut in half

½ cup (120 ml) olive oil*

1 large yellow onion,* thinly sliced on a mandoline

1½ teaspoons ground cumin

1½ teaspoons ground coriander

½ teaspoon ground turmeric

1 (14-ounce/400 g) can crushed tomatoes*

FOR THE RICE

1 tablespoon Diamond Crystal kosher salt

2 cups (360 g) good-quality sela or basmati rice

10 ounces (280 g) fresh baby spinach*

FOR THE KACHUMBER AND SALTED YOGURT

1 small yellow onion,* thinly sliced

Juice of 1 lemon*

2 green bird's-eye chilis or 1 jalapeño, seeds removed if desired, sliced

¼ cup (35 g) cherry tomatoes, halved, optional

1 teaspoon Diamond Crystal kosher salt, divided

¾ cup (180 ml) plain whole-milk yogurt

In its purest form, the inspiration for this dish, wali ya mboga (Swahili for "rice and vegetables"), is simple—literally just a mix of sauteed vegetables and rice. This riff on the Khoja version I grew up eating is reflective of my roots in both East Africa and India. Sure, rice and vegetables are still present in the form of long-grain rice swirled with ribbons of spinach, but there's also tender yogurt-marinated chicken that braises in a spice-forward, aromatic tomato curry made with lots of sweet, frizzled onions, making this version closer to a biryani. Finish each serving with a dollop of creamy salted yogurt and a helping of sharp and tart lemon-dressed onions known as kachumber, and you'll have a wonderfully balanced meal. Or, for a similar effect, try my Pickled Kachumber (page 198) or Lemony Cucumber Salad with Salted Yogurt (page 60) to serve alongside instead.

You'll find this recipe can be prepared with two cooking methods: on the stovetop or in the oven. While traditional wali ya mboga the way I know it is prepared in the oven, the stovetop option is great for a quick and satisfying dish. Granted, though, something magical happens when the tomato-y masala chicken and long-grain rice marry together, encompassed by the oven's heat. The oven method is also a convenient opportunity to prep ahead and warm through if you're preparing the dish for a large party. But, trust me, whichever method you choose, it will be delicious.

METHOD

To marinate the chicken: In a large bowl or resealable bag, combine the yogurt, half of the garlic, the ginger, salt, and ½ teaspoon of the chili powder. Add the chicken and stir in the bowl or move it around in the bag to combine thoroughly, making sure to coat each piece of chicken. Marinate for 30 minutes at room temperature or up to overnight in the fridge.

Heat the olive oil in a large high-sided skillet over medium-high heat. Add the very thinly sliced onion and fry, stirring occasionally, until deeply browned, 15 to 20 minutes. If desired, using a fork or slotted spoon, remove about ¼ cup of the onion and transfer to a paper towel to drain and crisp up as a garnish. Add the remaining garlic, the cumin, coriander, turmeric, and remaining ½ teaspoon chili powder. Add the marinated chicken and cook for 1 to 2 minutes—it's OK if the onions appear nearly burnt at this stage. Add the crushed tomatoes, stir to combine, and bring to a simmer. Partially cover and cook, stirring occasionally, until the chicken is cooked through and the curry has thickened and darkened in color, 30 to 35 minutes.

Meanwhile, prepare the rice using the pasta method: Bring a large pot of water with the salt to a boil. Add the rice to the boiling water and cook until almost tender, testing grains of rice for doneness every few minutes, between 5 and 15 minutes depending on the quality and brand of rice (cooking time varies significantly brand by brand). Add the spinach, stir, and cook until the spinach is tender and the rice is fully cooked through, another minute or two. Drain the rice and spinach through a colander and return to the pot. Cover to keep warm.

*INSTEAD OF...

Kashmiri red chili powder, use ¾ teaspoon paprika plus ¼ teaspoon cayenne pepper

Yellow onion, use red onion

Olive oil, use vegetable oil

Crushed tomatoes, use tomato sauce

Baby spinach, use chopped mature spinach, kale, or Swiss chard

Lemon juice, use 2 tablespoons white vinegar and a splash of water

Meanwhile, make the kachumber: Combine the onion, lemon juice, chilis, tomatoes, and ½ teaspoon of the salt in a small bowl. Toss with a fork to combine, separating the onion rings. Let the kachumber sit at room temperature for at least 5 minutes, then chill until ready to serve.

Whisk the yogurt and the remaining ½ teaspoon salt in another small bowl. Taste and adjust to your preference. Chill until ready to serve.

For the stovetop assembly method, while the rice and chicken are both still warm, add the chicken to the pot with the rice and roughly toss to combine. There should be some rice stained by the chicken and some rice completely untouched.

For the oven method, preheat the oven to 325°F (165°C). Return to the rice and fluff it with a fork. Spread one-third of the rice over the bottom of a large (9 × 13–inch works well here), oven-safe serving bowl or casserole dish. Top with the chicken and finish with the remaining rice. Cover with foil and bake for 30 to 40 minutes, until the rice is warmed through and tender.

Top the dish with the reserved frizzled onions and serve with the salted yogurt and kachumber.

WEEKNIGHT DAAL

Serves 4 to 6
1 hour

1½ cups (285 g) red lentils

¼ cup (60 ml) olive oil*

1 large yellow onion,* thinly sliced

3 teaspoons Diamond Crystal kosher salt, divided, plus more as needed

5 garlic cloves,* finely grated

1½ teaspoons ground cumin

1 teaspoon ground coriander

½ teaspoon Kashmiri red chili powder*

½ teaspoon ground turmeric

2 medium russet potatoes, peeled and cut into 2-inch pieces

3 tablespoons double-concentrated tomato paste*

6 cups (1.4 L) chicken broth,* plus more as needed

1 tablespoon fresh lemon juice,* plus wedges for serving

Long-grain rice or crusty bread, for serving

Carrot Sambharo (page 190), for serving, optional

*INSTEAD OF...

Olive oil, use vegetable oil

Yellow onion, use red onion

Garlic cloves, use a 2-inch piece ginger, grated

Kashmiri red chili powder, use ¼ teaspoon cayenne pepper plus ½ teaspoon paprika

Tomato paste, use ½ cup canned crushed tomatoes or 2 large Roma tomatoes, chopped

Chicken broth, use beef broth or water

Lemon, use lime

The daal I grew up eating on weeknights is most certainly not the kind of daal that I would make on a weeknight now. I don't have a pressure cooker and I refuse to purchase one—the old-school ones scare me and the electric ones take up too much counter space.

To enjoy this spicy wholesome lentil stew on a weeknight, I use red lentils only, instead of the traditional fifty-fifty blend of red lentils and split chickpeas I grew up seeing. Not only do they cook much faster than other varieties, but red lentils are also a lot easier to source at your average grocery store, making this labor of love truly weeknight-friendly.

If you're looking for more protein, one of my lovely cross-testers suggested stirring in greens to wilt and poaching eggs directly onto the daal before serving.

METHOD

Put the lentils in a fine-mesh sieve. Rinse under cool water until the water runs mostly clear. Set aside.

Heat the olive oil in a large pot over medium heat. Add the onion and 1 teaspoon of the salt. Cook, stirring often, until the onion is softened, 6 to 8 minutes. Add the garlic, cumin, coriander, chili powder, and turmeric. Stir to coat the onions in the spices and cook until fragrant, about 30 seconds. Add the potatoes and tomato paste and cook, stirring often, until the tomato paste is darkened in color, about 3 minutes. Add the broth, rinsed lentils, and remaining 2 teaspoons salt and stir. Bring the lentil mixture to a boil, then reduce the heat to medium-low and simmer, uncovered, stirring occasionally, until the lentils are very tender and the curry is almost creamy, 30 to 35 minutes. If the broth has absorbed quickly, add more as needed. Stir in the lemon juice. Taste for salt and adjust the seasoning to your preference.

Serve over long-grain rice or with a piece of crusty bread for dipping, with lemon wedges for squeezing.

Store leftover daal in an airtight container in the refrigerator for up to 7 days. Reheat in a pot over medium heat until simmering, adding water as needed to reach its original consistency, or in the microwave in 1-minute increments until warm.

MAKE IT BETTER

(188—203)

Condiments and accompaniments

Chutney Butter (194)
Green Chutney (196)

CARROT SAMBHARO

Makes 1½ cups (about 340 g)
15 minutes

3 medium carrots, peeled and cut into 2-inch-long matchsticks

2 to 3 green bird's-eye chilis,* halved lengthwise

1 teaspoon Diamond Crystal kosher salt, plus more as needed

1 tablespoon vegetable oil*

2 curry leaves (optional)

½ teaspoon black mustard seeds (optional)

3 tablespoons tomato paste

½ teaspoon ground turmeric

2 garlic cloves, finely grated

2 tablespoons fresh lemon juice,* plus more as needed

*INSTEAD OF...

Bird's-eye chilis, use thinly sliced jalapeño

Vegetable oil, use any neutral oil

Lemon juice, use lime juice

If you ask me, carrots aren't typically the most exciting ingredient; only occasionally do they have the star power to take center stage, which is probably why they end up chilling in the back of the crisper drawer most of the time. Rather than making a mirepoix or slicing them up to snack on, do what I do and make this crunchy, punchy condiment with origins in Gujarat, India. The pairing options are endless: served alongside a big bowl of rice and daal (see Weeknight Daal, page 185), as a flavorful finish to my Spiced Short Ribs and Potatoes (page 160), or my personal favorite, sandwiched between two slices of soft bread for a surprisingly delicious and simple lunch with lots of crunch. Carrots, I take back anything bad I ever said about you.

METHOD

Put the carrot sticks in a medium bowl, add the chilis, and sprinkle with the salt to season and draw out some of the moisture. Set aside.

Meanwhile, heat the vegetable oil in a small pot over medium heat with the curry leaves and mustard seeds, if using. Once the oil is nice and warm and the mustard seeds are just beginning to pop, add the tomato paste, turmeric, and garlic. Stir everything together and cook until the tomato paste gets a little darker and the oil is tinted red, 5 minutes or so.

Add the tomato paste mixture to the salted carrots and chilis, squeeze over the lemon juice, and toss everything together. The salty liquid released from the carrots will mix with the lemon juice and tomato paste to create the perfect viscosity to coat the carrots. If things are looking a little thick, just add a splash of water and mix until the carrots are coated.

Taste for salt and lemon juice and add more to your preference. I usually transfer it to a container to chill in the fridge for a few hours, but you can definitely eat it immediately.

Store in an airtight container in the refrigerator for up to 10 days.

CHILI CRISP

Makes about 2 cups (450 ml)
1 hour, plus cooling time

2 large shallots, very thinly sliced
6 garlic cloves, thinly sliced
1 cinnamon stick, optional
½ teaspoon black peppercorns
½ teaspoon Szechuan peppercorns*
1½ to 2 cups (360 to 480 ml) vegetable oil*
¼ cup (24 g) red pepper flakes
2 teaspoons smoked paprika*
1½ teaspoons soy sauce*
1 teaspoon sugar
Flaky sea salt*

*INSTEAD OF...
Szechuan peppercorns, use more black peppercorns
Vegetable oil, use any neutral oil
Smoked paprika, use regular paprika
Soy sauce, use tamari
Flaky sea salt, use Diamond Crystal kosher salt

If it isn't obvious by now, I love this recipe.

I was living on Long Island when chili crisp was having its mainstream media moment a few years ago, and finding a jar at a local supermarket back then was near impossible. Sure, I could've ordered it online, but I happen to enjoy cooking (crazy, I know), so developing my own version was a welcome undertaking. I had seen my grandmother make a red pepper flake-based chili oil condiment in the past, and I liked the idea of controlling the flavor in my own version and using an easily accessible chili flake. After several years of perfecting this recipe, I have now developed an inconvenient love for it; I cannot have a savory breakfast without it, and I feel a void in my fridge when this crispy chili oil isn't in it. It's the perfect accompaniment to eggs, avocado, soups, and rice.

I won't pretend you can do it with your eyes closed or that it takes no time at all, but I will vehemently uphold that it is very worth it—the flavor is nuanced but bold, making it an everyday luxury worth bragging about. If you do want to speed things up, use a mandoline to slice the garlic and shallots and process the paprika and chili flakes in a food processor or not at all (the texture will be slightly compromised, but it's a trade-off worth considering if you're tight on time). Plus, it keeps well when stored in the fridge.

METHOD

Combine the shallots, garlic, cinnamon stick, if using, and the black and Szechuan peppercorns in a small saucepan. Pour over the vegetable oil, making sure to use enough to cover the garlic and shallots. Bring the oil to a simmer over medium heat. Using a fork, gently break up the shallots out of their rounds. Cook, stirring occasionally but not often, until the garlic and shallots have turned a deep golden brown, 15 to 25 minutes. Keep an eye on them once they start to turn golden—they'll brown quickly from that point.

Meanwhile, combine the red pepper flakes and smoked paprika in a mortar and pestle and grind until the red pepper flakes are finer in texture. Transfer to a medium heatproof bowl and add the soy sauce and sugar. Place a metal mesh sieve over the bowl.

Remove the oil from the heat and carefully pour it through the sieve. Transfer the browned shallot and garlic pieces that remain in the sieve to a paper towel-lined plate, season with flaky salt, and leave to cool completely.

Stir the oil and red pepper flake mixture together and leave to cool completely, about 1 hour.

Once the oil mixture has cooled, stir in the crispy shallots and garlic. Transfer the chili crisp to an airtight jar, discarding the cinnamon stick if it doesn't fit in the jar, and store in the refrigerator for up to 1 month.

CHUTNEY BUTTER

Makes about 1 cup (250 g)
15 minutes, plus chill time

1½ cups (45 g) fresh cilantro, tender stems and leaves*
½ cup (15 g) fresh mint leaves*
1 cup (2 sticks/225 g) unsalted butter, divided (1 stick melted, 1 stick softened)
3 garlic cloves
Zest and juice of 1 lime*
1 to 2 green bird's-eye chilis*
1 teaspoon flaky sea salt, plus more as needed
Radishes and/or sourdough bread, for serving

*INSTEAD OF . . .
Cilantro and mint, use any other tender herb combination
Lime, use half a lemon
Bird's-eye chilis, use jalapeños

A very versatile hybrid of two already very versatile things: rich creamy butter and bright, herbaceous green chutney. Serve with bread or crudites, use it to cook eggs or baste steak, or even use it to finish stir-fries, sauces, soups, and curries.

METHOD

Bring a small pot of water to a boil. Blanch the cilantro and mint until just wilted, 30 seconds to 1 minute. Using a slotted spoon or tongs, transfer the herbs to an ice bath and then into a kitchen towel and squeeze hard to expel excess water. While it is optional, blanching the herbs like this helps to retain that vibrant green color for longer.

Transfer the blanched herbs to a blender along with the melted butter, garlic, lime zest and juice, and the chilis. Blend on high speed until bright green and fully emulsified. Transfer to a bowl and mix with the softened butter and flaky salt until evenly combined. Chill in the refrigerator until set, about 20 minutes.

Serve with sourdough and/or radishes. It will keep refrigerated for up to 2 weeks.

DATE CHUTNEY

Makes about ½ cup (170 g)
20 minutes

- 2½ ounces (4 to 5/70 g) pitted Medjool dates, torn in half
- ⅓ cup (75 ml) boiling water
- ½ teaspoon Diamond Crystal kosher salt, plus more as needed
- ¼ cup (60 ml) fresh lemon juice
- 1 garlic clove, finely grated
- ½ teaspoon Kashmiri red chili powder,* plus more depending on spice tolerance

*INSTEAD OF...
Kashmiri red chili powder, use ¼ teaspoon cayenne pepper plus ½ teaspoon paprika

Ambli, a tamarind and date chutney, is a staple South Asian condiment. But seeing that I never have tamarind around yet almost always have dates on hand, this ambli dupe does the trick. Similarly sweet, tangy, and spicy, it's perfect for when you want to add a little sweet, savory *umph* to whatever it is you're eating.

I'm typically not a fan of knockoffs, but, when it comes to this, I'll make an exception.

METHOD

Lay the date halves in a small, shallow bowl in an even layer and cover with the boiling water. Leave for 10 to 15 minutes. Don't drain the water; use a fork to mash the dates into a paste. You can also do this in a food processor or with a mortar and pestle. Stir in the salt, lemon juice, garlic, and chili powder. Taste and add more chili powder if you're craving more heat. Chill until ready to use.

Store in an airtight container in the refrigerator for up to 10 days.

GREEN CHUTNEY

Makes about 1 cup (115 g)
10 minutes

1 medium bunch cilantro,* leaves and tender stems, roughly chopped

2 garlic cloves

3 to 4 tablespoons fresh lemon juice,* from 1 lemon

1 teaspoon extra virgin olive oil

2 to 4 green bird's-eye chilis,* depending on spice tolerance

1 teaspoon Diamond Crystal kosher salt, or to taste

*INSTEAD OF...

Cilantro, use a combination of mint and cilantro

Lemon juice, use lime juice

Bird's-eye chilis, use 1 or 2 jalapeño or serrano chilis

Herb-forward condiments are common all over the world. Green chutney, a South Asian classic, is usually made from mint or cilantro, and often a combination of the two. The one I'm most accustomed to is cilantro-only and very bright, thanks to lots of lemon juice and salt. You'll find it in my Cucumber and Chutney Sandwiches (page 48) and as a serving suggestion in so many other recipes.

METHOD

Combine the cilantro, garlic, lemon juice, olive oil, chilis, and salt in a blender or small food processor. Blend until smooth, stopping to scrape down the sides of the blender and adding water by the tablespoonful to help the blender along as needed. Taste and adjust with more lemon juice as needed. It should be bright, salty, and tangy.

Store in an airtight container in the refrigerator for up to 2 weeks, or in the freezer for up to 3 months. Thaw frozen chutney in the refrigerator overnight; stir to combine before serving.

HOMEMADE HOT SAUCE

Makes about ¼ cup (60 ml)
5 minutes

¼ cup (60 ml) fresh lemon juice
2 teaspoons Kashmiri red chili powder,* plus more to taste
¾ teaspoon Diamond Crystal kosher salt

*INSTEAD OF...
Kashmiri red chili powder, use ¾ teaspoon cayenne plus 1¼ teaspoons paprika

My maternal uncle, Rizwan, insists that he's the inventor of this brilliant little hot sauce. I can't quite be sure if he's pulling my leg (his words, not mine) or not, but just in case, I'll give credit where credit is due. I can't remember a time when this hot sauce, referred to as mitu, mirchu, and limbu (a direct translation of the ingredient list: salt, chili, and lemon), wasn't in the fridge growing up. Used as both a hot sauce and a dipping sauce, it hits all the right notes without being overly spicy. I like using Kashmiri red chili powder alone, but my mom and grandmother will sometimes opt for a fifty-fifty blend of Kashmiri red chili and the more common Indian red chili powder, which is a bit spicier. So, if this feels a little too mild for your preference, feel free to use that technique or add a bit of cayenne pepper to bring up the spice factor.

METHOD

Combine the lemon juice, chili powder, and salt in a jar or small bowl. Shake or mix to combine. Adjust with chili powder to your desired spice level.

Store in an airtight container in the refrigerator for up to 3 weeks.

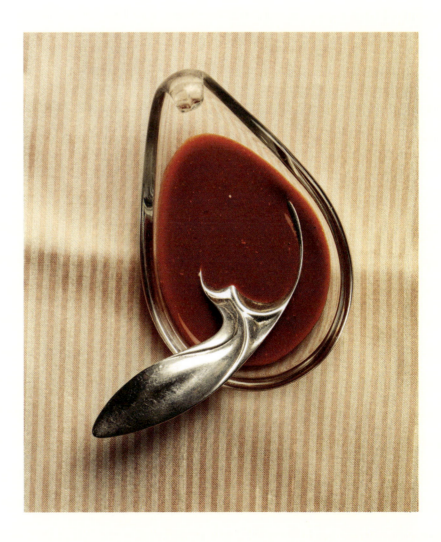

PICKLED KACHUMBER

Makes 1 (16-ounce/480 ml) jar
20 minutes

3 medium lemons, juiced (about ⅔ cup/150 ml), plus more as needed
1¼ teaspoons Diamond Crystal kosher salt
1 large red onion,* thinly sliced
2 green bird's-eye chilis,* halved

*INSTEAD OF...
Red onion, use yellow onion
Bird's-eye chilis, use jalapeño or serrano chilis, or ½ teaspoon red pepper flakes

You'll find classic kachumber speckled throughout this book: it's a salty, tart onion "salad" (I use the term loosely for lack of a better word) served as a punchy accompaniment to lots of rich, rice-forward traditional dishes. Versions vary, sometimes dressed with vinegar for acid, but the one I grew up on relied solely on lemon juice (usually Real Lemon, which may be real, but it's no substitute for fresh lemon juice). While onion remains the star, variations of kachumber may include tomatoes, chilis, cucumbers, and sometimes carrots.

Once you've entered the convenient world of having pickled onions on hand to zhuzh up meals at a moment's notice, there's really no going back. Considering the sour, sharp kind of pickled-ish kachumber I grew up on, it's no surprise that the typically vinegary, sweetened kind often available at the grocery store doesn't really appeal to me all that much. This version of pickled onions, featuring lots of lemon juice, does, and the classically appealing fuchsia colorway remains true to the original.

Use it the same way you would traditional pickled onions: on salads and sandwiches, with stews and soups, or, my preference, over rice dishes like Rishma's Pilau (page 143), Wali Ya Mboga, Sorta (page 182), and Farzana's Biryani (page 108).

METHOD
Put the lemon juice and salt in a very clean 16-ounce (480 ml) jar and swirl to combine. Tightly pack the onion and chilis into the jar. Screw on the lid and shake to coat the onions. Let stand for 20 minutes. Using a spoon, press the onions down to make sure they are submerged in the lemon juice (use more lemon juice if needed to fully cover). Chill for at least 1 hour before serving.

The kachumber will keep, refrigerated, for up to 3 weeks.

MAKE IT BETTER 199

White Sauce (203)
Shortcut Lemon Achaar (202)

SHORTCUT LEMON ACHAAR

Makes about 2 cups (480 ml)
20 minutes

4 medium preserved lemons (about 250 g), preferably Mina brand
1 tablespoon ground turmeric
2 tablespoons red pepper flakes*
¼ cup (60 ml) preserved lemon brine
¾ cup (180 ml) fresh lemon juice, from 3 large lemons

*INSTEAD OF...

Red pepper flakes, use Kashmiri red chili powder or 3 to 4 green bird's-eye chilis, halved

I've watched my grandmother make lemon achaar one too many times. A rather arduous process for a condiment, it starts by covering lemons in salt, turmeric, and chilis and requires monitoring them for days, then waiting for weeks until the lemons have softened so the pith is palatable. Call me impatient, but committing to that process is a hard no from me. I grew up watching Sandra Lee on Food Network, and I have no shame in my "semi-homemade" game. The shortcut: using an ingredient I've been known to rave about, preserved lemons.

Popularly used in Moroccan tagines, preserved lemons as they're sold are salty, briny, and tender. Add the chili and turmeric and the job's done. Use it the same way you would any other salty, briny, pickled thing. The best part? You can have them with dinner tonight, and they'll only get better with time.

Use them like you would most other pickled things—in sauces, soups, and marinades, on toast, or as a condiment. And feel free to adjust the spice to your liking. I'd say this amount of chili results in a pretty spicy lemon achaar.

METHOD

Cut the preserved lemons into quarters and remove the seeds. Cut each quarter into 1-inch pieces. Transfer to a small bowl and add turmeric, red pepper flakes, preserved lemon brine, and lemon juice. Stir to coat. Transfer to a sterile jar and press down to make sure the lemons are completely submerged in the liquid; you may need more lemon juice depending on the size of your preserved lemons and your jar. Store in the refrigerator for up to 1 year.

WHITE SAUCE

Makes 1 cup (about 330 g)
10 minutes

1 cup (240 ml) plain whole-milk yogurt
¼ cup (60 ml) mayonnaise
½ teaspoon sugar
2 garlic cloves, finely grated
1 tablespoon fresh lemon juice*
1 teaspoon Diamond Crystal kosher salt
Freshly cracked black pepper

*INSTEAD OF...
Lemon juice, use white vinegar or lime juice

Inspired by the creamy, herby, and garlicky sauces sometimes served alongside American Afghani and Persian dishes, this versatile condiment is perfect to serve with meats and rice. Think of it as similar to a ranch dressing—it's good with veggies, rice, barbecued meats, and my Halal Cart Salad (page 124). I consider this a great base recipe for white sauce, so feel free to adjust it to your liking by adding dried or fresh herbs. I'll often stir in some dried mint or fresh dill, depending on what I've got on hand.

METHOD
Whisk together the yogurt, mayonnaise, sugar, garlic, lemon juice, and salt in a small bowl. Season with pepper.

The white sauce will keep, covered and refrigerated, for up to 1 week.

SOMETHING SWEET

(206—249)

*Baked goods, desserts,
and the like*

Banana Cake with Tahini Fudge (214)
Fruit and Nut Biscotti (233)

Ashraf's
BAKLAVA

Serves 40 to 50 (150 to 200 pieces of baklava)
2 hours 30 minutes

Weddings in my family are incomplete without a tray of my grandmother's sweet and flaky homemade baklava. Ideal for serving a crowd, one tray makes more than 150 pieces of baklava. You might be thinking, "Who would ever need to feed that many people?" Well, Ashraf does. It's not unusual for my grandmother to find herself in situations where she needs to feed many mouths. Weddings in our family have upwards of three hundred people, and feeding them home-cooked food is just her way of spreading the celebratory joy. If you read about my grandmother in the headnote of her Tomato Saag recipe (page 94), you'll know her cooking style lends itself perfectly to a project-y recipe like this one.

A dessert with roots in the Ottoman Empire and with many regional variations, baklava is essentially a syrup-soaked flaky pastry filled with crushed nuts. My grandmother's version combines Greek, Armenian, and Syrian techniques, featuring a simple syrup infused with honey and whole spices and a blend of nuts including pistachios, walnuts, and almonds.

Making baklava might seem intimidating, but the components individually are pretty straightforward, and once you get the hang of the rolling method, it becomes almost cathartic—a simple repetition that's incredibly satisfying to see come to fruition.

Phyllo dough is extremely thin, and therefore prone to drying (ergo breakage), so try to buy the freshest box you can find by checking expiration dates, and consider buying two boxes in case one has one too many unusable sheets. Assembling directly in the tray you bake in means you don't have to move around those nut-filled logs and risk damaging them. The recommended brand, Apollo, produces sheets of baklava the perfect size for a standard rimmed baking sheet, and while you can definitely use other brands, using a different size of phyllo dough sheets might make things challenging logistically.

Serve with Turkish tea or espresso to balance the sugar high.

SOMETHING SWEET 209

FOR THE FILLING

2⅓ cups (465 g) plus 3 tablespoons sugar, divided

Zest of 1 large lemon, plus 2 teaspoons fresh lemon juice, divided

5 whole cloves

¼ cinnamon stick

1 tablespoon honey

¼ teaspoon saffron threads

1 cup (160 g) almonds

⅓ cup (50 g) shelled pistachios, plus more (optional) for serving

3 cups (340 g) walnut halves

¼ teaspoon ground cinnamon

FOR ASSEMBLY

36 to 40 (12 × 17-inch) sheets Apollo brand phyllo pastry (#4 weight/2 pounds/908 g), thawed

1½ cups (3 sticks/340 g) unsalted butter, melted

METHOD

Start by making the syrup for the baklava: Combine 2⅓ cups (465 g) of the sugar, 1½ cups (360 ml) water, the lemon zest, cloves, and cinnamon stick in a small pot. Bring to a simmer over medium-low heat and cook, stirring occasionally, until slightly thickened but still pourable, 18 to 22 minutes. Remove from the heat and stir in the lemon juice and honey. Strain the syrup through a fine-mesh sieve into a large measuring cup. Discard the cloves and cinnamon stick; it's OK if some lemon zest remains in the syrup. Add the saffron threads to the syrup and let steep and cool completely while you make the baklava.

While the syrup boils, prepare the nut mixture: Process the almonds in a food processor, pulsing until coarse crumbs form (similar in texture to panko breadcrumbs—it's OK if they're not processed completely evenly). Transfer to a medium bowl and repeat with the pistachios and then the walnuts. Add the remaining 3 tablespoons sugar and the ground cinnamon to the bowl and mix to distribute evenly. Optional: Process an additional 2 tablespoons pistachios into a fine crumb for serving; set aside.

Place a rack in the middle of the oven and preheat to 350°F (175°C).

Carefully unroll the thawed phyllo pastry sheets onto a large cutting board or work surface. Cover the stack with a tea towel to prevent drying out through the process.

Place a standard baking sheet (18 × 13-inch) in front of you on a countertop, positioned vertically (portrait).

Carefully transfer 2 sheets of phyllo to the baking sheet and use a pastry brush to spread a thin, even layer of melted butter over the top. Working with ¼ cup of the nut mixture at a time, arrange the mixture by the spoonful in a horizontal, 1-inch-thick line about 2 inches from the bottom edge of the phyllo. Drizzle 2 teaspoons of melted butter over the line of nuts. Fold up the bottom edge of the phyllo over the nut mixture to cover, then start rolling it up tightly into a log and push the log to the far edge of the baking sheet.

Repeat the entire process with the remaining phyllo (two sheets at a time), nut mixture, and butter. You can lay the phyllo sheets over the finished logs of baklava on the baking sheet as you work. You may need to re-melt the butter a few times to keep it viscous. Once the tray is filled with rows of baklava logs, brush any remaining melted butter over the top. You should have 15 to 18 logs in total. Cut the logs vertically, crosswise (or down the length of the pan) into 1½-inch pieces. Bake for 38 to 43 minutes, until golden brown.

Remove from the oven and immediately drizzle the syrup over the hot baklava. Let stand for at least 20 minutes at room temperature before serving.

Sprinkle with the reserved fine pistachio crumbs, if using.

Store in an airtight container at room temperature or in the refrigerator for up to 10 days, between sheets of parchment or waxed paper if stacking.

BAKLAVA GRANOLA

Makes about 8 cups (455 g)
1 hour

1 large egg white
⅔ cup (165 ml) ghee
⅔ cup (165 ml) honey
1½ teaspoons Diamond Crystal kosher salt
1½ teaspoons ground cinnamon
2 tablespoons orange zest, from 1 large or 2 medium oranges, optional
4 cups (360 g) rolled oats
¾ cup (70 g) walnut halves and pieces, roughly chopped*
¾ cup (95 g) shelled salted pistachios*

*INSTEAD OF...

Walnut halves and pieces, use more pistachios or another nut

Shelled salted pistachios, use more walnuts or other nut plus ¼ teaspoon Diamond Crystal kosher salt

One of the great things about being a recipe developer is that you can create things exactly as you wish they'd be. I'm not a huge fan of dried fruit in granola; I like it very crunchy and only kind of clustery—I don't want to break my teeth on it, I don't want it too chewy, I want to be able to taste the salt, I want deeply toasted oats, I'd like it to be nut-forward so I can get some healthy fats and protein in, and I want some spice, but not too much. Is that really too much to ask?

Introducing my ideal granola: Inspired by the flavors of baklava, this granola is heavy on the nuts, featuring a blend of walnuts and pistachios, and it gets a ton of flavor from the honey, ghee, cinnamon, and orange zest, all common ingredients in baklava varieties. You can adjust the salt and spices to your liking, and even swap some of the nuts out for seeds, but be sure to maintain the ghee to honey to mix-in (nuts and oats) ratio. If dried fruit feels like a nonnegotiable for you, I'd recommend chopped dates, chopped dried apricots, dried cherries, or dried cranberries. Stir them in just after the granola comes out of the oven.

Egg white in granola usually makes people raise an eyebrow, but it's a tested, tried-and-true trick to ensure extra-crunchy clusters of oats.

I hesitate to suggest that people make small things that are easy to buy, but if you ask me, this (and my Chili Crisp on page 192) are absolutely worth the effort, especially considering their yield and lasting power.

METHOD

Preheat the oven to 350°F (175°C). Line a baking sheet with parchment paper.

Put the egg white in a large bowl, tilt the bowl, and whisk until foamy and loose, about 30 seconds.

Melt the ghee in a microwave-safe liquid measuring cup for 15 seconds (the ghee should be melted but not hot). Pour any extra ghee (if there's more than ⅔ cup/165 ml) back into the ghee jar. Transfer to the large bowl. Tip: Use the same measuring cup to measure the honey—the residual ghee will make it easier to pour into the bowl.

Add the honey, salt, cinnamon, and orange zest to the bowl and stir to combine. It'll appear thickened and coagulated—that's OK. Add the rolled oats, walnuts, and pistachios to the bowl and stir until completely combined.

Transfer to the prepared baking sheet using a spatula to form an even layer and bake for 27 to 30 minutes, until golden brown. Halfway through baking, remove the pan from the oven and toss the granola to ensure even browning, encouraging the mixture back into an even layer before returning to the oven. Remove the baking sheet from the oven and increase the oven temperature to 400°F (205°C). Once again, toss the granola and spread it out into an even layer. Bake for 3 to 7 minutes more, until deep golden brown all over.

Let cool on the baking sheet for at least 40 minutes, until crisp, before touching. Break the granola into clusters with a spoon and transfer to an airtight container, where it will keep for up to 4 weeks.

BANANA CAKE WITH TAHINI FUDGE

Serves 8 to 10
1 hour

Rotting bananas had a constant presence in our kitchen island's fruit bowl. My mother, who is adamant against food waste of any kind, would absolutely never throw them away. Instead, she'd pull out her Betty Crocker binder, remove the banana bread recipe, and hand it over to one of my sisters, usually Fatema, who'd always add chocolate chips in addition to the recipe's recommendation for chopped walnuts. There's still no banana bread recipe I prefer more than that one, and believe me I've tried to develop a better one.

This banana *cake*, however, is different from basic banana bread. Slightly more airy and spongy in texture, it doesn't have the denser crumb structure of a typical loaf cake. So, when I find myself staring at some near-rotten bananas sitting on the counter, I'll make this cake instead of a regular old loaf (sorry, Betty). The tahini fudge couldn't be easier to make and has the most luxurious mouthfeel while maintaining those nutty, chocolaty flavor notes from the original inspo. If you love chocolate fudge sauce, double the recipe and keep some in the fridge to reheat for later and enjoy with vanilla ice cream and flaky sea salt.

FOR THE BANANA CAKE

2 to 3 large overripe bananas

1 cup (130 g) all-purpose flour

1 teaspoon baking powder

1 teaspoon baking soda

¾ teaspoon Diamond Crystal kosher salt

⅓ cup (75 g) unsalted butter*

¾ cup (150 g) sugar

2 large eggs

1 teaspoon vanilla extract

FOR THE TAHINI FUDGE AND ASSEMBLY

¼ cup (60 ml) heavy cream

¼ cup (45 g) semisweet chocolate chips*

¼ cup (50 g) sugar

¼ teaspoon Diamond Crystal kosher salt

2 tablespoons well-stirred tahini*

Flaky sea salt, optional

Toasted sesame seeds, optional

Vanilla ice cream, optional

*INSTEAD OF . . .

Unsalted butter, use salted butter; reduce the salt in the recipe to ¼ teaspoon

Semisweet chocolate chips, use bittersweet chocolate

Tahini, use natural peanut butter

METHOD

To make the cake: Preheat the oven to 350°F (175°C). Line the bottom and sides of an 8 × 8-inch baking dish with parchment paper.

Mash the bananas on a cutting board with a fork. You should have about 1 cup of mashed banana (about 215 g).

Whisk the flour, baking powder, baking soda, and kosher salt in a medium bowl.

Cream the butter and sugar together in a large mixing bowl using a stand or handheld mixer on medium speed until pale and airy, 1 to 2 minutes. Add the eggs, one at a time, and mix until well combined. Add the vanilla and bananas and mix until combined. Add the dry ingredients and mix until no spots of dry flour remain. Scrape the batter into the baking dish; smooth out the top with a spatula.

Bake the cake until a tester inserted into the center comes out mostly clean, 20 to 25 minutes. Transfer to a wire rack and cool the cake to the touch in the pan, about 20 minutes. Invert the cake onto a platter and remove the parchment paper. Turning the cake bottom side up ensures a nice flat surface for glazing.

Meanwhile, make the tahini fudge: Pour the heavy cream and ¼ cup (60 ml) water into a small liquid measuring cup and set aside. Combine the chocolate chips, sugar, and kosher salt in a small heavy pot. Place the pot over medium-low heat and add a few tablespoons of the watered-down heavy cream. Whisk until the chocolate chips have melted (it's OK if the sugar is still grainy at this point). Keep adding the heavy cream, a few tablespoons at a time, stirring constantly until incorporated before adding more. Once all the heavy cream is combined, add the tahini, continuing to whisk. Keep cooking, whisking often, until thickened but still pourable. This whole process usually takes 6 to 10 minutes. Transfer to a heatproof jug or jar. Set aside until ready to use.

Pour the glaze over the cake and spread to the edges with an offset spatula. Sprinkle with flaky salt and sesame seeds. Serve with a scoop of vanilla ice cream, if you'd like.

Both the fudge and the cake can be made up to 2 days in advance. Keep the fudge in the fridge and reheat it in 20-second increments in the microwave. Wrap the cake very well in plastic wrap and store it at room temperature. Assemble just before serving.

CHEWY GINGER COOKIES

24 cookies
1 hour

2 sticks (1 cup/230 g) unsalted butter*

2½ cups (312 g) all-purpose flour

1 teaspoon baking soda

1½ teaspoons Diamond Crystal kosher salt

3-inch piece organic ginger

¾ cup (150 g) packed dark brown sugar

¾ cup (150 g) granulated sugar

1 large egg, cold from the fridge

1 tablespoon vanilla extract

1 cup (210 g) demerara or raw sugar, for rolling, optional

*INSTEAD OF...

Unsalted butter, use salted butter; reduce the salt in the recipe by ½ teaspoon

The snack cabinet at my parents' house was always filled to the brim with South Asian and East African snacks. One of the few "normal" sweets we had was a beige bag of Stauffer's Ginger Snaps stuffed into a zip-top freezer bag to preserve their freshness. While I do love the short crispiness and spice-forward quality of a traditional ginger snap, I'm a chewy cookie girl at heart. Plus, making traditional ginger cookies from scratch generally requires molasses—an ingredient I seldom use and therefore object to purchasing. Instead of using molasses for depth, this recipe leans on dark brown sugar (which is already heavy on the molasses), deeply browned (nearly burnt) brown butter, lots of vanilla extract, and fresh organic ginger for a subtle lingering kick, resulting in a cookie akin to a sugar cookie, but more interesting. The pre-bake roll in demerara sugar is entirely optional, although the sparkle really makes them feel special, especially during the winter holiday season.

If you want a cookie that's cakier in texture, increase the dark brown sugar to 1 cup (200 g) and decrease the white sugar to ¼ cup (50 g). If you're planning ahead or don't want to bake the whole batch at once, you can freeze the dough balls for up to 3 months. Roll the frozen dough in demerara sugar and increase the bake time to 12 to 15 minutes.

METHOD

Arrange an oven rack in the center of the oven, and preheat to 350°F (175°C). Line 2 baking sheets with parchment paper.

Put the butter in a small skillet over medium-high heat. Cook, stirring often and scraping the sides and bottom of the skillet, until the milk solids have separated and turned deep brown (nearly burnt), 5 to 7 minutes. Pour into a large bowl and set aside.

Meanwhile, whisk the flour, baking soda, and kosher salt in a medium bowl.

Grate the ginger using a Microplane or crush it into a paste with a mortar and pestle and set aside. You should have ¼ cup ginger.

Once the brown butter is just warm to the touch, add the dark brown sugar and granulated sugar and whisk until combined, making sure to work out any larger lumps from the brown sugar. Add the egg, vanilla, and ginger and whisk until well combined. Mix in the dry ingredients using a rubber spatula until just combined. If the mixture won't hold together, let it stand for 15 to 30 minutes before proceeding.

Portion out the dough into 2-tablespoon (35 g) balls. If time allows, chill the dough for 8 to 24 hours for better flavor. (As they chill, they'll also get deeper in color once baked.)

Roll the dough balls in the demerara sugar, if using. Set the dough balls on the prepared baking sheets, spaced about 2 inches apart, and bake one sheet at a time for 10 to 12 minutes. Remove the sheets from the oven and let the cookies cool completely on the sheets.

Store the cookies in an airtight container for up to 1 week.

CHOCOLATE CAKE WITH CHAI BUTTERCREAM

Serves 10 to 12
2 hours, plus cooling time

FOR THE CAKE

Butter or neutral oil, for greasing the pan
1 cup (120 g) Dutch-process cocoa powder*
2 teaspoons cornstarch
2 cups (255 g) all-purpose flour
2 teaspoons baking soda
1½ teaspoons baking powder
1½ teaspoons Diamond Crystal kosher salt
1 cup (240 ml) buttermilk*
2 cups (400 g) granulated sugar
½ cup (120 ml) olive oil*
2 large eggs
2 large egg yolks
1 cup (240 g) warm water*

FOR THE FROSTING AND ASSEMBLY

1½ cups (360 ml) heavy cream
¾ teaspoon Diamond Crystal kosher salt
1 tablespoon vanilla extract
2 tablespoons loose black tea
1½ teaspoons ground cinnamon
1½ teaspoons ground cardamom
3-inch piece ginger, finely grated
3 sticks (1½ cups/345 g) unsalted butter, at room temperature
6 cups (600 g) powdered sugar
Flaky sea salt, for serving

(continued)

Chocolate cake will always be my favorite. And whenever I think of it, I remember the iconic chocolate fudge cake from the movie *Matilda*. When I thought of developing a chocolate cake recipe, I knew it needed to be fudgy and tender. Cocoa powder has a tendency to dry things up, but from a few small additions, like oil instead of butter, cornstarch to prevent much gluten from forming, extra egg yolks for richness, and buttermilk for an extra-moist crumb, this perfect chocolate cake was born.

While I often use a chocolatey cream cheese frosting to ice this cake, this chai-spice buttercream has been quick to replace it. Remarkably like the chai I know and love (see Karak Chai, page 256), its spicy, floral flavor pairs incredibly well with the intense and deep chocolate. This technique for creating a heavy cream–based flavor concentrate is a good one to experiment with to make the unique buttercreams of your dreams. Try different teas, coffees, and spices to suit your preference.

If a layered cake doesn't quite fit the occasion, feel free to divide the cake recipe in half and the frosting by a third (you won't need nearly as much if you're not covering the sides and center).

METHOD

Preheat the oven to 350°F (175°C).

Line two 9-inch cake pans with parchment paper and grease them with butter or oil to ensure the cake doesn't stick.

To make the cake: Whisk the cocoa powder, cornstarch, flour, baking soda, baking powder, and kosher salt in a medium bowl. Make sure to work through any lumps of cocoa powder.

Combine the buttermilk, sugar, olive oil, eggs, and egg yolks in a large bowl and whisk well until combined. Add the dry ingredients and mix well to combine. The batter will be very thick at this stage, but it's much easier to mix in the dry ingredients and ensure no clumping this way. Mix in the warm water. It's OK if there are a few small lumps.

Divide the batter between the prepared cake pans and tap them on the counter to release any excess air bubbles. Bake for 25 to 30 minutes, until a skewer inserted into the center comes out with a few moist crumbs. Remove the cakes from the oven and let them cool completely.

Meanwhile, make the buttercream frosting. To make a chai concentrate, combine the heavy cream, kosher salt, vanilla, black tea, cinnamon, cardamom, and ginger in a small pot. Place over medium heat and cook, stirring continuously, until the mixture has thickened but is looser than pudding and bubbles are gurgling, 5 to 7 minutes. The mixture should be milky brown in color. Remove from the heat and let stand for 1 to 2 minutes.

Set a mesh strainer over a small bowl and pour the chai concentrate through the sieve. Use a spatula to help work the cream through the strainer—much of the ginger and black tea will be left behind. Discard it. Let the cream stand to cool completely.

Combine the softened butter (it's super important that your butter is fully softened and at room temperature so your buttercream doesn't break) and powdered sugar in the bowl of a stand mixer fitted with the

*INSTEAD OF...

Dutch-process cocoa powder, use unsweetened cocoa powder

Buttermilk, use 1 tablespoon lemon juice or white vinegar plus enough whole milk to measure 1 cup

Olive oil, use vegetable oil

Warm water, use 1 cup (240 ml) warm coffee or black tea

whisk attachment. Mix together on Stir, or the lowest setting on your mixer, to combine the butter and sugar, then increase the speed to medium (setting 4 on most stand mixers). Whip the sugar and butter until lighter in color and thick, 5 to 6 minutes (don't be alarmed if it doesn't come together at first—just keep it going). I usually stop halfway through to scrape down the sides of the bowl to ensure all the butter is combined evenly. Add the reserved chai cream and continue to whip on medium speed, scraping down the sides of the bowl as needed, until light, fluffy, and completely combined, another 2 to 3 minutes. Remove the whisk attachment and stir manually with a rubber spatula, pushing the frosting against the sides of the bowl to release any air pockets. You can also do this by switching to the paddle attachment and mixing on Stir for 2 minutes. Transfer to an airtight container until the cake has cooled completely.

Once the cakes are cooled, invert the cake pans over a large cutting board and peel off the parchment paper bottom. Level the cakes with a serrated knife if they've domed. Trim a piece of parchment into four 2- to 3-inch strips. Lay them to form a square with overlapping edges on top of a cake stand or serving plate. Transfer a cake layer to the stand or platter, laying it over the parchment strips. This is a trick to help keep the plate clean; after you frost the cake, simply shimmy off those parchment strips to reveal an untouched surface. Transfer one-third of the frosting to the top of the cake layer and, using an offset spatula, spread to the edges in an even layer. Top with the next cake layer, ensuring the even, flat bottom of the cake layer is now the top of the layered cake. Spread the remaining frosting evenly over the top and sides. Sprinkle with flaky salt and serve.

Do-ahead: The cakes and frosting can be made up to 2 days ahead. Store the cakes wrapped in plastic wrap at room temperature. Store the frosting in an airtight container in the refrigerator. Bring to room temperature and stir vigorously until smooth and airy before frosting.

SOMETHING SWEET 221

MALL CINNAMON ROLLS

Makes 10 to 12 rolls
3 hours 30 minutes

FOR THE DOUGH
- ¾ cup (180 ml) plus ⅓ cup (75 ml) 2% or whole milk, divided
- 2¾ cups (343 g) plus 2 tablespoons all-purpose flour, divided
- 1 large egg
- 1 packet (7 g) instant yeast
- ¼ cup (50 g) granulated sugar
- 1½ teaspoons Diamond Crystal kosher salt
- ¼ cup (½ stick/55 g) unsalted butter, cut into cubes, at room temperature, plus more for the pan

FOR THE FILLING
- ¼ cup (½ stick/55 g) unsalted butter, at room temperature, plus more for the pan
- ½ cup (110 g) packed dark brown sugar
- 1 tablespoon ground cinnamon
- ¼ teaspoon Diamond Crystal kosher salt
- 1 tablespoon heavy cream, optional

FOR CARAMEL DRIZZLE
- 2 tablespoons unsalted butter
- ¼ cup (55 g) packed dark brown sugar
- ¼ cup (60 ml) heavy cream
- ¼ teaspoon Diamond Crystal kosher salt

(continued)

Oh, the mall. A place I spent much time at during my childhood, either with my clothing-obsessed sisters and aunt or sale-loving mother. A mandatory stop at every mall visit: Cinnabon. While I've always preferred a simpler, more classic American-style cinnamon roll, my mother loves to pull out all the stops, and in her honor, so does this recipe. To mimic her Cinnabon order, these fluffy cinnamon rolls get topped with a classic cream cheese icing, sweet caramel drizzle, and crunchy pecans for texture (the flaky sea salt is a personal preference, which I bet you could've guessed).

When I call these buns fluffy, I really do mean it. Taking the lead from Asian bread doughs, I employ the popular tangzhong technique of cooking off some of the flour with milk to create a roux of sorts that acts as a thickening agent, allowing the dough to hold onto more water (aka moisture) than a dough without one. Otherwise, everything else in this recipe is pretty standard, in a good way. You'll be left with the platonic ideal of a cinnamon roll.

If you want, split the process into two days: Make the dough the night before and let it rise in the fridge for about 8 hours. Proceed with the recipe the next day.

METHOD
To prepare the dough: Combine ⅓ cup (75 ml) of the milk and 2 tablespoons of the flour in a small saucepan over medium heat. Cook, whisking constantly, until a thick paste forms, 2 to 3 minutes. Transfer the paste to the bowl of a stand mixer. Let cool until warm to the touch, about 5 minutes, then add the remaining ¾ cup (180 ml) milk, the egg, instant yeast, granulated sugar, and kosher salt. Whisk until combined. Add the remaining 2¾ cups (343 g) flour to the bowl and fit the stand mixer with the dough hook attachment. Stir on low speed until combined. Increase the speed to 3 or 4 and knead until the dough is smooth and elastic, 15 to 18 minutes. Add the butter and continue to knead until it is fully incorporated and the dough is smooth and elastic, about 4 minutes. Cover with a damp tea towel and let rise in a warm place until doubled in size, 60 to 75 minutes.

Meanwhile, make the filling: With a spatula, combine the butter, brown sugar, cinnamon, and kosher salt in a medium bowl. Add the heavy cream for a filling that's on the gooier side after baking.

Once the dough has risen, punch the dough down to release the gas. Transfer the dough to a clean, lightly oiled surface and roll out into a rectangle about 16 × 22 inches as thinly as possible without breaking it. It's OK if your rectangle isn't quite this big—it won't affect the taste or the bake very much. Spread the filling over the dough in an even layer and roll it tightly into a log. Using floss, cut the dough into 10 to 12 pieces that are about 1½ inches thick. Lay the rolls flat into the greased baking dish, usually 3 rolls across, 4 rolls down, and cover with a damp tea towel. Let them rise one more time, until the rolls have grown in size and spring back when gently pushed, 30 to 45 minutes.

Meanwhile, preheat the oven to 350°F (175°C). Grease a 9 × 13-inch baking dish with butter and set aside.

FOR THE FROSTING

¼ cup (½ stick/55 g) unsalted butter, at room temperature

8 ounces (225 g) cream cheese, at room temperature

1¼ cups (138 g) powdered sugar, plus more as needed

1 tablespoon heavy cream, plus more as needed

¼ teaspoon Diamond Crystal kosher salt

FOR ASSEMBLY

Pecans, for serving

Flaky sea salt, for serving

After the final rise, bake the rolls for 20 to 30 minutes, until golden brown on the surface and puffed up. Bake toward the longer end of the timeframe if you prefer a crispy, bready roll or shorter if you prefer a doughy, soft texture. Don't worry if the centers of the rolls rise significantly. You can push them down with a spoon when they come out of the oven. Remove from the oven and let the rolls cool until warm to the touch, about 10 minutes.

While the rolls are baking, prepare the caramel drizzle: Melt the butter in a small saucepan over medium heat and cook until beginning to brown and smell fragrant and nutty, 2 to 3 minutes. Add the brown sugar and stir to combine. Cook until the sugar melts and turns slightly darker in color, about 1 minute. Add the heavy cream and stir vigorously until smooth. Immediately remove from the heat (be careful not to leave it on the stove for too long at this point). Stir in the kosher salt and set aside.

To prepare the frosting: Using an electric mixer, beat the butter and cream cheese on medium speed, scraping down the sides of the bowl as needed, until combined. You can also do this by hand with a whisk. Add the powdered sugar, heavy cream, and kosher salt and beat until the mixture is smooth and the sugar is incorporated. Taste and beat in more powdered sugar (up to ¾ cup/83 g), if desired. Thin with more cream as needed, a teaspoonful at a time, until the frosting is thick but spreadable.

To serve, spread the frosting over the warmed rolls, drizzle with the caramel, and sprinkle with the pecans and flaky salt.

COCONUT AND CARDAMOM CAKE

Serves 8
2 hours, plus cooling time

FOR THE CAKE

½ cup (1 stick/115 g) unsalted butter, at room temperature, plus more for the pan

1⅓ cups (170 g) all-purpose flour

1¼ teaspoons baking powder

1 teaspoon Diamond Crystal kosher salt

½ teaspoon ground cardamom

1 cup (200 g) granulated sugar

2 large eggs

2 tablespoons vegetable oil

1 teaspoon vanilla extract

½ teaspoon coconut extract

½ cup (120 ml) whole milk

FOR THE FROSTING OPTION

1 cup (85 g) sweetened shredded coconut

½ cup (1 stick/115 g) unsalted butter, at room temperature

2 cups (220 g) powdered sugar

¾ teaspoon Diamond Crystal kosher salt

½ teaspoon coconut extract

¼ cup (60 ml) heavy cream, plus more as needed

(continued)

Inspired by the nutty and mildly floral cardamom flavors of East African mkate mimina, a bouncy yeasted coconut and rice cake, this version of a classic, American-style yellow cake is made with a kiss of coconut extract and ground cardamom. The cake gets topped with a simple coconut-infused American buttercream and toasted coconut flakes to double down on the coconutty-ness. Think of the toasted coconut flakes that blanket the tender cake like you would sprinkles on steroids, adding flavor and tons of crunchy-chewy texture.

Some top tips: For an exceptionally tender and soft cake, I'll always add a liquid fat (aka oil) to cakes even when butter is the main fat. And make sure the butter for the buttercream is nice and soft and all ingredients are the same temperature so the sugar can incorporate evenly and the buttercream can whip up into a soft, airy texture without splitting.

Considering the inspiration for this cake, I mostly think of it as a warm-weather treat. But when late spring rolls around, I prefer a fruit-forward, fresh topping, so I've given you a second option: a strawberry rhubarb compote and whipped cream to make the most of the season. The compote also makes a great accompaniment to pancakes, yogurt bowls, and toast.

To turn this into a double-layer cake, simply double the cake recipe and scale up the frosting by three so you have enough for a layer in the center and to cover the top and sides.

METHOD

To make the cake: Place a rack in the middle of the oven and preheat to 325°F (165°C). Grease an 8-inch cake pan with butter and line with a parchment paper round.

Whisk the flour, baking powder, kosher salt, and cardamom in a medium bowl to combine. Set aside.

In the bowl of a stand mixer fitted with the paddle attachment, beat the granulated sugar and butter on medium speed until light and fluffy, about 3 minutes. Add the eggs, one at a time, beating until incorporated and scraping down the sides of the bowl with a rubber spatula as needed. Add the vegetable oil and vanilla and coconut extracts and beat until combined. Reduce the speed to low and gradually pour in the milk, beating until incorporated. Scrape down the sides of the bowl and mix to combine. Add the dry ingredients and gently fold in with a spatula just until no dry spots remain.

Scrape the batter into the prepared cake pan and smooth out the surface. Bake the cake for 45 to 50 minutes, until a tester inserted in the center comes out clean. Transfer the pan to a wire rack and let cool for 1 to 2 hours.

While the cake is cooling, prepare the frosting and toppings, choosing between the coconut frosting or strawberry rhubarb compote.

For the coconut frosting, heat a dry small skillet over medium heat, add the shredded coconut, and toast, stirring often, until mostly golden brown, 5 to 7 minutes. Immediately transfer to a small bowl and let cool (the coconut will continue to darken slightly as it cools).

FOR THE COMPOTE AND CREAM OPTION

1 pound (455 g) strawberries, hulled and halved or quartered if large

1 pound (455 g) rhubarb, roughly chopped

¼ teaspoon Diamond Crystal kosher salt

½ cup (100 g) granulated sugar

1 cup (240 ml) heavy cream

1 tablespoon sugar

½ teaspoon vanilla bean paste

Extra virgin olive oil, for serving

Flaky sea salt, for serving

Using an electric mixer on medium speed (resist the urge to use high speed to ensure your emulsion stays together), beat the butter in a medium bowl until light and fluffy, about 3 minutes. Add the powdered sugar in two additions, beating until combined after each addition. Add the kosher salt and coconut extract and beat until incorporated. Reduce the mixer speed to medium-low and beat, scraping down the sides of the bowl as needed, until the mixture is very light and fluffy, about 5 minutes. Add the heavy cream and beat until the frosting is smooth and spreadable. If it's too thick, beat in more cream, 1 tablespoon at a time. If the mixture still splits, remove about ⅓ cup (75 ml) of the frosting and warm it in the microwave until melted. Return to the rest of the buttercream and whisk; the heat should help form a stable buttercream.

To assemble, invert the cake onto a platter and unmold, carefully removing the parchment paper. As always, make sure the cake has cooled completely before frosting it. Using an offset spatula, spread the frosting evenly over the top and sides of the cake. Sprinkle the toasted shredded coconut over to coat the top and sides. Press gently to adhere. Slice and serve.

Alternatively, if you're making the compote and cream, combine the strawberries, rhubarb, kosher salt, and granulated sugar in a large skillet over medium-high heat. Cook, stirring often, until the fruit has broken down and the mixture has thickened, about 10 minutes. Let cool to room temperature and refrigerate until ready to assemble. In another large bowl, using an electric mixer or a whisk, whisk the heavy cream, sugar, and vanilla bean paste until soft peaks form. Top slices of cake with a dollop of whipped cream followed by a dollop of compote. Drizzle with olive oil and finish with a gentle sprinkle of flaky salt.

Do-ahead: The cake can be made up to 2 days ahead. Wrap in plastic wrap and store at room temperature. The frosting can also be made up to 2 days ahead. Cover and chill. Bring to room temperature, then beat until fluffy again before using. The compote can be made up to 3 days ahead. Cover and refrigerate. The whipped cream can be made up to 1 day ahead. Cover and refrigerate. You may need to re-whip it just before serving.

COFFEE CAKE MUFFINS

Makes 24 muffins
1 hour 15 minutes

FOR THE STREUSEL TOPPING

1¼ cups (160 g) all-purpose flour

1 cup (220 g) packed dark brown sugar

4 teaspoons ground cinnamon

½ teaspoon Diamond Crystal kosher salt

½ cup (1 stick/115 g) unsalted butter, melted and cooled

FOR THE CINNAMON SWIRL

½ cup (110 g) packed dark brown sugar*

1 teaspoon ground cinnamon

FOR THE BATTER

2 cups (255 g) all-purpose flour

¾ teaspoon baking soda

¾ teaspoon baking powder

½ teaspoon Diamond Crystal kosher salt

½ cup (1 stick/115 g) unsalted butter, at room temperature

1 cup (200 g) granulated sugar

2 large eggs

2 teaspoons vanilla extract

1½ cups (360 ml) sour cream

*INSTEAD OF...

Dark brown sugar, use light brown sugar

My dad has a very real addiction . . . to Dunkin' Donuts. His order: a medium hot coffee with skim milk, no sugar, and a coffee cake muffin. If you've never experienced a coffee cake muffin from Dunkin' Donuts, its sheer size sets it apart from any other variety I've ever known. A soft, cakelike, cinnamon-swirl muffin base sits below its crunchy, crumbly sweet muffin top (my dad's favorite part, and understandably so). This fondness has been passed down to his children, and now we all love them deeply.

Making a coffee cake muffin good enough to stand up to the nostalgia of our suburban Dunkin' runs means a very tender muffin crumb and a streusel topping that's nice and crisp. The batter relies on sour cream to keep it moist but still sturdy, and the technique for only kind of mixing together the ingredients for the streusel topping is key to big, crispy bits. I stuck to a standard muffin tin for the sake of accessibility, but if you adapt the recipe to the jumbo tins, you'll be left with a result even closer to the classic.

Serve with your favorite cup of joe.

METHOD

Preheat the oven to 350°F (175°C). Line 2 standard muffin tins with parchment liners.

To make the streusel: Whisk the flour, brown sugar, cinnamon, and salt in a medium bowl. Pour the melted butter over the mixture. Using a fork, gently combine to form crumbles. Do not overmix—it's OK if the ingredients don't appear evenly distributed. Set aside.

To make the cinnamon swirl: Combine the brown sugar and cinnamon in a small bowl and set aside.

To make the batter: Whisk the flour, baking soda, baking powder, and salt in a small bowl. Using a stand mixer fitted with the paddle attachment, cream the butter and granulated sugar on medium speed for 3 minutes, or until well combined and fluffy. Mix in the eggs, one at a time, until completely combined, stopping to scrape down the sides of the bowl as needed. Add the vanilla and mix until combined. Remove the bowl from the mixer and stir in the sour cream. Fold in the dry ingredients until mostly combined—it's OK if some lumps remain.

Divide half of the batter among 24 muffin cups, filling each liner one-quarter of the way up. Divide the cinnamon swirl among the muffin cups, then divide out the remaining batter over the top, leaving about ⅓ inch of space from the top. Divide the streusel mixture evenly over the top and bake for 18 to 22 minutes, until light golden and a toothpick inserted in the center comes out with a few moist crumbs. Let cool completely before serving.

Store the muffins in an airtight container or zip-top bag at room temperature for up to 3 days.

DATE AND DARK CHOCOLATE COOKIES

Makes 22 cookies
1 hour, plus chill time

2¼ cups (285 g) all-purpose flour
1 teaspoon baking soda
1 teaspoon cornstarch
1 teaspoon Diamond Crystal kosher salt
9 Medjool dates (165 g), pitted and chopped
8 ounces (225 g) 70% cacao bittersweet chocolate,* roughly chopped
2 large eggs
½ cup (110 g) extra virgin olive oil
¼ cup (60 g) well-mixed tahini
2 teaspoons vanilla extract
¾ cup (150 g) granulated sugar
¾ cup (150 g) packed light brown sugar*
Flaky sea salt

*INSTEAD OF...

Bittersweet chocolate, use semisweet chocolate

Light brown sugar, use dark brown sugar

Just a few months into my time as a food editor at *Bon Appétit*, a story highlighting the Islamic month of Ramadan was given the green light—a truly unique opportunity considering mainstream media rarely sheds a positive light on Islamic culture and tradition. In the month of Ramadan, dates play a significant role in the food tradition: After long days of fasting, Muslims break their fast with a date to quickly restore blood sugar levels, following the practice of our Prophet Muhammad. To spotlight the versatility of this holy fruit, we published a multirecipe ingredient explainer in the magazine alongside a profile on a Muslim date farmer in California's Coachella Valley. This recipe is my favorite of my contributions to the bunch (the Shawarma-Spiced Carrots on page 75 is a close second).

Like most people, my ideal cookie has crispy edges and a chewy center. Thanks to the tahini and olive oil–based dough, these deliver on that while also lending an exceptional sweet-savory balance, another quality I look for in a good dessert. To get the cookies just right, measure the ingredients by weight (tahini can be tricky to measure, so it really does help), use good-quality chocolate bars, and keep the pieces pretty big for oozy pools of melty chocolate. Oh, and finishing with flaky sea salt is a must. For a softer, less crisp cookie, reduce the oven temperature to 350°F (175°C) and bake for a few extra minutes.

METHOD

Whisk the flour, baking soda, cornstarch, and kosher salt in a medium bowl. Stir in the dates and chocolate to evenly distribute.

Using an electric mixer, beat the eggs, olive oil, tahini, and vanilla on medium speed until creamy and emulsified, about 2 minutes. Beat in the granulated sugar and brown sugar until combined, about 45 seconds. Reduce the mixer speed to low and mix in the dry ingredients, scraping down the sides of the bowl as needed, just until combined, about 30 seconds. Using a 2-ounce (60 ml) cookie scoop or ¼-cup measuring cup, portion the dough onto a plate. Cover and chill for at least 3 hours and up to 72 hours.

Place a rack in the middle of the oven and preheat to 375°F (190°C). Line 2 baking sheets with parchment paper.

Divide the dough balls between the prepared baking sheets spaced about 3 inches apart.

Put one baking sheet in the oven and bake until golden brown around the edges, 11 to 13 minutes. Remove from the oven and carefully but firmly bang the baking sheet against the counter to deflate the centers (to create a chewier cookie). Sprinkle with flaky salt. Bake the second sheet of cookies in the same way. Let the cookies cool on the baking sheets for 10 minutes before serving.

Store in an airtight container for up to 5 days. Reheat in the microwave for 15 seconds. You can freeze unbaked dough balls for up to 3 months; thaw overnight in the refrigerator or bake from frozen for 3 to 5 minutes longer.

SOMETHING SWEET

FRUIT AND NUT BISCOTTI

Makes 14 biscotti
1 hour 30 minutes

½ cup (1 stick/115 g) unsalted butter, at room temperature

¾ cup (150 g) sugar

3 large eggs

2 teaspoons vanilla extract

½ teaspoon almond extract*

2 cups (250 g) all-purpose flour

2 teaspoons baking powder

¾ teaspoon Diamond Crystal kosher salt

½ cup (50 g) toasted sliced almonds*

4 ounces (115 g) semisweet chocolate,* cut into small pieces

¼ cup (35 g) dried cherries,* cut into small pieces if large

*INSTEAD OF...

Almond extract, use coconut extract or ½ teaspoon ground cinnamon

Toasted sliced almonds, use sliced or chopped toasted hazelnuts, peanuts, pecans, or pistachios

Semisweet chocolate, use milk, dark, or white chocolate

Dried cherries, use raisins, dates, apricots, figs, or cranberries

Lucky for me, my mom was never an "almond mom" (Google it). I think of her more as a "Cadbury mom": the kind that can annihilate an entire family-sized bar of Cadbury chocolate by herself in one sitting.

For context, my mom spent her teenage years in London, where Cadbury chocolate is the reigning brand of choice. Whenever we'd travel there growing up, she'd bring back bars and bars of the purple foil-wrapped chocolate bars—either Whole Nut (milk chocolate with roasted hazelnuts) or Fruit & Nut (milk chocolate with almonds and raisins), which eventually became the inspiration for this recipe. The other inspiration: Nonni's chocolate and almond biscotti, the chai accompaniment of choice at my house. My take features a combination of both: toasted, sliced almonds, dried cherries, and semisweet chocolate (because milk chocolate just isn't for me).

If you don't have whole roasted, salted almonds to chop up for this, sliced almonds will work well. Just be sure to toast them to extract maximum flavor by baking them in a rimmed baking sheet 350°F (175°C) until golden brown, 8 to 10 minutes.

METHOD

Place a rack in the middle of the oven and preheat to 325°F (165°C). Line 2 baking sheets with parchment paper.

Combine the butter and sugar in a stand mixer fitted with the paddle attachment. Cream together on medium-low speed until lightened in color, about 3 minutes. Alternatively, use a large bowl and electric beaters or a whisk (just expect to use a little more elbow grease). Add the eggs, one at a time, and mix, scraping down the sides until well combined. Add the vanilla and almond extracts and mix to incorporate. On low speed, add the flour, baking powder, salt, sliced almonds, chocolate chips, and dried cherries and mix until evenly combined. The dough will be quite wet and will not hold together like a typical cookie dough.

Do your best to transfer the dough to the center of one of the prepared baking sheets and use damp hands to shape it into an 11 × 4-inch log (this will help keep the dough from sticking to your hands too much). Bake until puffed and very lightly browned around the edges, 25 to 30 minutes. Remove from the oven and cool for 5 to 10 minutes, until cool enough to handle. Cut crosswise using a straight-edged knife into 12 to 14 slices of biscotti that are 1 inch thick. Transfer to the second prepared baking sheet cut side up. Bake again until lightly browned, 18 to 22 minutes. Remove from the oven and let cool completely.

Store in an airtight container or zip-top bag for up to 2 weeks.

GAHWA SUNDAE

Serves 4
10 minutes

Vanilla, pistachio, or chocolate ice cream*
10 whole green cardamom pods,* crushed well
3 whole cloves*
⅛ teaspoon saffron
2 tablespoons finely ground medium or dark roast coffee
4 Medjool dates,* pitted and chopped
4 tablespoons (30 g) shelled salted pistachios,* roughly chopped
4 Maraschino cherries, for serving, optional

*INSTEAD OF...

Ice cream, use gelato, your choice of flavor

Whole green cardamom pods, use ½ teaspoon ground cardamom

Whole cloves, use ⅛ teaspoon ground cloves

Dates, use dried cherries, apricots, or cranberries

Pistachios, use another salted nut

Arabic coffee, called qahwah or gahwa in the Emirati dialect, is a very fragrant black coffee made with spices and traditionally served in small cups, similar to a shot of espresso, with dates alongside.

Inspired by Italian affogato, espresso is replaced by a splash of aromatic, spiced Arabic coffee to add an intriguing twist. You can leave it at just ice cream and qahwah and have a delicious version of an affogato, but this dessert is more akin to the sundaes I grew up eating, thanks to the addition of chewy dates (to replace gummy bears) and chopped pistachios (to replace peanuts).

The outlined method below is a riff on the traditional gahwa preparation for accessibility and ease, but if you can get your hands on good Arabic coffee and a roaster, please be my guest. Feel free to adjust the flavors to your liking; sometimes I'll even add ginger to amp up the warm spice factor. Use finely ground coffee, the kind you'd add to a coffee machine or moka pot to extract maximum flavor during the boiling.

METHOD

Remove the ice cream from the freezer. Let it stand to soften slightly and make scooping easier.

Bring 1½ cups (360 ml) water to a boil in a small pot over medium heat. Add the cardamom, cloves, saffron, and coffee and boil for 5 minutes. Remove from the heat and let stand for 2 minutes to allow the coffee grounds and spices to settle.

Meanwhile, put 2 scoops of ice cream into each of 4 small bowls or large coupe glasses.

Return to the coffee, and strain it through a fine-mesh sieve over a small liquid measuring cup. You should have about 1 cup (240 ml) of gahwa.

Divided the gahwa over the bowls of ice cream. Sprinkle the chopped dates on top and finish each bowl with 1 tablespoon chopped pistachios and a maraschino cherry, if using.

Gulzar's SUGAR PUFFS

Makes 24 sugar puffs
1 hour 30 minutes

3¼ cups (415 g) all-purpose flour, plus more for rolling and brushing

3 tablespoons neutral oil, plus more for brushing and deep-frying

¾ teaspoon table salt

½ cup (100 g) sugar

Our old mosque in Woodside, Queens, had a very particular way about it, and I loved it. So deeply familiar and habitual, it's a place that brought my creature-of-habit self so much comfort. Every time I'd walk in, usually late from the traffic on the FDR Drive, I'd dart left though the double doors and straight through to the very last sufro line: a paper runner that lined the length of the mosque where people would gather to sit and eat on the carpeted floor. My mom had her spot next to her friend, on the wall (a luxury reserved for elders), and I would sit between my two best friends. Right across from me, also on the wall, sat my best friend's mom, Shabnam, and her mother, Gulzar Meghji.

Gulzar Aunty, or Nani (abbreviated from Nani Ma, meaning *little mother*), as I refer to her casually now, is my childhood best friend, Asiya's, maternal grandmother. Fatiha, the tradition of a snack shared with others in honor of one's departed loved ones, is a common Ramadan practice in my community. Gulzar Aunty would always bring something homemade, passing it up and down the sufro line to anyone who wanted to try one. My favorite of her passed snacks were the sugar puris. Unique to her as far as I'm concerned, this take on a classic puri, a deep-fried puffed bread, is so sugary and crisp, making it perfect with a cup of our shared tea of choice: moori chai (Gujarati for unsweetened chai).

A master of all trades, Gulzar Aunty has served as our community chairlady for many terms, is an excellent self-taught seamstress (a talent I've always admired), an avid crossword player, and a seasoned cook. She's one of the few people I've encountered in my life who intimidates me. She doesn't talk too much or express much emotion, but she always shows up for what she cares for: her family and her community. I've always admired Gulzar Aunty's unwavering support for her daughter and her family. Despite being widowed at a young age, she's raised a family of exceptionally capable and smart women like herself.

When I asked Gulzar Aunty to teach me to make her special sugar puffs, she immediately obliged, and we quickly scheduled a date and time to meet. My friend was out of town that day, so it was just the two of us. When I entered her home in Queens, she had already laid the foundation for the work to begin. Most notably, she laid newspaper down to protect her counters and make cleanup fast and easy (a tip I've carried into my own kitchen)—an efficient woman indeed.

Her method is fairly simple but incorporates a layering technique and a dip in sugar straight out of the fryer that's unique to this version, creating an extra flaky and indulgent puri.

METHOD

Mix the flour, neutral oil, salt, and ¾ cup (180 ml) water in a large bowl with your hands until combined. If the dough is very dry, add more water by the tablespoonful, mixing between each addition, until all the flour is hydrated. Turn out onto a clean work surface and knead by hand until the dough is smooth and elastic, 5 to 8 minutes. Divide it into 4 portions, and then divide each portion into 6 pieces (about 1 ounce/25 g each). Roll each piece into a ball between your palms, set them aside, and keep them covered with a kitchen towel as you work.

On a lightly floured work surface, roll out each ball into 4-inch flat rounds. Brush the surface of each round with vegetable oil and dust with flour. Fold the sides of each round in toward each other, overlapping in the center both ways to form a neat square, then flatten each square by pressing down on it with your fingertips. Repeat with all the pieces of dough. Freeze the dough at this stage if you're planning to store it for later.

Roll each piece of dough into a 3-inch square. Try to avoid reflouring the work surface to avoid cloudy oil when frying.

Put the sugar on a small plate and set aside. Line a plate with paper towels.

Heat a large wok or karahi over medium heat and fill it with 2 inches of vegetable oil for deep-frying. Once the oil is hot (about 350°F/175°C), working in batches of 4 to 6, deep-fry the puris until light golden on both sides, agitating the puris in the oil so they puff slightly as they cook, 1 to 2 minutes per side. Remove the puris from the oil and transfer them to the paper towel–lined plate and let them rest for about 1 minute. Dip one side of the puris in sugar and transfer to a plate for serving.

ALMOND MOCHA BLONDIES

Makes 9 to 12 squares
1 hour

1 cup (130 g) all-purpose flour

¼ teaspoon baking soda

½ teaspoon Diamond Crystal kosher salt

2 tablespoons warm water

2 tablespoons instant coffee, preferably Nescafé Dark Roast

½ cup (1 stick/115 g) unsalted butter, melted

¼ cup (50 g) granulated sugar

½ cup (100 g) packed dark brown sugar*

1 large egg yolk

½ cup (70 g) roasted, salted almonds,* roughly chopped

¾ cup (130 g) semisweet chocolate chunks*

Whipped cream or crème fraîche, for serving, optional

Cocoa powder, for serving, optional

Flaky sea salt, for serving, optional

*INSTEAD OF...

Dark brown sugar, use light brown sugar

Almonds, use another roasted salted nut

Semisweet chocolate chunks, use milk or bittersweet chocolate chunks or chips

My dad's working hours kept him away from home for long hours, so he rarely came home before 9:00 p.m. His absence was a thing of requirement, not preference. I'll never know if this tradition was born of guilt, but every Friday night, no matter the time (my mom was not thrilled with this), he would drive me and whichever siblings were around to the local twenty-four-hour Dunkin' Donuts Baskin-Robbins to buy ice cream before movie night. I'd almost always order Jamoca ice cream, occasionally Jamoca Almond Fudge. Nowadays I can't have a single bite of ice cream without remembering our weekly tradition and, moreover, I'll always hold a special place for Jamoca Almond Fudge.

While developing this recipe, I felt compelled to finally find out where the name Jamoca comes from. It's probably common knowledge to most, but I learned that it's a combination of Java and mocha, and they are the primary flavors of this blondie-cookie hybrid. For crunch, and to stay true to the inspiration, roasted salted almonds join the party. If you don't have whole roasted, salted almonds to chop up for this, sliced almonds will work well—just be sure to toast them to extract maximum flavor by baking them in a rimmed baking sheet at 350°F (175°C) until golden brown, 8 to 10 minutes.

METHOD

Place a rack in the center of the oven and preheat to 350°F (175°C). Line an 8 × 8-inch baking pan with parchment paper.

Meanwhile, whisk the flour, baking soda, and kosher salt in a small bowl.

In a large bowl, combine the warm water and instant coffee and whisk to dissolve the coffee. Add the melted butter, sugars, and egg yolk and whisk very well to aerate. Add the dry ingredients, almonds, and chocolate chunks and use a rubber spatula to mix until no dry spots remain.

Transfer the batter to the prepared pan and use an offset spatula to spread it into an even layer. Bake for 25 to 30 minutes, until golden, papery, and puffed on the surface. Remove from the oven and let cool completely. Then transfer to a cutting board, discard the parchment, and cut into even squares.

If desired, serve with a dollop of whipped cream or crème fraîche, a dusting of cocoa powder, and a sprinkle of flaky salt.

SOMETHING SWEET 239

JUGU SCONES WITH BUTTER AND JAM

Makes 12 scones
1 hour 30 minutes

½ cup (1 stick/115 g) cold unsalted butter

¾ cup (115 g) salted roasted peanuts*

2½ cups (315 g) all-purpose flour

¼ cup (50 g) sugar, plus up to ½ cup (100 g) more

1 tablespoon baking powder

½ teaspoon kosher salt

1 large egg

¾ cup (180 ml) cold heavy cream, plus more for brushing*

Flaky sea salt

Salted French butter, for serving

Strawberry jam,* for serving

*INSTEAD OF . . .

Peanuts, use another roasted salted nut, or forgo the nuts entirely for ½ cup (65 g) extra flour and ½ teaspoon more salt

Heavy cream for brushing, use egg wash (1 egg beaten)

Strawberry jam, use another flavor

Jugu cake, an East African peanut rusk, was always in abundance in our snack cabinet growing up. Stale and crumbly in texture (similar to biscotti yet somehow drier), you absolutely needed to have it with a cup of tea or coffee to avoid a Sahara Desert dry mouth. If that description isn't obvious enough, I'll be clearer: I never really preferred it. I did, however, like peanut butter and jelly sandwiches. Meet my happy medium: a flaky scone made with crushed roasted peanuts and served with butter and jam.

METHOD

Grate the cold butter on the large holes of a box grater onto a small plate. Transfer to the freezer and chill for 15 minutes.

Meanwhile, put the peanuts in a food processor and pulse until a coarse crumb is formed and no whole peanuts remain. Remove 2 tablespoons of the peanuts and set aside for garnish. Continue pulsing until the peanuts are finely ground and sand-like, about 30 seconds, making sure to stop before the peanuts turn to peanut butter.

Put the ground peanuts into a large bowl, add the flour, sugar, baking powder, and kosher salt, and whisk to combine. Add the grated butter and toss to coat the butter in the flour mixture.

In a separate bowl, whisk together the egg and heavy cream. Pour the wet mixture into the dry mixture and stir until the dough just begins to come together. It'll be a bit dry. Transfer the dough to a lightly floured cutting board and flatten down to ¾ inch thick (the shape doesn't matter). Using a knife, cut into 4 pieces, stack the pieces on top of each other, and flatten the dough into a ¾-inch-thick, 9-inch square (this process will create flaky layers when the scones are baked). Cut the dough in half lengthwise, then cut each half into thirds crosswise to form six 3-inch squares. Cut each square in half on a diagonal to make 12 triangles total. Alternatively, you can use a 2½-inch-diameter biscuit cutter to punch out scones. Gather the scraps and repeat, patting and cutting, until you have 12 scones. Chill the scones, uncovered, for 15 to 20 minutes.

Meanwhile, preheat the oven to 400°F (205°C) and line a baking sheet with parchment paper.

Transfer the scones to the prepared baking sheet and brush with heavy cream using a pastry brush. Sprinkle with the remaining coarse peanut crumbs and some flaky salt. Bake for 17 to 20 minutes, until the tops of the scones are golden. Allow to cool slightly on the baking sheets until just warm.

The scones should easily split in half. Top with a thick slab of salted butter and a swoosh of strawberry jam.

Store the scones in an airtight container at room temperature for up to 3 days.

MELON SORBET

*Serves 6 (24 ounces sorbet)
30 minutes, plus 7 to 12 hours chill time*

1 medium ripe cantaloupe* (about 3 pounds/1.3 kg), cut in half, seeded, flesh scooped out and cut into 1-inch cubes, divided

2 tablespoons good-quality honey, plus more to taste

2 tablespoons boiling water, plus more as needed

½ teaspoon Diamond Crystal kosher salt

Lemon or lime wedges, for serving

Flaky sea salt, for serving

Aleppo chili flakes, for serving

Extra virgin olive oil, for serving

*INSTEAD OF...

Cantaloupe, use another melon or ripe summer fruit

I've always loved very cold, icy things like Slurpees, slushies, sorbet, and Italian ice. This melon sorbet was born out of wanting an even colder way to enjoy one of my favorite summertime snacks: ripe melon with chili powder, salt, and lemon or lime juice.

This technique for making sorbet is very easy and yields a shockingly ideal sorbet texture, not too hard and frosty but not too wet and melty thanks to the honey syrup inhibiting crystallization when freezing. Choosing to completely freeze only half of the cantaloupe makes the blending process much smoother and keeps things in sorbet territory rather than granita, although that would also be lovely. I find cantaloupe's firm flesh to be ideal for this, but this technique will work on watermelon, honeydew, and even mango or berries, but manage your textural expectations accordingly (watermelon probably will be a little on the icier side, while mangos and berries probably will be a little softer and creamier); just make sure to keep the ratio as is, starting with 1½ pounds (680 g) of prepared fruit.

Freezing tends to mellow out flavors, so when you taste the puree, make sure it tastes a little more intense than where you'd want it to be from a sweetness perspective. This really isn't an issue when you're using in-season melon, but since it's not summer all year round where I live, it's worth noting.

METHOD

Spread half of the cubed cantaloupe on a baking sheet in an even layer. Freeze until solid, 4 to 6 hours. Set the remaining cantaloupe aside for later.

Put the honey and boiling water in a small bowl and stir to combine. Let stand until cooled to room temperature.

Put the remaining cantaloupe in a high-speed blender (preferably one with a tamper) or a food processor and add the kosher salt, honey syrup, and frozen cantaloupe. Blend until smooth and Frostee-like in texture and on the sweet side (the sweetness will mellow as it freezes). If it's not sweet enough for you, make more honey syrup using the same 1:1 honey to boiling water ratio and add it in at this phase. Transfer to a loaf pan. Cover with plastic wrap and freeze until solid, 3 to 5 hours.

To serve, scoop into bowls using a warm ice cream scoop. Finish with a squeeze of lemon or lime, flaky salt, chili flakes, and a drizzle of olive oil.

Freeze, covered in plastic wrap, or in an airtight container, for up to 3 months. Thaw at room temperature for 15 minutes before scooping and serving.

PINEAPPLES AND GHEE

Serves 2
15 minutes

¼ cup (55 g) packed dark brown sugar*

2 tablespoons ghee*

¼ teaspoon Diamond Crystal kosher salt

7 ounces (200 g) fresh pineapple,* cut into ½-inch cubes (about 1¼ cups)

1¼ cup (300 ml) plain whole-milk Greek yogurt*

⅔ cup (80 to 90 g) granola,* homemade (page 212) or store-bought

*INSTEAD OF...

Dark brown sugar, use light brown sugar or granulated sugar

Ghee, use butter (omit the salt if using salted butter)

Pineapple, use another hearty fruit like banana, apple, papaya, strawberries, orange, or persimmon

Greek yogurt, use skyr or plain yogurt

Granola, use 2 tablespoons roughly chopped nuts per serving

Ghee kera is a hot caramelized banana dish that my mother would excitedly prepare to eat with roti on mornings when the fruit bowl bananas had one too many spots. While I, too, am a fan of dessert for breakfast on occasion, I'll be honest, I never really liked how mushy and cloyingly sweet ghee kera is. Another of my mother's sweet treats I grew up on: pineapple supreme, a creamy, simple cold dessert of pineapple, sweetened whipped cream, and crunchy chopped nuts. Now, that's a dessert I'd be excited to eat for breakfast. The marrying of those two dishes results in an indulgent, satisfying breakfast of warmed, caramel-y pineapple paired with cold, creamy yogurt, best served with a crisp granola (see Bakalava Granola, page 212). The resulting ghee syrup is perfect for spooning over the top of yogurt to sweeten it, like you would with honey on a traditional breakfast parfait.

While I mostly enjoy this as a solo morning breakfast, you can scale it up and make it ahead for a crowd and use any slightly acidic fruit. I've made this with out-of-season strawberries, citrus, and even apples (with a sprinkle of cinnamon and cardamom). This would also work very well over oatmeal instead of yogurt if you're not into a hot-cold breakfast moment.

METHOD

Heat a small skillet over medium heat until warm. Add the brown sugar, ghee, salt, and pineapple and stir to combine. Cook, stirring often, until the sugar dissolves and melts into the ghee and the pineapple is warmed through and crisp tender, about 5 minutes. Don't worry if the sugar appears clumpy or crystallized in the first few minutes of cooking—just keep stirring and it'll eventually become a homogeneous sauce.

Divide the yogurt, pineapple mixture and sauce, and granola between 2 bowls. Serve immediately.

Store any leftover or unused pineapple mixture or sauce refrigerated in an airtight container for up to 5 days. Reheat in the microwave in 30-second bursts or in a skillet over medium heat until warm and bubbly.

SALTED BROWN BUTTER PECAN SHORTBREAD

Makes 16 shortbread biscuits
1 hour 30 minutes, plus resting time

1½ cups (3 sticks/345 g) good-quality unsalted butter*

1 cup (100 g) pecan halves,* roughly chopped

⅔ cup (140 g) sugar

1¼ teaspoons Diamond Crystal kosher salt

2 teaspoons good-quality vanilla extract

3⅓ cups (425 g) all-purpose flour

Flaky sea salt

*INSTEAD OF...

Unsalted butter, use salted butter; reduce the salt in the recipe by ¾ teaspoon

Pecan halves, use another roughly chopped nut

Unassuming but incredibly flavorful, these Scottish shortbread-inspired cookies are really something special. Having lived her adolescent years in London, my mother introduced us to the wonderful world of Walker's Shortbread biscuits early on. Their salty, buttery quality has always been so delightful to me.

I've mentioned my Baskin-Robbins ice cream order (see Almond Mocha Blondies, page 238), but anywhere else, I order butter pecan. The creamy, crunchy, salty, buttery elements just work so well together, so I applied them here—in an already buttery, salty cookie.

Toasting both the nuts and the milk solids from the butter ensures an ultra-rich, nutty, and buttery flavor that you can really taste, but if you're short on time or don't love brown butter, use 2½ sticks (285 g) cold unsalted butter, cut into small cubes, and proceed with the recipe.

If you have a nut allergy or don't enjoy nuts, omit the pecans and reduce the salt by ¼ teaspoon.

METHOD

In a large light-colored skillet or medium pot, melt the butter over medium heat. Add the pecans and toast, stirring frequently, until the milk solids in the butter have separated from the fat and have turned dark brown, 5 to 7 minutes. Carefully pour the pecan butter into the bowl of a stand mixer and chill until the butter is firm and cold to the touch, about 1½ hours.

Meanwhile, line an 8 × 8-inch square baking pan with parchment paper, leaving an overhang on all sides, and prepare your other ingredients.

Once the butter is chilled, fit a standing mixer with the paddle attachment. Add the sugar, kosher salt, and vanilla to the butter and mix on medium-low speed until the butter is light and fluffy, about 1 minute. Scrape down the sides of the bowl to make sure all the butter is completely incorporated. Add the flour and mix on low speed to combine; the dough should come together, while being easy to crumble apart. Depending on your altitude and the humidity, you may need an extra tablespoon or so of flour to achieve that texture.

Transfer the dough to the prepared baking pan and spread it into an even layer. I like to do this by covering the dough with another sheet of parchment and, using the bottom of a small glass, pushing to distribute the dough in the pan into an even layer. You can also use your fingers or an offset spatula. Peel off the top layer of parchment (if you used it) and dock the dough by pricking it all over with a fork. Chill in the freezer while the oven preheats, about 10 to 20 minutes.

Meanwhile, place a rack in the middle of the oven and preheat to 350°F (175°C).

Bake for 45 to 50 minutes, until lightly browned on top. Remove from the oven. Sprinkle with flaky salt and run a knife or offset spatula along the edges of the shortbread to loosen the parchment. Let cool in the pan completely.

Using the parchment paper overhang, remove the shortbread from the pan and transfer it to a cutting board. Discard the parchment. Cut the shortbread into sixteen 4 × 1–inch fingers. I strongly recommend letting these rest uncovered overnight before biting into one for the ideal texture and flavor.

Store in an airtight container for up to 2 weeks. Alternatively, freeze between layers of parchment paper for up to 3 months and leave to thaw on the counter overnight before serving.

SOMETHING SWEET 247

STRAWBERRY DELIGHT

Serves 4 to 6
25 minutes

1 pint (290 g) ripe strawberries,* hulled and quartered

¼ cup (25 g) plus ⅓ cup (35 g) powdered sugar, divided, plus more as needed

¼ teaspoon Diamond Crystal kosher salt

1 tablespoon fresh lemon juice,* from about ½ a lemon

1 cup (240 ml) heavy cream, divided

½ teaspoon vanilla extract

1 (8-ounce/226 g) package cream cheese,* at room temperature

Zest of 1 lemon*

1 sleeve Ritz crackers,* very roughly crushed

*INSTEAD OF...

Strawberries, use another berry, citrus, or stone fruit

Cream cheese, use mascarpone

Lemon juice and zest, use another citrus juice and zest

Ritz crackers, use another salted cracker

I happened to make the final version of this recipe while at my parents' house for dinner. As I anxiously awaited their feedback on a dessert that took only fifteen minutes to make, I could tell they weren't expecting much. My mom took a bite and made an audible "Mmm" sound, followed by "You should name this strawberry delight." I laughed at the time, but as usual she was right, and here we are. There really isn't quite a better name to describe this easy, indulgent dessert.

The inspiration for this recipe comes from so many places, so you're going to need to walk with me through this one. The flavors come from a snack my mom used to make for us after school: Ritz crackers topped with cream cheese and jam (so good, please try them). Inspiration number two and one of my all-time favorite summertime treats: in-season berries served with some Chantilly cream for dipping. Third: the no-bake cheesecake cups that frequently graced the dessert displays thirteen-year-old me put together for friends and family gatherings. And, finally: mille-feuille, one of my favorite French pastries.

Put all that together and we have strawberry delight: a mildly sweet, texture-forward dessert of juicy berries, airy cream, and salty, buttery crackers to provide a little crunch. This really is a very flexible dessert, so you can and should use the recipe as a set of guidelines.

METHOD

Put the strawberries, ¼ cup (25 g) of the powdered sugar, the salt, and lemon juice in a medium bowl. Toss to combine until the powdered sugar dissolves, about 30 seconds. Taste a berry and check for sweetness. Adjust to your preference depending on how ripe the berries are by adding 1 tablespoon of powdered sugar at a time. Let rest in the refrigerator to macerate, at least 15 minutes or up to overnight.

Meanwhile, put ¾ cup (180 ml) of the heavy cream, the remaining ⅓ cup (35 g) powdered sugar, and the vanilla in a large bowl or the base of a stand mixer. Whip on medium speed until thick and foamy, just shy of soft peaks.

Add the cream cheese (make sure it's very soft) and lemon zest and mix on low speed until the cream cheese is well incorporated and no lumps remain, about 1 minute. The mixture may be very stiff at this stage. Add the remaining ¼ cup (60 ml) heavy cream and mix on medium speed until incorporated and the mixture is thick and airy and like sour cream in texture, 30 seconds or so. Stir in more cream by the tablespoonful as needed to achieve that texture.

Divide half of the Ritz cracker bits among 4 to 6 coupe glasses or dessert bowls. Divide half of the cream mixture over the top and spoon half of the strawberry mixture over that. Repeat with the remaining cracker bits, cream, and strawberry mixture.

Do-ahead: The cream and berries can be made up to 12 hours in advance. Transfer the cream and berries into separate airtight containers and chill until ready to assemble and serve.

SIPS

(252–263)

*Beverages, smoothies, and,
of course, chai*

A DIFFERENT DATE SHAKE

Serves 2 to 4 (makes 4 cups)
10 minutes

3 Medjool dates, pitted
1 tablespoon Dutch-process cocoa powder
1 tablespoon instant coffee granules,* such as Nescafé
1 teaspoon vanilla extract
½ teaspoon Diamond Crystal kosher salt
1¼ cups (180 g) frozen banana pieces, from about 2 medium bananas
1 cup (155 g) frozen blueberries*

*INSTEAD OF...

Instant coffee granules, use 1½ cups (360 ml) chilled coffee (omit the water) or 1½ teaspoons instant espresso powder

Frozen blueberries, use another frozen berry

A shake worth getting out of bed for.

A date shake, akin to a milkshake, in its traditional preparation, consists simply of dates, milk, and ice cream. While it's delicious, it doesn't exactly scream "balanced breakfast." So, to make this dessert-for-breakfast a little more fruitful (pun intended), I've reimagined the classic with the addition of blueberries, bananas, and coffee.

Even though this is technically a smoothie, I didn't want to use the name because it is so much more complex in flavor than what comes to mind when I think of one. While it's fruit forward, it's deeper and richer than your average smoothie thanks to the salt, vanilla, and cocoa powder (try to use Dutch-process; it really does make a difference). Salt and vanilla in a smoothie are non-negotiables for me—they take any smoothie to an irresistible, milkshake-like place.

As someone who can't start their day without caffeine, coffee in a morning smoothie just makes sense. Nescafé instant coffee granules are easy to find and are always in my pantry, so I developed this recipe using those, but feel free to use 1½ cups (360 ml) of your favorite chilled or cooled coffee instead and forgo the water from the ingredient list. You can absolutely throw everything into the blender and give it a good whirl, but blending the dates before adding any frozen fruit ensures a smooth drink with no chewy bits of floating dates.

METHOD

Combine the dates, cocoa powder, instant coffee, vanilla, salt, and 1½ cups (360 ml) water in a blender and blend on high speed until smooth, about 1 minute. Add the frozen bananas and frozen blueberries and blend on high speed until smooth. Taste and thin with more water as needed to your desired consistency.

GINGER LIME SPRITZ

Serves 4
30 minutes

8 ounces (225 g) fresh ginger, roughly chopped
¾ cup (150 g) granulated sugar
¾ teaspoon Diamond Crystal kosher salt
¼ cup (60 ml) fresh lime juice, from about 2 limes
Ice cubes
About 24 ounces (720 ml) chilled sparkling water
Lime wedges or wheels, for serving

Stoney's Tangawizi, a spicy ginger beer popular throughout East Africa, inspired this refreshing ginger soda made with lots of fresh ginger root (use organic for an even better, spice-forward flavor), plenty of fresh lime juice to tame the heat, and a good amount of salt for complexity. Let the crushed ginger steep in the syrup the full fifteen minutes to allow the residual heat to continue to extract its flavor.

METHOD

To make the syrup, crush the ginger with a mortar and pestle or further chop the ginger into fine bits. In a medium skillet, combine the ginger, sugar, salt, and ¾ cup (180 ml) water and bring to a boil over medium-high heat. Cook, stirring occasionally, until the sugar is dissolved and the syrup has reduced slightly, about 3 minutes. Remove from the heat and let stand for 15 minutes.

Strain the syrup through a fine-mesh sieve into a heatproof measuring glass. Discard the ginger and stir in the lime juice.

Divide the syrup among four 8-ounce glasses. Add ice, then top off each glass with about 6 ounces (180 ml) sparkling water. Garnish with lime wedges or wheels.

The syrup can be made up to 3 days ahead. Transfer to an airtight container and refrigerate.

KARAK CHAI

Serves 6
35 minutes

4 Tetley brand tea bags,* ideally Orange Pekoe or British Blend
13 cardamom pods, cracked
3-inch cinnamon stick
3 tablespoons granulated sugar,* plus more to taste
1 teaspoon vanilla extract, optional
2 tablespoons unsweetened cocoa powder, optional
1 cup (240 ml) evaporated milk

*INSTEAD OF...
Tetley tea bags, use PG Tips or 4 teaspoons loose black tea leaves
Granulated sugar, use cane sugar or light brown sugar

A socially acceptable upper in our community, it could be the caffeine in this traditional milky tea that makes it so addictive, but it's more likely the low and slow cook, the rich evaporated milk, and all the aromatic spices.

Karak chai, also called Kadak chai, is a variant of the South Asian masala chai very popular in the Middle East where the tea is cooked until it's strong (for reference, *kadak* means "hard" or "harsh" in Hindi). The spices used can vary from household to household—some recipes even include ginger, but cardamom is essential. The vanilla extract is a personal preference—it's mostly for aroma and entirely optional. Sometimes I'll add cocoa powder to make something more akin to a hot chocolate, an East African variant called cocoa chai.

The evaporated milk is signature to this tea, resulting in a drink so luscious it's sometimes a little too rich for my mood. When I want something lighter, I'll replace half of the evaporated milk with 1% or 2% milk.

This amount of sugar feels like the minimum for a pleasant drinking experience, but feel free to adjust it depending on who you're serving it to, or simply serve the tea with a bowl of sugar alongside with spoons for people to sweeten to their liking. Fair warning, someone will absolutely use the dry sugar spoon to mix their chai and return it to the now-clumpy sugar bowl. That's when I have to remind myself to breathe—it's all part of the experience.

METHOD
Combine 6 cups (1.4 L) water, tea bags, cardamom, cinnamon, sugar, vanilla, and cocoa powder, if using, in a stove-safe tea kettle or medium pot. Place over medium-high heat and bring to a boil. Stir in the evaporated milk and return to a boil, watching carefully to ensure the tea doesn't boil over—once the milk is introduced, boiling over is common at a rolling boil. Once just boiling, reduce the heat to medium-low and simmer until thick, creamy, and caramel in color, about 25 minutes. The longer the tea simmers, the stronger and creamier it will be, although it will also reduce in volume. Taste for desired sweetness and add more sugar to your taste.

Strain the chai through a fine-mesh sieve into mugs; discard the spices and tea bags. Serve with additional sugar on the side.

The Pink Drink (260)
Preserved Limonata (260)

THE PINK DRINK

Serves 8 to 10
10 minutes

1 (14-ounce/397 g) can sweetened condensed milk

4 (12-ounce/354 ml) cans evaporated milk

4 cups (960 ml) cold water

½ cup (165 ml) Rooh Afza rose syrup, plus more to taste

¼ teaspoon Diamond Crystal kosher salt

⅓ cup (45 g) almonds, finely chopped

⅓ cup (45 g) shelled pistachios, finely chopped

While Starbucks may claim the Pink Drink title, the original pink drink that I grew up on is called sharbat: a fragrant, milky drink topped with crushed nuts with origins in India. As the beverage most associated with indulgence in my culture, we drink this during times of celebration (and otherwise) and serve it with a generous spirit. Its pink color comes from Rooh Afza, a South Asian rose-infused syrup, which imparts a strong floral flavor. Crushed pistachios and almonds add to the luxury of this pink drink, and it's best served very cold.

Since you're investing in the bottle of Rooh Afza (for its size more so than price), know that there will be a high yield on your return. A quick mix with a glass of milk before bedtime or a drizzle over vanilla ice cream topped with crushed nuts (basically a Hershey's chocolate syrup alternative) is a quick sweet evening treat that feels just as indulgent as sharbat, in a fraction of the time. And, if you're feeling fancy, blend some with frozen watermelon for a floral and refreshing summertime sip. It's also a great addition to a matcha or regular latte. Use it like you would most other flavored syrups.

METHOD

Combine the condensed milk, evaporated milk, cold water, rose syrup, and salt in a punch bowl. Stir to dissolve the condensed milk. Add the nuts and stir to combine; they will float to the top. Taste and add more rose syrup to reach your desired sweetness and color. Chill and serve or divide among glasses filled with ice.

PRESERVED LIMONATA

Serves 4
10 minutes

3 tablespoons chopped preserved lemon, plus more, thinly sliced, for serving

3 tablespoons fresh lemon juice, from 1½ to 2 lemons

Ice, for serving

Chilled tonic water,* for serving

*INSTEAD OF...
Tonic water, use sparking water plus simple syrup to taste

Like lemonade but more sophisticated. Partially inspired by classic Italian sparkling lemonade, limonata, this version is complex and dynamic thanks to the funky preserved lemon. Using bittersweet tonic water as the mixer here helps to balance the sourness of fresh lemon and the brininess of preserved lemon, but sparkling water and a bit of simple syrup will work, too. It's perfect for sipping poolside or serving as a mocktail.

METHOD

Crush the preserved lemon to a paste with a mortar and pestle or the flat side of a chef's knife. Transfer to a small bowl and stir in the lemon juice.

Divide the mixture among 4 highball glasses. Fill with ice, then top off with tonic water. Garnish with preserved lemon slices.

SLIGHTLY
SALTY
MANGO LASSI

Serves 2 to 4 (3 cups/720 ml)
15 minutes

- 2 very ripe Champagne (also known as Ataulfo) mangos* (about 12 ounces/340 g), peeled, pit removed, and flesh scooped out
- ¾ cup (180 ml) plain whole-milk yogurt
- ½ cup (120 ml) whole milk*
- 2 tablespoons honey, plus more as needed*
- Heaping ¼ teaspoon kosher salt
- ⅛ teaspoon ground cardamom*
- Ice, for serving, optional

*INSTEAD OF...
- Champagne mangos, use another variety of equal weight or canned mango pulp (omit honey if using sweetened mango pump)
- Whole milk, use any dairy-free alternative or water (if using water, your lassi will be slightly less creamy)
- Honey, use sugar or maple syrup
- Ground cardamom, use the seeds from 2 green cardamom pods, crushed in a mortar and pestle

I've always been indecisive (see Pasta Day Pasta, page 137), so when a waiter asks, "Lassi, salted or mango?" I find myself at a crossroads, wanting both but only able to order one. I generally alternate between the two when dining out. But not at home. At home, I bask in the glory of a slightly sweet, slightly salty combination, resulting in the perfect lassi for me. A heaping ¼ teaspoon salt is ideal: a level ¼ teaspoon and you can't quite taste the salt, but ½ teaspoon will be too salty for most.

METHOD

Combine the mangos, yogurt, milk, honey, salt, and cardamom in a blender and blend on high speed until smooth. Adjust the viscosity by blending in water ¼ cup (60 ml) at a time and adjust the sweetness with honey to your preference. Chill before serving or divide between glasses over ice.

Karak Chai (256)
Fruit and Nut Biscotti (233)
Date and Dark Chocolate Cookies (230)

ACKNOWLEDGMENTS

Where do I even begin? One thing's for sure: It really does take a village, and the sheer length of this list proves it. Whether you're on this list because you've contributed directly to this book or because in some moment you've offered me a word of encouragement or advice, I can genuinely say that without each and every one of you, this book wouldn't be what it is. Thank you.

Mikhail Khalfan

Ebrahim Issa
Rishma Issa
Ashraf Dinani
Riffat Khalfan

Denise Comley
Fatema Issa Asharia
Nicole Tourtelot
Holly Dolce
Lisa Silverman
Sebit Min
Michael Graydon
Nikole Herriott
Pearl Jones
Rebecca Bartoshesky

Yekaterina Boytsova
Hannah Braden
Ava Chambers
Christian Ern
Chis Johnson
Christine Quach
Ali Park
Tia Rotolo
Emilie Saulter
Leda Scheintaub
Deb Wood
Danielle Youngsmith

Shenaz Chevel
Gulzar Ebrahim
Sukayna Essa
Rumina Khalfan
Layla Ladha
Gulzar Meghji

Sakina Issa
Ali Manekia
Shabbar Asharia
Mikaeel Issa
Mazhar Khalfan
Farzana Khalfan
Zaynab Khalfan
Fatemah Khalfan
Mehnaz Khimji
Hasnain Khimji
Alia Khalfan
Siraj Khalfan

Ferwa Khalfan
Aliza Abarbanel
Hana Asbrink
Inés Anguiano
Sabrina Azizi
Sarah Azizi
Natalie Bade
Andy Baraghani
Tanya Bush
Christina Chaey
Nadia Chatoo
Sonia Chopra
Dawn Davis
Farhan Davdani
Kerry Diamond
Ali Hussein Dinani
Asiya Dinani
Irfan Dinani
Rizwan Dinani
Sameer Ladha Dinani
Shafina Dinani
Justine Doiron
Abdul Essa
Serena Goh
Rachel Gurjar
Zahra Imran
Aejaaz Issa
Asiya Jaffer
Fatim Jaffer
Kaniz Jaffer
Khatija Jaffer
Nishat Jessa
Maleeha Khalfan
Nasim Lahbichi
Edy Massih
Chris Morocco
Nadir Nahdi
Romilly Newman
Vivian Nguyen
Olivia Noceda
Dan Pelosi
Natasha Pickowicz
Arsh Raziuddin
Woldy Reyes
Meryl Rothstein
Zainab Shah
Amanda Shapiro
Emily Schultz
Anisha Sisodia
Ivana Somorai

Tahsine
Aleksandar Tosic
Shilpa Uskokovic
Kendra Vaculin
Noreen Wasti

Arunima Agarwal
Sarah Ahmad
Asnia Akhtar
Alana Al-Hatlani
Neeli Amin
Abena Anim-Somuah
Talene Appleton
Brittany Arnett
Beatrice Azzolina
Oset Babür-Winter
Shawn Barreiro
Bianca Betancourt
Vidushi Bhargava
Lizzy Briskin
Gina Bruno
Katie Calton
Kristiana Chancy
Victoria Chardiet
Pamelia Chia
Jessica Chou
Matthew Ciampa
Jasmyn Crawford
Londyn Crenshaw
Farhan Davdani
Alexia Derkasch
Julie Dumas
Salma El-Sahhar
Jade Farhat
Gonzalo Fernández
Sera Filiz
Lottie Frick
Sean Gallagher
Devan Grimsrud
Nazlee Habibi
Kurtis Hashimoto
Sarah Hussaini
Haneen Iqbal
Zainab Jabri
Emma Jacobson
Caro Jelert
Sanaa Jeraj
Zoe Johnston
Chala June
Salwa Khan

Ayesha Khan
Aamina Khan
Fatima Khawaja
Bhavna Kolakaluri
Gabrielle Lamontagne
Clare Langan
Maia Lauria
Patty Lee
Jocette Lee
Callie Longenecker
Miranda Madrazo
Fatma Masaud
Willa Moore
Abeer Najjar
Sarah Nasser
Maya Okindo
Cassidy Olsen
Aditya Palacharla
Manu Patel
Hanisha Patel
Vanessa Pham
Angela Pizzimenti
Brianna Plaza
Jamie Rothenberg
Shabnam Sabur Dinani
Yina Shan
Kayla Sherman
Muna Shikaki
Ananya Singh
Armin Tehrani
Sezen Tokadam
Toral Vaidya
Salma Valimohamed

INDEX

A.

achaar, 20
    Achaar, Egg, and Cheese, *88*, 89
    Shortcut Lemon Achaar, *201*, 202
adobo sauce, 96, *97*
Aleppo chili flakes. *See* chili flakes
almonds
    Almond Mocha Blondies, 238, *239*
    Ashraf's Baklava, 208, *209–10*, 211
    Fruit and Nut Biscotti, *207*, *232*, 233, *262*, 263
    The Pink Drink, *258*, 259, 260
American food, defining, 8, 11
Arrogant Tomato Toast, 92, *93*
Artichoke Dip, TGIF, *82*, 82–83
arugula, 164, *165*
Ashraf's Baklava, 208, *209–10*, 211
Ashraf's Tomato Saag, 94, *95*
author, about, 8, *10*, 11, *263*
avocado
    Carthage Must Be Destroyed, *102*, 103

B.

baklava
    Ashraf's Baklava, 208, *209–10*, 211
    Baklava Granola, 212, *213*
bananas
    Banana Cake with Tahini Fudge, *206*, *214*, 214–15
    A Different Date Shake, 252, *253*
basil, 118, *119*
    Pasta Day Pasta, *136*, 137
    Summer on a Plate, 76, *77*
    Thai-Style Crispy Salmon and Rice, *172*, 173
Batata Vada (Kachori), 40–41, *41*
beef. *See also* steak
    Beef Samosas, 70, *71–72*, 73
    Koobideh Meatballs with Minty Yogurt, 126–27, *127*
    Rishma's Pilau, 143, *144*, 145, *145*
    Rumina's Kebabs and Coconut Chutney, 66–67, *67*
    salami, 52, *53*
    Samosa-Spiced Burgers, 148, *149*
    Spiced Short Ribs and Potatoes, 160, *161–63*
bird's-eye chili, 20
    Batata Vada, 40–41, *41*
    Carrot Sambharo, 190, *191*
    Chevro Chips, 42, *43*
    Chicken Kitchri, *104*, 104–5
    Chutney Butter, *189*, 194
    Green Chutney, *189*, 196, *196*
    Lemony, Herby Shrimpies, 130, *131*
    Lemony Cucumber Salad with Salted Yogurt, 60, *61*
    Pickled Kachumber, *12*, 198, *199*
    Potato Samosas, 70, *71–72*, 73
    Rishma's Pilau, 143, *144*, 145, *145*
    Rumina's Kebabs and Coconut Chutney, 66–67, *67*
    Samosa-Spiced Burgers, 148, *149*
    Thai-Style Crispy Salmon and Rice, *172*, 173
    Wali Ya Mboga, Sorta, 182–83, *183*
Biryani, Farzana's, 108–9, *110–11*
Biscotti, Fruit and Nut, *207*, *232*, 233, *262*, 263
B-L-D Tomatoes and Eggs, *98*, 99
blueberries
    A Different Date Shake, 252, *253*
bok choy, 114, *115*
bread (ingredient). *See also* sandwiches and burgers
    Arrogant Tomato Toast, 92, *93*
    Grape and Fennel Salad, 52, *53*
    Rumina's Kebabs and Coconut Chutney, 66–67, *67*
    Shawarma Salad Wrap, 150–51, *151*
breadcrumbs
    Fish Fillet, *112*, 112–13
    Koobideh Meatballs with Minty Yogurt, 126–27, *127*
    Smashed Black Bean Burgers, 96, *97*
    TGIF Artichoke Dip, *82*, 82–83
broccoli rabe
    Gochujang Tahini Noodles, 118, *119*
broth, about, 18
burgers. *See* sandwiches and burgers
butter, 240, *241*. *See also* ghee
    Chili Butter, 54
    Chutney Butter, *189*, 194
    Salted Brown Butter Pecan Shortbread, 246–47, *247*
buttermilk
    Chocolate Cake with Chai Buttercream, *218*, 219–20, *221*

C.

cacao
    Date and Dark Chocolate Cookies, *37*, 230, *231*, *262*, 263

Calabrian Chili Chicken with Caper Raita, 100, *101*
cantaloupe
   Melon Sorbet, 242, *243*
   Summer on a Plate, 76, *77*
capers
   Caper Raita, 100, *101*
   A Great Tuna Melt, 174, *175*
   One Pan(try) Pasta, 134, *135*
cardamom, 19, 108–9, *110–11*
   Chocolate Cake with Chai Buttercream, *218*, 219–20, *221*
   Coconut and Cardamom Cake, 225–26, *227*
   Gahwa Sundae, 234, *235*
   Karak Chai, 256, *257*, *262*, 263
   Rishma's Pilau, 143, *144*, 145, *145*
carrots, 116, *117*, 158, *159*
   Carrot Sambharo, 190, *191*
   Shawarma-Spiced Carrots, *74*, 75
Carthage Must Be Destroyed, *102*, 103
Chai, Karak, 256, *257*, *262*, 263
cheese. *See also* cream cheese; feta cheese
   Achaar, Egg, and Cheese, *88*, 89
   Grape and Fennel Salad, 52, *53*
   A Great Tuna Melt, 174, *175*
   Parmesan, *82*, 82–83, 134, *135*
   pecorino romano, 180, *181*
   Samosa-Spiced Burgers, 148, *149*
   Smashed Black Bean Burgers, 96, *97*
   TGIF Artichoke Dip, *82*, 82–83
cherries, dried
   Fruit and Nut Biscotti, *207*, 232, 233, *262*, 263
Chevro Chips, 42, *43*
Chewy Ginger Cookies, 216, *217*
chicken
   Calabrian Chili Chicken with Caper Raita, 100, *101*
   Chicken Kitchri, *104*, 104–5
   Coronation Chicken Pastries, 46, *47*
   Gully's Gajjar Chicken, 122–23, *123*
   Halal Cart Salad, *124*, 124–25
   An Iconic Chicken Pot Pie, *90*, 90–91
   Red, Hot Tandoori Wings, 78, *79*
   Riffat's Kuku Paka, *140*, 141–42
   Shenaz's Chicken Haleem, 152, *153*, 154–55
   Wali Ya Mboga, Sorta, 182–83, *183*
chickpea flour, 18

Batata Vada, 40–41, *41*
Peppery Potato Pakoras, 64, *65*
chickpeas
   Spiced Chickpea Soup, 158, *159*
chili crisp, 20
   Hot and Sour Tomatoes, 58, *59*
   recipe, 192, *193*
   Spiced Chickpea Soup, 158, *159*
chili flakes, 18
   B-L-D Tomatoes and Eggs, *98*, 99
   Shortcut Lemon Achaar, *201*, 202
   Spiced Chickpea Soup, 158, *159*
   Summer on a Plate, 76, *77*
   Turkish-ish Eggs, *178*, 179
   Za'atar and Maple Kettle Corn, 62, *63*
chili paste, 20
   One Pan(try) Pasta, 134, *135*
chili powder, 19
   Ashraf's Tomato Saag, 94, *95*
   Batata Vada, 40–41, *41*
   Chevro Chips, 42, *43*
   Gully's Gajjar Chicken, 122–23, *123*
   Homemade Hot Sauce, 197, *197*
   Shenaz's Chicken Haleem, 152, *153*, 154–55
   Spiced Short Ribs and Potatoes, 160, *161–63*
   Steak Sandwich with Date Chutney, 164, *165*
   Tandoori Tacos, 170, *171*
chilis. *See also* bird's-eye chili
   Farzana's Biryani, 108–9, *110–11*
   Sukayna's Omelet, 166, *167*
   Tandoori Tacos, 170, *171*
   Tarka Olives, 80, *81*
chipotle peppers, 96, *97*
chocolate
   Almond Mocha Blondies, 238, *239*
   Banana Cake with Tahini Fudge, *206*, 214, 214–15
   Chocolate Cake with Chai Buttercream, *218*, 219–20, *221*
   Date and Dark Chocolate Cookies, *37*, 230, *231*, *262*, 263
   Fruit and Nut Biscotti, *207*, 232, 233, *262*, 263
chutney. *See also* Green Chutney
   Chutney Butter, *189*, 194
   Coconut Chutney, 66–67, *67*
   Cucumber and Chutney Sandwiches, 48, *49*
   Date Chutney, 195, *195*
cilantro, 78, 108–9, *110–11*
   Beef Samosas, 70, *71–72*, 73

Chutney Butter, *189*, 194
Coconut Chutney, 66–67, *67*
Coconutty Corn, 44, *45*
Cucumber and Chutney Sandwiches, 48, *49*
Green Chutney, *189*, 196, *196*
Samosa-Spiced Burgers, 148, *149*
Tandoori Tacos, 170, *171*
Thai-Style Crispy Salmon and Rice, *172*, 173
cinnamon
   Chocolate Cake with Chai Buttercream, *218*, 219–20, *221*
   Coffee Cake Muffins, 228, *229*
   Karak Chai, 256, *257*, *262*, 263
   Mall Cinnamon Rolls, 222, *223*, 224, *224*
citric acid, 18
cloves, 108–9, *110–11*
   Ashraf's Baklava, 208, *209–10*, 211
   Gahwa Sundae, 234, *235*
   Rishma's Pilau, 143, *144*, 145, *145*
cocoa powder, 19
   Chocolate Cake with Chai Buttercream, *218*, 219–20, *221*
   A Different Date Shake, 252, *253*
coconut
   Coconut and Cardamom Cake, 225–26, *227*
   Coconut Chutney, 66–67, *67*
coconut milk
   Coconutty Corn, 44, *45*
   Riffat's Kuku Paka, *140*, 141–42
coffee
   Almond Mocha Blondies, 238, *239*
   A Different Date Shake, 252, *253*
   Gahwa Sundae, 234, *235*
Coffee Cake Muffins, 228, *229*
corn
   Coconutty Corn, 44, *45*
   Coronation Chicken Pastries, 46, *47*
cranberries, dried
   Coronation Chicken Pastries, 46, *47*
cream
   Chocolate Cake with Chai Buttercream, *218*, 219–20, *221*
   Coconut and Cardamom Cake, 225–26, *227*
   Strawberry Delight, 248, *249*
cream cheese
   Cucumber and Chutney Sandwiches, 48, *49*
   Mall Cinnamon Rolls, 222, *223*, 224, *224*

Strawberry Delight, 248, *249*
TGIF Artichoke Dip, 82, *82–83*
cucumber, 100, *101*, 108–9, *110–11*. *See also* raita
    Cucumber and Chutney Sandwiches, 48, *49*
    Fruity Fattoush, 50, *51*
    Lemony Cucumber Salad with Salted Yogurt, 60, *61*
    Thai-Style Crispy Salmon and Rice, *172*, 173
Cumin Fried Rice, 106, *107*
curry leaves
    Chevro Chips, 42, *43*
    Potato Samosas, 70, *71–72*, 73
curry paste, 138, *139*
curry powder, 18–19, 46, *47*
    Super-Savory Chicken Noodle Soup, 116, *117*

D.
dates, 19
    Date and Dark Chocolate Cookies, 37, 230, *231*, *262*, *263*
    Date Chutney, 195, *195*
    A Different Date Shake, 252, *253*
    Gahwa Sundae, 234, *235*
    Herb Salad, 75
    Steak Sandwich with Date Chutney, 164, *165*
Diamond Crystal kosher salt, 19, 22, *23*
A Different Date Shake, 252, *253*
dill, *178*, 179
    Tartar Sauce, *112*, 112–13

E.
eggplant
    Not So Norma Pasta, 132, *133*
    Roasted Eggplant Sandwich, 146, *147*
eggs, 106, *107*
    Achaar, Egg, and Cheese, 88, *89*
    B-L-D Tomatoes and Eggs, *98*, 99
    Carthage Must Be Destroyed, *102*, 103
    Green Eggs and Hummus, *120*, 120–21
    Sukayna's Omelet, 166, *167*
    Turkish-ish Eggs, *178*, 179
    Udon Carbonara, 180, *181*
English muffins
    Achaar, Egg, and Cheese, 88, *89*
equipment, 21

F.
Farzana's Biryani, 108–9, *110–11*
fennel bulb
    Grape and Fennel Salad, 52, *53*
feta cheese
    Calabrian Chili Chicken with Caper Raita, 100, *101*
    Herby, Garlicky Pasta Salad, 56, *57*
    Summer on a Plate, 76, *77*
    Tarka Olives, 80, *81*
fish
    Fish Fillet, *112*, 112–13
    A Great Tuna Melt, 174, *175*
    Thai-Style Crispy Salmon and Rice, *172*, 173
fish sauce, 20, *172*, 173
French Onion Ramen, 114, *115*
fridge staples, 20
fruit, dried, 46, *47*
    Fruit and Nut Biscotti, *207*, *232*, 233, *262*, 263
Fruity Fattoush, 50, *51*

G.
Gahwa Sundae, 234, *235*
gajjar masala, 122–23, *123*
garam masala, 19
    Samosa-Spiced Burgers, 148, *149*
    Samosas Two Ways, 70, *71–72*, 73
garlic, 166, *167*, *192*, *193*
    Garlicky Labneh, 54, *55*
    Gully's Gajjar Chicken, 122–23, *123*
    Herby, Garlicky Pasta Salad, 56, *57*
    Shenaz's Chicken Haleem, 152, *153*, 154–55
ghee, 212, *213*
    Pineapples and Ghee, *244*, 245
    Shenaz's Chicken Haleem, 152, *153*, 154–55
ginger, 70, *71–72*, 73, 100, *101*, 138, *139*, 166, *167*
    Chewy Ginger Cookies, 216, *217*
    Chocolate Cake with Chai Buttercream, *218*, 219–20, *221*
    Ginger Lime Spritz, 254, *255*
    Rumina's Kebabs and Coconut Chutney, 66–67, *67*
    Shenaz's Chicken Haleem, 152, *153*, 154–55
    Super-Savory Chicken Noodle Soup, 116, *117*
goat
    Rishma's Pilau, 143, *144*, 145, *145*

Gochujang Tahini Noodles, 118, *119*
granola
    Baklava Granola, 212, *213*
    Pineapples and Ghee, *244*, 245
Grape and Fennel Salad, 52, *53*
A Great Tuna Melt, 174, *175*
Green Chutney, *189*, 196, *196*
    Farzana's Biryani, 108–9, *110–11*
Green Eggs and Hummus, *120*, 120–21
greens. *See* lettuce and greens
Gully's Gajjar Chicken, 122–23, *123*
Gulzar's Sugar Puffs, 236–37, *237*
Gyoza with Garlicky Labneh and Chili Butter, 54, *55*

H.
halal diet, 18, 96, 112
    Halal Cart Salad, *124*, 124–25
haleem masala, 152, *153*, 154
herbs. *See also specific herbs*
    Herb Salads, 75, 78
    Herby, Garlicky Pasta Salad, 56, *57*
    Lemony, Herby Shrimpies, 130, *131*
Homemade Hot Sauce, 197, *197*
hosting, menus for, 32, 34–35
Hot and Sour Tomatoes, 58, *59*
hot sauce
    Homemade Hot Sauce, 197, *197*
    Red, Hot Tandoori Wings, 78, *79*
hummus
    Green Eggs and Hummus, *120*, 120–21
    Roasted Eggplant Sandwich, 146, *147*

I.
ice cream
    Gahwa Sundae, 234, *235*
An Iconic Chicken Pot Pie, *90*, 90–91

J.
jalapeños
    Coconutty Corn, 44, *45*
    Cucumber and Chutney Sandwiches, 48, *49*
    Herb Salad, 75
    Jugu Scones with Butter and Jam, 240, *241*

K.

Kachori. *See* Batata Vada
kachumber
    Farzana's Biryani, 108–9, *110–11*
    Pickled Kachumber, *12*, 198, *199*
    Rishma's Pilau, 143, *144*, 145, *145*
    Wali Ya Mboga, Sorta, 182–83, *183*
kale, 54, *55*, *120*, 120–21
Karak Chai, 256, *257*, *262*, 263
Kebabs and Coconut Chutney, Rumina's, 66–67, *67*
Kewpie mayo. *See* mayonnaise
Khoja heritage, 8, *10*, 11
Koobideh Meatballs with Minty Yogurt, 126–27, *127*

L.

labneh, 20
    Arrogant Tomato Toast, 92, *93*
    Garlicky Labneh, 54, *55*
    Herb Salad, 75
    Turkish-ish Eggs, *178*, 179
lamb
    Spicy Lamb and Cumin Noodles, 156, *157*
Last-Minute Tahdig, 128, *129*
lavash bread, 150–51, *151*
lemon, preserved, 20
    Lemony, Herby Shrimpies, 130, *131*
    Preserved Limonata, *259*, 260
    Shortcut Lemon Achaar, *201*, 202
    Tortellini en Preserved Lemon Brodo, 176, *177*
lemon zest and juice, 195–96, *201*, 202
    Lemony Cucumber Salad with Salted Yogurt, 60, *61*
    Tarka Olives, 80, *81*
lentils
    Chicken Kitchri, *104*, 104–5
    Weeknight Daal, *184*, 185
lettuce and greens, 114, *115*, 164, *165*
    Fruity Fattoush, 50, *51*
    Grape and Fennel Salad, 52, *53*
    Green Eggs and Hummus, *120*, 120–21
    Gyoza with Garlicky Labneh and Chili Butter, 54, *55*
    Halal Cart Salad, *124*, 124–25
    Shawarma Salad Wrap, 150–51, *151*
lime
    Ginger Lime Spritz, 254, *255*

M.

Mall Cinnamon Rolls, 222, *223*, 224, *224*
mangos
    Slightly Salty Mango Lassi, 261, *261*
mayonnaise, 20
    Halal Cart Salad, *124*, 124–25
    Shawarma Salad Wrap, 150–51, *151*
    Tartar Sauce, *112*, 112–13
    TGIF Artichoke Dip, *82*, 82–83
    White Sauce, *201*, 203
melon
    Melon Sorbet, 242, *243*
    Summer on a Plate, 76, *77*
menus
    for hosting specific events, 32, 34–35
    mood-based, 29–31
milks. *See also* coconut milk; cream
    buttermilk, *218*, 219–20, *221*
    Karak Chai, 256, *257*, *262*, 263
    The Pink Drink, *258*, 259, 260
mint, 78
    Chutney Butter, *189*, 194
    Fruity Fattoush, 50, *51*
    Gully's Gajjar Chicken, 122–23, *123*
    Koobideh Meatballs with Minty Yogurt, 126–27, *127*
    Samosa-Spiced Burgers, 148, *149*
    Shenaz's Chicken Haleem, 152, *153*, 154–55
    Spicy Lamb and Cumin Noodles, 156, *157*
miso paste
    French Onion Ramen, 114, *115*
mood, cooking for, 29–31
mushrooms. *See* shiitake mushrooms

N.

noodles. *See* pasta and noodles
Not So Norma Pasta, 132, *133*
nuts. *See also* almonds; peanuts; pistachios; walnuts
    pecans, 246–47, *247*
    pine nuts, 54, *55*

O.

oats
    Baklava Granola, 212, *213*
olives, 20
    Green Eggs and Hummus, *120*, 120–21
    Herby, Garlicky Pasta Salad, 56, *57*
    Tarka Olives, 80, *81*
One Pan(try) Pasta, 134, *135*
onions, 94, *95*, 146, *147*. *See also* kachumber
    French Onion Ramen, 114, *115*
    fried, 108–9, *110–11*, 152, *153*, 154
    Pickled Kachumber, *12*, 198, *199*
    Sukayna's Omelet, 166, *167*
    Udon Carbonara, 180, *181*
orzo pasta, 138, *139*
oyster sauce, 106, *107*

P.

panko. *See* breadcrumbs
pantry staples, *16–17*, 18–19
paprika, smoked, 54, *98*, 99, 156, *157*, 158, *159*
Parmesan cheese, *82*, 82–83, 134, *135*
pasta and noodles
    French Onion Ramen, 114, *115*
    Gochujang Tahini Noodles, 118, *119*
    Herby, Garlicky Pasta Salad, 56, *57*
    Not So Norma Pasta, 132, *133*
    One Pan(try) Pasta, 134, *135*
    Pasta Day Pasta, *136*, 137
    Red Curry Orzotto with Mushrooms and Peas, 138, *139*
    Spicy Lamb and Cumin Noodles, 156, *157*
    Sungold and Saffron Spaghetti, 168, *169*
    Super-Savory Chicken Noodle Soup, 116, *117*
    Tortellini en Preserved Lemon Brodo, 176, *177*
    Udon Carbonara, 180, *181*
peanuts
    Jugu Scones with Butter and Jam, 240, *241*
    Thai-Style Crispy Salmon and Rice, *172*, 173
peas
    Red Curry Orzotto with Mushrooms and Peas, 138, *139*
pecans
    Salted Brown Butter Pecan Shortbread, 246–47, *247*
pepperoncini, 52, *53*, 150–51, *151*
peppers, hot. *See* bird's-eye chili; chili variations; chipotle peppers; jalapeños

Peppery Potato Pakoras, 64, *65*
perfectionism, 27
phyllo pastry
    Ashraf's Baklava, 208, *209–10*, 211
Pickled Kachumber, *12*, 198, *199*
pickles
    Tartar Sauce, *112*, 112–13
Pineapples and Ghee, *244*, 245
pine nuts, 54, *55*
The Pink Drink, *258*, 259, 260
pistachios
    Ashraf's Baklava, 208, *209–10*, 211
    Baklava Granola, 212, *213*
    Gahwa Sundae, 234, *235*
    The Pink Drink, *258*, 259, 260
pita chips, 50, *51*, *124*, 124–25
pomegranate molasses, 19, 50, *51*
    Roasted Eggplant Sandwich, 146, *147*
popcorn
    Za'atar and Maple Kettle Corn, 62, *63*
potato chips
    Chevro Chips, 42, *43*
potatoes
    Batata Vada, 40–41, *41*
    Farzana's Biryani, 108–9, *110–11*
    An Iconic Chicken Pot Pie, *90*, 90–91
    Peppery Potato Pakoras, 64, *65*
    Rishma's Pilau, 143, *144*, 145, *145*
    Spiced Short Ribs and Potatoes, 160, *161–63*
    Weeknight Daal, *184*, 185
presentation principles, *26*, 26–27, 32
Preserved Limonata, *259*, 260
puff pastry
    Coronation Chicken Pastries, 46, *47*
    An Iconic Chicken Pot Pie, *90*, 90–91
    Salty Little Hearts, 68, *69*

R.
radishes
    Green Eggs and Hummus, *120*, 120–21
raita
    Caper Raita, 100, *101*
    Farzana's Biryani, 108–9, *110–11*
ramen noodles
    French Onion Ramen, 114, *115*
recipes, guide to, 24–25
Red Curry Orzotto with Mushrooms and Peas, 138, *139*
Red, Hot Tandoori Wings, 78, *79*
red pepper flakes. *See* Chili Crisp; chili flakes
rhubarb
    Coconut and Cardamom Cake (variation), 225–26, *227*
ribs, 160, *161–63*
rice, 18
    Chicken Kitchri, *104*, 104–5
    Cumin Fried Rice, 106, *107*
    Farzana's Biryani, 108–9, *110–11*
    Last-Minute Tahdig, 128, *129*
    Rishma's Pilau, 143, *144*, 145, *145*
    Thai-Style Crispy Salmon and Rice, *172*, 173
    Wali Ya Mboga, Sorta, 182–83, *183*
Riffat's Kuku Paka, *140*, 141–42
Rishma's Pilau, 143, *144*, 145, *145*
Roasted Eggplant Sandwich, 146, *147*
rose syrup
    The Pink Drink, *258*, 259, 260
Rumina's Kebabs and Coconut Chutney, 66–67, *67*

S.
saffron, 19, 208, *209*, 210–11
    Farzana's Biryani, 108–9, *110–11*
    Sungold and Saffron Spaghetti, 168, *169*
salami, 52, *53*
salmon
    Thai-Style Crispy Salmon and Rice, *172*, 173
salt, choosing, 19, 22, *23*
Salted Brown Butter Pecan Shortbread, 246–47, *247*
Salty Little Hearts, 68, *69*
sambal oelek, 166, *167*
Samosa-Spiced Burgers, 148, *149*
Samosas Two Ways, 70, *71–72*, 73
sandwiches and burgers
    Achaar, Egg, and Cheese, *88*, 89
    Cucumber and Chutney Sandwiches, 48, *49*
    A Great Tuna Melt, *174*, 175
    Roasted Eggplant Sandwich, 146, *147*
    Samosa-Spiced Burgers, 148, *149*
    Smashed Black Bean Burgers, 96, *97*
    Steak Sandwich with Date Chutney, 164, *165*
scones, 240, *241*
serveware, 27
sesame oil, toasted, 106, *107*
    Gochujang Tahini Noodles, 118, *119*
shawarma spice
    Shawarma Salad Wrap, 150–51, *151*
    Shawarma-Spiced Carrots, *74*, 75
Shenaz's Chicken Haleem, 152, *153*, 154–55
shiitake mushrooms
    French Onion Ramen, 114, *115*
    Red Curry Orzotto with Mushrooms and Peas, 138, *139*
Shortcut Lemon Achaar, *201*, 202
shrimp
    Lemony, Herby Shrimpies, 130, *131*
Slightly Salty Mango Lassi, 261, *261*
Smashed Black Bean Burgers, 96, *97*
Sorbet, Melon, 242, *243*
soups
    Spiced Chickpea Soup, 158, *159*
    Super-Savory Chicken Noodle Soup, 116, *117*
    Tortellini en Preserved Lemon Brodo, 176, *177*
sour cream
    Coffee Cake Muffins, 228, *229*
    TGIF Artichoke Dip, *82*, 82–83
sparkling water, 254, *255*
Spiced Chickpea Soup, 158, *159*
Spiced Short Ribs and Potatoes, 160, *161–63*
Spicy Lamb and Cumin Noodles, 156, *157*
spinach
    TGIF Artichoke Dip, *82*, 82–83
    Wali Ya Mboga, Sorta, 182–83, *183*
spring roll pastry
    Samosas Two Ways, 70, *71–72*, 73
staples, ingredient, *16–17*, 18–20
steak
    Cumin Fried Rice, 106, *107*
    Steak Sandwich with Date Chutney, 164, *165*
    Tandoori Tacos, 170, *171*
strawberries
    Coconut and Cardamom Cake (variation), 225–26, *227*
    Fruity Fattoush, 50, *51*
    Strawberry Delight, 248, *249*
strawberry jam, 240, *241*
styling, *26*, 26–27, 32

success, guide for, 14
Sugar Puffs, Gulzar's, 236–37, *237*
Sukayna's Omelet, 166, *167*
sumac, 19, 146, *147*
Summer on a Plate, 76, *77*
Sungold and Saffron Spaghetti, 168, *169*
sweet potatoes
   Calabrian Chili Chicken with Caper Raita, 100, *101*

T.
Tacos, Tandoori, 170, *171*
tahini, 150–51, *151*
   Banana Cake with Tahini Fudge, *206*, *214*, 214–15
   Date and Dark Chocolate Cookies, *37*, 230, *231*, *262*, 263
   Gochujang Tahini Noodles, 118, *119*
Tandoori Tacos, 170, *171*
Tanzania, 8
Tarka Olives, 80, *81*
Tartar Sauce, *112*, 112–13
tea, black, 18
   Chocolate Cake with Chai Buttercream, *218*, 219–20, *221*
   Karak Chai, 256, *257*, *262*, 263
TGIF Artichoke Dip, *82*, 82–83
Thai-Style Crispy Salmon and Rice, *172*, 173
"third culture," defined, 8
tikka seasoning, 122–23, *123*
tomatoes, 126–27, *127*, 143, *144*, 145, *145*
   Arrogant Tomato Toast, 92, *93*
   Ashraf's Tomato Saag, 94, *95*
   B-L-D Tomatoes and Eggs, *98*, 99
   Carthage Must Be Destroyed, *102*, 103
   Farzana's Biryani, 108–9, *110–11*
   Fruity Fattoush, 50, *51*
   Green Eggs and Hummus, *120*, 120–21
   Halal Cart Salad, *124*, 124–25
   Herby, Garlicky Pasta Salad, 56, *57*
   Lemony Cucumber Salad with Salted Yogurt, 60, *61*
   Pasta Day Pasta, *136*, 137
   Riffat's Kuku Paka, *140*, 141–42
   Summer on a Plate, 76, *77*
   Sungold and Saffron Spaghetti, 168, *169*
tomato sauce/paste, 158, *159*, 190, *191*

Gully's Gajjar Chicken, 122–23, *123*
Not So Norma Pasta, 132, *133*
Shawarma Salad Wrap, 150–51, *151*
Spiced Short Ribs and Potatoes, 160, *161–63*
Weeknight Daal, *184*, 185
tonic water, *259*, 260
tools, 21
Tortellini en Preserved Lemon Brodo, 176, *177*
tortillas
   Tandoori Tacos, 170, *171*
Turkish-ish Eggs, *178*, 179

U.
Udon Carbonara, 180, *181*

V.
vanilla, 216, *217*, *218*, 219–20, *221*
vegetables, mixed
   An Iconic Chicken Pot Pie, *90*, 90–91
vegetarian, menu for, 34

W.
Wali Ya Mboga, Sorta, 182–83, *183*
walnuts
   Ashraf's Baklava, 208, *209–10*, 211
   Baklava Granola, *212*, *213*
watermelon
   Summer on a Plate, 76, *77*
Weeknight Daal, *184*, 185
wheat
   Shenaz's Chicken Haleem, 152, *153*, 154
White Sauce, *201*, 203

Y.
yogurt, *104*, 104–5, 182–83, *183*. *See also* labneh; raita
   Farzana's Biryani, 108–9, *110–11*
   Gully's Gajjar Chicken, 122–23, *123*
   Halal Cart Salad, *124*, 124–25
   Koobideh Meatballs with Minty Yogurt, 126–27, *127*
   Last-Minute Tahdig, 128, *129*
   Pineapples and Ghee, *244*, 245
   Rishma's Pilau, 143, *144*, 145, *145*
   Slightly Salty Mango Lassi, 261, *261*

Tandoori Tacos, 170, *171*
White Sauce, *201*, 203

Z.
za'atar, 19, 56, *57*, 92, *93*
   Green Eggs and Hummus, *120*, 120–21
   Za'atar and Maple Kettle Corn, 62, *63*
   Za'atar and Maple Kettle Corn, 62, *63*

EDITOR:
Holly Dolce
DESIGNER:
Sebit Min
DESIGN MANAGER:
Danielle Youngsmith
MANAGING EDITOR:
Lisa Silverman
PRODUCTION MANAGER:
Larry Pekarek

ASSISTANT COPYWRITER:
Fatema Issa Asharia
AUTHOR'S ASSISTANT:
Tia Rotolo
FOOD STYLIST:
Pearl Jones
FOOD STYLIST'S ASSISTANTS:
Ava Chambers
Christine Quach
PHOTOGRAPHERS:
Michael Graydon
Nikole Herriott

PHOTOGRAPHER'S ASSISTANTS:
First assistant: Chris Johnson
Second assistant: Christian Em
PROP STYLIST:
Rebecca Bartoshesky
PROP STYLIST'S ASSISTANT:
Uma Tufekcic

Library of Congress
Control Number: 2024941002

ISBN: 978-1-4197-7007-4
eISBN: 979-8-88707-114-5

Text copyright © 2025
Zaynab Issa
Photographs copyright © 2025
Graydon Herriott

Cover © 2025 Abrams

Published in 2025 by Abrams, an imprint of ABRAMS. All rights reserved. No portion of this book may be reproduced, stored in a retrieval system, or transmitted in any form or by any means, mechanical, electronic, photocopying, recording, or otherwise, without written permission from the publisher.

Printed and bound in China
10 9 8 7 6 5 4 3 2 1

Abrams books are available at special discounts when purchased in quantity for premiums and promotions as well as fundraising or educational use. Special editions can also be created to specification. For details, contact specialsales@abramsbooks.com or the address below.

Abrams® is a registered trademark of Harry N. Abrams, Inc.

ABRAMS The Art of Books
195 Broadway, New York, NY 10007
abramsbooks.com